Before the New Deal

 Before the New Deal

*Social Welfare in the South,
1830–1930*

EDITED BY ELNA C. GREEN

The University of Georgia Press · Athens & London

© 1999 by the University of Georgia Press
Athens, Georgia 30602
All rights reserved
Designed by Kathi Morgan
Set in Minion by G&S Typesetters, Inc.
Printed digitally

Library of Congress Cataloging in Publication Data
Before the New Deal : social welfare in the South,
1830–1930 / edited by Elna C. Green.
    p. cm.
   Includes bibliographical references and index.
   ISBN 0-8203-2091-9 (alk. paper)
   0-8203-2114-1 (pbk.: alk. paper)
   1. Public welfare—Southern States—
History. 2. Social service—Southern States—
History. 3. Socially handicapped—Services
for—Southern States—History. 4. Southern
States—Social policy—History. I. Green, Elna C.
HV98.S9B4   1999
361.975′09′034—dc21   98-39166

British Library Cataloging in Publication Data available
Paperback ISBN-13: 978-0-8203-2114-1
2017 hardcover reissue ISBN-13: 978-0-8203-5212-1

CONTENTS

vii   Introduction

ONE   State Policies

3   Laissez Faire and the Lunatic Asylum: State Welfare Institutions in Georgia—The First Half-Century, 1830s–1880s · *Peter Wallenstein*

24   Confederate Pensions as Southern Social Welfare · *Kathleen Gorman*

40   Regulating the Poor in Alabama: The Jefferson County Poor Farm, 1885–1945 · *James H. Tuten*

61   We Take Care of Our Womenfolk: The Home for Needy Confederate Women in Richmond, Virginia, 1898–1990 · *Susan Hamburger*

TWO   Local Case Studies

81   National Trends, Regional Differences, Local Circumstances: Social Welfare in New Orleans, 1870s–1920s · *Elna C. Green*

100   Are You or Are You Not Your Sister's Keeper?: A Radical Response to the Treatment of Unwed Mothers in Tennessee · *Mazie Hough*

120   Anxious Care and Constant Struggle: The Female Humane Association and Richmond's White Civil War Orphans · *E. Susan Barber*

138   I Certainly Hope That You Will Be Able to Train Her: Reformers and the Georgia Training School for Girls · *Lee S. Polansky*

160   The Colors of Social Welfare in the New South: Black and White Clubwomen in South Carolina, 1900–1930 · *Joan Marie Johnson*

181   Disease, Disorder, and Motherhood: Working-Class Women, Social Welfare, and the Process of Urban Development in Atlanta *Georgina Hickey*

209   Selected Bibliography

215   List of Contributors

217   Index

INTRODUCTION

One of the purposes of this book is to draw attention to the South's overlooked social welfare history. Scholars in social welfare history in general have neglected the South; southern scholars in general have neglected social welfare history.[1] Moreover, when new books are published on topics that should properly be considered southern social welfare history, they have been designated (and reviewed as) southern history rather than social welfare history.[2] This book should change these attributions by firmly linking social welfare history with southern history. The intersection of these two dynamic fields offers some exciting possibilities for new research that might also address older questions. Social welfare scholarship can tackle the issue of southern distinctiveness, for example, from a new perspective: Was the South's experience in evolving social welfare policies uniquely southern? Or are the differences more a matter of degree rather than of kind? How deeply into the South did national trends and policies seep? What role did the South (and southerners) play in shaping social welfare policy in the nation at large?

The essays collected here suggest that the South did have a different historical experience in providing for its poor and other dependents. Yet, this book does not explore this question systematically; that is, we do not take each historical epoch and test for differences and similarities. I would like to think, however, that this book will stimulate just that kind of research agenda in the future. Instead, these essays explore several discrete topics from the nineteenth and early twentieth centuries based on the work currently under way in the field.

The essays included in this book were not chosen because they hold a particular point of view nor because they utilize a particular methodology. The reader will notice that the authors disagree with one another, and with me, on some fundamental interpretations of both southern history and social welfare history. Instead, essays were selected for their ability to give definition to this emerging field. The essays that follow point out some of the rich, untouched documentary sources available to scholars in southern social welfare history, they demonstrate the most prominent methodologies in current use, and they illuminate, by default, topics still waiting to be explored.

The Field of Social Welfare History

Social welfare history began to coalesce as a subdiscipline in the late 1950s and early 1960s, driven, in part, by interest in contemporary reform efforts that resulted in the Great Society's war on poverty.[3] Social welfare historians were especially interested in the charitable institutions that Americans had created in the past, hoping that understanding those institutions would inform the efforts to create new, alternative institutions under construction as they wrote. They examined orphanages, insane asylums, reformatories, and settlement houses.[4] They scrutinized the evolution from private charity to public provision.[5] And they paid a great deal of attention to the development of professional social work and the impact that professionalization had on reform efforts.[6]

Responding to the domestic upheavals of the 1960s and the radical analyses of American history that emerged in their wake, social welfare scholarship in the late 1960s and early 1970s generally took a much more critical view of past social policy. Scholars focused on the motivations behind private charity and public welfare: Did charity/welfare serve to control the activities and values of the working class, regardless of the providers' own conscious goals? Or did it serve to broaden economic opportunities and expand democracy, as its providers had intended?[7] This debate over the question of social control energized the field of social welfare history, giving it a crisp edge that drove the scholarship for nearly twenty years.[8]

All of this scholarship (both the social control debate and its predecessors) had started from the point of view of the providers: the middle class, the reformers, the social workers, the intellectuals. But, under the influence of the new social history of the 1970s, scholars began attempting to look at social welfare from the bottom up. They began to examine the role of race,[9] gender,[10] and class and ethnicity,[11] in shaping the distribution of society's resources. Moreover, in a trend that has not yet seen completion, social welfare historians have attempted to uncover the ways in which the poor, the working class, and the marginal have resisted the efforts to control their behavior often implicit in social provision. These scholars find agency among the dispossessed and family strategies for survival quite distinct from those institutions created to support them.[12]

Many scholars of social welfare and social policy writing in the late 1980s and 1990s have been influenced by the concept of state formation. Stimulated in part by current concerns about economic globalization and its effects, historians and historical sociologists have been reexamining the origins of social welfare policy in the context of state formation. Much of this recent literature has been comparative, and it contrasts the United States with other Western industrial democracies that have developed different systems of social provision.[13]

Another stimulus to social welfare research in the 1990s has been the contemporary debate about public provision in the United States. As politicians have debated ways to dismantle the welfare state apparatus, scholars have been reexamining the origins and evolution of our current system of public assistance. Recent public discussions about foster care, orphanages, institutionalization, and dysfunctional families have sent historians scurrying to the archives hoping to contribute to the public debate and evolving public policy. These debates have served to give social welfare scholarship a more overtly political edge and have helped to make the field vigorous and expansive.[14]

Thus the field of social welfare history has seen a boom in interest during the 1990s, and the scholarship has been produced at an impressive, and impassioned, pace. But this new generation of social welfare history, as rich as it is, has almost wholly ignored the U.S. South. This oversight is important, for the evolution of social welfare policy in the South has often taken a different trajectory than elsewhere in the United States, and the differences can be significant in understanding current public debate on welfare. Attention to the South's differences can help illuminate national trends not otherwise visible. One of the goals of this anthology is to point out the importance of the South in understanding social welfare history in the United States and to encourage the incorporation of regional differences into our larger analyses.

Southern Social Welfare History

Although there is no general study of southern social welfare history yet in print, the outlines of the region's social policy can be assembled from works already published.[15] The summary of the current literature that follows is heavily reliant on a handful of monographs and points out the work still to be done.

English settlers of the southern colonies brought with them a set of assumptions about social relations. The English poor laws, which mandated local support for the needy, became the basis of southern colonial social welfare policy. The colony of Virginia established parishes (the local governing bodies responsible for caring for the poor) even before the House of Burgesses was created. Virginia passed a general poor law in 1642–43, defining the duties of the vestrymen in caring for the poor. This act acknowledged that sickness and old age prevented many colonists from working, thus producing want.[16] Parish vestry books indicate that substantial portions of the parish taxes went to poor relief, even in the seventeenth century. And as early as 1668, some Virginians were asking that each county should be compelled to build a workhouse for the instruction of poor children in useful trades.[17] Similarly, South Carolina passed its first colonywide poor law in 1695, appointing a board of commissioners to administer a voluntary poor fund. Three years later, the poor tax was made compulsory.[18]

Some mixture of auctioning off the poor to the lowest bidder, outdoor relief (direct payments to those who lived outside of public institutions), and poorhouses (or indoor relief) were the common methods of dealing with poverty throughout the American colonies, although auctioning may have been less common in the South.[19] The poor and other dependents might be cared for in private homes or given outdoor relief if they remained in their own homes. But in the eighteenth century, larger communities especially began to feel the pressure of rising numbers of needy and began building workhouses or almshouses to house the indigent.[20] Charleston's leaders petitioned the provincial assembly for a workhouse in 1734, a request that was promptly granted.[21] In 1755 the colonial assembly of Virginia authorized the parishes to build or buy buildings to house the poor; and by 1760 most parishes in the colony had an almshouse. The almshouse then became the colony's primary method of caring for the poor.[22]

Did these early efforts in the southern colonies differ from those found elsewhere in the American colonies? At least one scholar has argued that they did. Virginia Bernhard compared attitudes and practices in Anglican Virginia with Puritan Massachusetts and suggested that Virginians accepted poverty as omnipresent and poor relief as an act of noblesse oblige that helped to establish the colonial gentry as the rightful rulers of the colony. Whereas Puritans might have interpreted poverty in their "city on the hill" as a sign of God's disfavor, Virginians saw poverty as providing planters with the opportunity "to play a familiar and comfortable role: that of the

English country gentleman."²³ Thus, from the earliest settlement, Bernhard suggested, southern social welfare ideology differed from that elsewhere in the American colonies.

Southern colonies and states also differed in their approach to the settlement or residency requirements. In New England lengthy residence in the colony or state was often required in order to obtain public support, while southern colonies and states tended to pass more lenient residency laws. One scholar has suggested that this difference should not be interpreted as a more tolerant attitude toward the poor in the South. Instead, it is likely that the sparsely settled region may have been more eager to promote migration of new laborers, and harsh residency requirements would have been a deterrent.²⁴

The institution of slavery complicated the question of public relief in the southern states. What little public provision existed was generally denied to blacks; slaves were the responsibility of their masters and were prohibited from receiving aid in most states. Free blacks, too, were usually denied public assistance and were forced to develop their own informal self-help mechanisms, setting in motion a trend that would last until the twentieth century.²⁵ Black churches began assuming the responsibility for supporting indigent members by establishing "poor saints funds" or other methods of caring for their own. Mutual assistance associations, which would become one of the cornerstones of black civic life later in the nineteenth century, provided the equivalent of death benefits, burial policies, and even unemployment insurance for those whom the state refused to assist.²⁶

The Revolution unleashed much popular distrust of the Church and led to an overhaul of much of the region's welfare system. The Church (represented by the parish vestrymen) was relieved of its authority over and responsibility for the poor and was replaced by the State. All four southern colonies dissolved the old vestry system and established overseers of the poor for each district of each county.²⁷ Elizabeth Wisner has argued that this change of authority did little to improve the quality of care for the poor, as county officials often failed to provide more adequate relief than had the Anglican vestrymen.²⁸

In most southern localities in the early national period, there were few institutions (almshouses and perhaps the local jail) to house the poor, the elderly, or dependent children. Outdoor relief, either in their own homes or in the homes of others, was the most important form of provision for the poor.²⁹ Moreover, according to Michael Katz, in the first decades of the nineteenth century, rural counties in the South often abandoned their previously built poorhouses, further reducing the availability of indoor relief.³⁰

However, state support for *some* dependent classes developed even as rural communities closed their almshouses. In 1792 Charleston opened the first municipal orphanage in the new republic. Attending to the needs of white children only, the orphanage had multiple agendas. Its founding viewed as an act of patriotism, the orphanage also served as an agency of racial definition. Slaves were used to serve the white orphans, who were taught the "proper" relationship between whites and blacks in society.³¹

Other institutions and asylums cropped up too, as the South shared the new national enthusiasm for reform by institutionalization (an area that is analyzed by David Rothman). Anticipating the trend considerably, Virginia had established a state hospital for the insane in 1769 at Williamsburg.³² In the Jacksonian period, the institutions multiplied rapidly. Kentucky and South Carolina established state institutions for the insane in 1824 and 1828, respectively. Virginia's state institution for the deaf, dumb, and blind was established in 1838. Georgia began construction of a state mental institution in 1837.³³

As Peter Wallenstein has demonstrated, however, the willingness of southern states to build these institutions during the antebellum period was sometimes dependent on the availability of nontax revenue. Georgia's profitable experiments with railroads and banks provided the funding for its expansion of social services, such as the state mental institution. When that revenue dried up, so did the state support for public welfare projects.³⁴

Like asylums elsewhere, southern institutions sought to control as well as to assist the poor. Wallenstein has argued that in Georgia the most coercive institutions opened first (such as the penitentiary, opened in 1817), while the more benevolent ones opened later (such as the schools for the deaf and blind, opened in the 1850s).³⁵ Similar analyses of other states are needed to determine if this is, in fact, a regional trend.

In addition to founding institutions, southerners also participated in the great groundswell of voluntary association, inspired by evangelical religiosity, sweeping the nation at the time. Focusing primarily on personal morality, the reform movement hoped to make the American people worthy of the great experiment in republicanism and democracy then under way. Bible societies, temperance unions, and moral reform clubs peppered the southern landscape, and many of them concentrated their energies on the urban poor. Richmond's Female Humane Society, established in 1805, operated an orphanage for poor white girls, among other benevolences. In New Orleans the Poydras Female Orphan Society provided a similar service. Charleston's Female Domestic Missionary Society, founded in 1818, hired preachers to minister to the city's poor.[36]

As these three examples suggest, many of the voluntary associations were founded by women. Like evangelical women elsewhere in the nation, southern women organized scores of local benevolent associations. An emerging urban middle class, with strongly religious motivations, began building a tradition of women's benevolency that would last to the twentieth century. Again, the question of southern distinctiveness arises: Did the South's experience with benevolent associations differ from the model common to the rest of the nation? At least one scholar has argued that southern antebellum women's benevolency did not produce the same kind of female consciousness and protofeminist solidarity that reform activism produced in the northeast. Gail Murray has argued that southern white female benevolence never moved into advocacy or reform activities. Instead, southern associations were limited to the vision "imposed by their race, class, and gender."[37]

While reformers attempted to aid, reform, and control the poor and dependent, southerners also joined in the national debate about the best ways to compel the poor to work. They experimented with work programs in the almshouses, the abolition of outdoor relief, and the reduction of public services. But like welfare institutions elsewhere, southern almshouses discovered that the dependent often were dependent because they were in fact unable to work. Poorhouse work projects regularly failed.[38]

Mirroring the urban experience elsewhere in the country, southern poorhouses also came to have significant immigrant populations. By the 1840s Irish immigrants were the predominant group in Charleston's poorhouse, and similar trends in other cities are likely to be uncovered through further research.[39]

It was the issue of slavery that most divided reformers into regional factions. Northern reformers insisted that abolitionism was part of the great reform spirit of the day, while southern reformers adamantly resisted the argument. (Dorothea Dix maintained her legitimacy and effectiveness in the South partly because she rejected the antislavery impulse.[40]) As Barbara

Bellows has argued, southerners found they could reconcile slavery with moral reform—good could coexist comfortably with evil.[41]

Although slaveholders often boasted that slavery was superior to free labor, in part because of its built-in social welfare system, slaves frequently became public dependents. Aged, infirm, or insane slaves could be found in jails, poorhouses, or chained in the basement of the county courthouse, sometimes with their owners contributing an annual fee to the county for their support.[42]

The Civil War produced poverty and dislocation on a new scale. Paul Escott has demonstrated that the Civil War also helped to produce a new view of government activism in the South, as southern whites willingly turned to both state and Confederate governments for relief. The war seemed to sweep away not only a labor system but also some fundamental assumptions about government: "Abandoning ideas of limited government, southerners demanded that the authorities undertake new responsibilities and provide relief." Ordinary citizens urged the Confederacy to regulate the economy, set prices, ration food, and run the railroads. Most of all, they wanted the government to provide direct assistance to those whom the war had impoverished. Although the poor laws were still in effect and should have been available to assist these newly destitute, their stigma made it unthinkable for the wives and children of soldiers to enter the poorhouse.[43]

Southern state governments began to spend unprecedented amounts on poor relief. Direct public aid on a grand scale became available, reversing temporarily the nineteenth-century trend toward charity.[44] According to one scholar, at least one-fourth of the white population of Alabama was receiving state or county assistance during the last two years of the war.[45] Yet expenditure did not match need: "In contrast to the relatively lavish benefits provided for the families of the Northern forces, all resources of relief for soldiers' families in the Confederate states were meager indeed."[46] Bread riots broke out in several southern cities, including Mobile and Richmond. The Confederate government began to provide direct relief, using the largess of the tax-in-kind to distribute food directly to the poor.[47]

The federal government also contributed to the relief efforts. As Confederate territory came under Union control, the U.S. Army attempted to provide assistance to the local population, usually in the form of rations. In New Orleans, for example, Gen. Benjamin Butler experimented with a public works program, putting one thousand unemployed men to work cleaning streets and wharves. In addition he made contributions of federal monies to the local orphanage and charity hospital.[48]

As the war ended, the Freedmen's Bureau and the U.S. Army both launched massive relief programs to prevent starvation in the region. In some of the larger cities, the bureau opened soup kitchens and in other places experimented with work relief projects.[49] Whites as well as blacks received assistance from the Freedmen's Bureau; in Alabama, whites received more aid than did blacks. Regardless of this fact, white landowners especially resented the relief efforts of the Freedmen's Bureau, claiming that the freedmen would not work so long as free rations were available.[50]

As John Hope Franklin has written, "One of the ironies of Confederate reconstruction is that those in the South who inveighed most bitterly against the federal government and its agencies were the beneficiaries of their largesse. Between 1865 and 1869 no Southern state provided as much public welfare in so many different areas as the federal government.... By 1867 there were forty-six Bureau hospitals serving whites as well as blacks [in addition to providing millions of rations of food]."[51]

Taking advantage of the relief provided by the federal government, state governments began to focus their attentions exclusively on veterans and their families, leaving problems of freedmen and other poor whites to the federal agencies. State governments launched vast programs for pensions, supported homes for veterans and their widows, and provided money for artificial limbs.[52] Relief of the civilian poor, in contrast, was a burdensome obligation that was evaded whenever possible. Disputes between different government agencies were common as each tried to establish that a given pauper was the responsibility of another jurisdiction.[53]

But while southern states tried to avoid direct relief to the poor, they did attempt to bolster white solidarity by a series of public welfare provisions that would benefit whites only. An obvious example, public schools established throughout the region were often used for the education of white children only. Many justified the exclusion of blacks from these public facilities on the grounds that the Freedmen's Bureau schools were taking care of the educational needs of southern blacks.[54]

The Civil War and Reconstruction undoubtedly changed the face of social welfare provision in the South. Hundreds of thousands of southerners—black and white—received public assistance for the first time in their lives. What is not yet clear is how that experience affected the South's views on welfare. Did the events of 1861 to 1877 convince southerners that government had a vital role to play in welfare? Did white southerners come to resent federal welfare (because it was seen to be helping blacks) and embrace state welfare instead (because it was largely directed at veterans)? What, if anything, was the long-term impact of the Civil War and Reconstruction on southern welfare policies? These questions await thorough investigation.

The social welfare history of the postbellum South is more complex, and its story has not yet been entirely reconstructed. Developments such as rapid industrialization, significant population shifts through migration, the growth of large urban centers, the emergence of a powerful middle class, and conflicts over segregation, disfranchisement, land tenure, and Democratic party hegemony left their mark on the provision of assistance to the poor and dependent. However, the scholarship on this period has yet to perform a systematic analysis of social welfare policies or practices in the South.

The postbellum South continued to struggle with the issue of race and social welfare institutions. Some states attempted to integrate facilities; for instance, Georgia admitted blacks to the previously all-white insane asylum in 1865. Other states, such as Virginia, Kentucky, Tennessee, and Texas, established separate institutions for their insane freedmen. But in many localities, the common practice was to put dangerously insane blacks in jail and let others wander at large.[55]

The county poorhouse continued to be a prominent feature of public welfare until the 1930s, but the characteristics of its inmates changed considerably over time. As specialized institutions for certain dependent classes continued to proliferate (orphanages, veterans' homes, maternity homes, institutions for the blind/deaf/insane), the almshouses slowly evolved into homes for the elderly, a population not served by as many asylums. Partly because the state, county, and local governments were helping to fund so many institutions, and partly because of the fear of giving money to support the undeserving poor, public funding for the poorhouses was miserly, and conditions in them were frequently horrific. In Alabama the state spent less per poorhouse inmate than did any other state studied in a national survey of 1923. Yet, as Wayne Flynt has observed, the state could find money for those things it considered important. In 1910 the legislature appropriated five hundred thousand dollars for relief of needy Confederate veterans and their widows and provided a soldiers' home so that veterans would not have to become residents of the poorly funded almshouses.[56]

Although postbellum city governments throughout the region spent considerable sums of money on poor relief in the form of direct payments, no scholarly research on this form of public aid yet has been published. And the investigation of state welfare policies in the South has barely begun. As a result, the appearance has been that southern social welfare was largely a function of private charity, with the notable exception of state-assisted Confederate veterans' homes and pension systems.[57] The record of private charities has been far better researched. We know a good deal about missionary societies, settlement houses, women's clubs, temperance unions, mutual benefit associations, labor unions, public health movements, free kindergartens, and other private endeavors.[58] It is understandable that scholars have assumed the absence of state aid.

Indeed, in the late nineteenth century, the system of charitable agencies and reformers became exceedingly complex. The states began to search for ways of ordering the anarchy in private and public philanthropy. After Massachusetts established the first state central authority in social welfare in 1863, other states followed suit. The first southern state to do so was North Carolina, where a Board of Public Charities was created by the General Assembly in 1869 to supervise all the charitable and penal institutions of the state. By World War I, six southern states had welfare boards, although those in existence had quite limited authority.[59]

In this, as in many other areas, southern practices grew more similar to social welfare policies elsewhere in the country. While southern social welfare continued to have distinct regional characteristics, the story of the twentieth century may well be the demise of southern distinctiveness. Steven Noll has suggested recently that national social welfare organizations worked hard to penetrate the South in the twentieth century and began to have a significant impact on the region's policies and practices. Progressive southerners "looked explicitly northward" for reform models, and northern philanthropists and social workers responded enthusiastically. Money and support from northern philanthropies, such as the Rockefeller and Sage Foundations, as well as pressure from national organizations, such as the National Association of Social Workers, helped to bring the South into the mainstream of standardized social welfare practice.[60]

Perhaps even more important in bringing the South in line with national social welfare trends was the powerful influence of the federal government through its New Deal programs. Although this volume does not cover the years of the New Deal, the importance of the New Deal to southern social welfare history in the twentieth century should be noted. Elizabeth Wisner has speculated that "in no section of the country has the impact of federal funds and federal standards in the administration of public assistance and child welfare programs been greater than in the Southern region." Moreover, federal programs such as the Social Security Administration preempted the traditional principle of local responsibility for the support of the poor.[61]

Before the New Deal

To date there has been no historiography of southern social welfare history. The most important historiography of southern history, *Interpreting Southern History*, had no entries for charity, social welfare, or welfare.[62] This anthology, then, will serve as both history and historiography.

Has the South's social welfare history been different from that of the rest of the country? Most scholars have assumed so. Wisner believed that "the economic and social institutions of the Old South set that region apart from the rest of the nation and cast a long shadow on those services of traditional concern to the social worker."[63] John Hope Franklin argued that "the South lagged behind the rest of the country in social reform generally because of its obsession with defending slavery and engaging in the struggle for power in national politics."[64] The essays in this book offer no firm consensus on the perennial question of southern distinctiveness. Peter Wallenstein's essay in this collection, for example, recognizes that both North and South experienced the Civil War but suggests that the South's experience was one of tremendous devastation that resulted in vastly increased needs in the realm of social welfare provision. For social welfare history, the Civil War had a different impact in the South than elsewhere in the country. By way of contrast, James Tuten's account of the evolution of the Jefferson County Poor Farm parallels the transition of poor farms and poorhouses in the United States generally, implying that the South's differences might qualify as degree rather than kind.

It should be immediately apparent that women's history has been an important influence on the essays in this volume. In fact, the majority might be considered essays in women's history. Susan Barber and Susan Hamburger, for example, examine institutions created by women for the benefit of other women. Other essays, such as those by Georgina Hickey and myself, utilize gender as a central analytic device. Clearly women's history has played a key role in fostering current social welfare history, as historians in this field have been taking insights gained from their own discipline and have been applying them to new topics.

Although interest in gender seems to permeate the volume, race and class are certainly not absent from the discussion. The authors in general presume that social welfare is a point of interclass contact and imply that social welfare is central to understanding the South's nineteenth-century class formation as well as twentieth-century class relations. Several of the essays, such as those by Wallenstein and Joan Marie Johnson, are directly concerned with the interactions of black and white southerners or with the impact of racism in the distribution of the region's resources. Other essays examine the contact, and the conflict, between middle-class reformers and working-class or poor southerners. Lee Polansky and Mazie Hough, for example, interpret the efforts to assist (and control) delinquent mill-village girls and unmarried mothers.

The majority of the essays are focused on the postbellum, or New South, period. There are good reasons for this concentration. Many of the institutions and movements of progressivism were effectively social welfare programs. Training schools, maternity homes, charity organization societies, orphanages, and settlement houses—the staples of progressivism—are also central to welfare in the period. In addition, documentary sources are more readily available for this period. This book highlights the fact that more attention is focused currently on social welfare in the postbellum years than in the antebellum period; still less attention has been devoted to the colonial era.

Several of the selections in this book might also be seen as representatives of a new form of institutional history. Rather than chronicling the establishment, development, official policies, and leadership of a given institution, these authors see the institution as a site where agendas meet, negotiate, and struggle, while simultaneously responding to external pressures, such as limited funding, changing labor markets, shifting political winds, and uncontrollable demographic trends. Essays by Tuten and Wallenstein use this approach, which makes the institution the setting rather than the topic.

These essays engage many of the common themes in social welfare history. The issue of social control versus humanitarianism, for example, appears in the following in much the same degree as it appears in current literature on nonsouthern topics. That is, the question of social control is no longer the central debate, but it continues to be a tertiary issue.

However, these essays also focus very clearly on regional distinctiveness. By examining the role of the South's unique political economy, the impact of slavery and racism on social institutions, and the region's experience of war and reconstruction, this volume insists that the South's social welfare story is no mere carbon copy of the nation's.

Future Directions

Because southern social welfare history is still an emerging field, there seems to be no limit to the topics waiting to be explored. The suggestions that follow are hardly an exhaustive list.

Although central to discussions of social policy in other regions, there appears to be little work under way on immigrants and social welfare in the South. Self-help efforts, such as mutual benefit societies by the working class (black and white), have yet to receive their full due either. Readers will notice that most of the scholarship here focuses either on public institutions or on private associations; few scholars are attempting to merge the two and treat them together. The bulk of current scholarship focuses on urban settings, while the rural South's social welfare history remains underexplored.

As this anthology demonstrates, there is an especially large void in southern colonial history. The scarcity of usual welfare history sources for this period makes research particularly challenging, and historians will have to stretch their imaginations in order to find usable documentation. But early parish records (as in the case of Virginia) seem a likely spot in which to look for evidence about support for dependent women and children, for example. Wills and probate records, housed in county courthouses throughout the region (and often copied and/or microfilmed for use in state archives and other regional research facilities) can offer a patient scholar sources of information regarding the southern extended family and its role in caring for dependents of all sorts, including the elderly. Some historical imagination applied to the vast body of Revolutionary War warrants and petitions for reimbursement for goods and services rendered might uncover evidence about contemporary southern views on citizenship and welfare in the new republic.

Use of nineteenth-century records is growing, but in some cases utilizing those records to the fullest will require a good deal of scholarly tenacity. Government records at all three levels (local, state, and federal) are available. County court records offer a great range of opportunities. Wills and estate records might be used to examine the question of how (and how well) planters actually cared for their elderly and infirm slaves. Dependent slaves also appear regularly in records of county poorhouses and other county institutions. The extensive records of the Freedmen's Bureau have scarcely been mined by scholars interested in social welfare in the South. Records of Overseers of the Poor and the Orphans Courts are logical, and underutilized, resources as well. The federal census of 1850 began providing data on pauper support in every state in the social statistics schedules. City council records, available for numerous southern communities for the later nineteenth century, can be studied for accounts of municipal relief, urban services and social welfare, and debates by southern city-builders over the proper role of public provision in the context of New South boosterism.

Unofficial records are plentiful as well, although they can be more difficult to locate. Church records, many of which have never been archived and remain with local churches, can be used to explore numerous topics, including foreign missions as southern charity, religious benevolency toward slaves, the use of charity for purposes of sectarian conversion, and Hebrew benevolent societies and southern Judaism. Records of numerous private charities and reform organizations are scattered in public libraries, state archives, and regional research facilities, such as the Southern Historical Collection at Chapel Hill. One of the challenges for southern scholars will be to reexamine topics in southern progressivism with social welfare in mind. Child labor, convict leasing, eugenics, public health crusades, mothers' pensions, and dozens of other subjects are waiting to be considered as problems of social welfare.

Records for national organizations that had southern branches or chapters tend to be overlooked as a source for southern social welfare history. The papers of the NAACP and the National Urban League, both held in the Library of Congress, offer plenty of opportunities to examine black self-help strategies as well as organizational efforts to overcome the segregation of social welfare provision.

The national welfare journals, which emerged in the 1890s to publish studies and polemics by social workers and social scientists, are filled with material on the South. Such journals as *Charities, Current Opinion,* and *Survey* are useful, as are *Literary Digest, Outlook,* and the *American Mercury.*

Finally a large number of theses for the master's degree in social work produced in the years between 1920 and 1950 can be valuable sources for historical researchers. The School of Social Work at Tulane University and the Richmond Professional Institute (and perhaps others as well) sent many students out to write theses on social welfare topics in the South. Although often concerned with different issues than those of historians in the 1990s, these works are nevertheless important resources.

Southern scholars have contributions to make to the discussion of state formation and the trajectory of the welfare state. The ideology of states' rights, for so long a near-southern monopoly, has received in the 1980s and 1990s new life outside the region as justification for the dismemberment of the welfare state. The language of welfare reform has often had a southern accent, as politicians speak of returning power to the states at the expense of the federal government. The South's history of social welfare seems all the more pertinent here. There is much work to be done. This anthology will have succeeded if it encourages others to follow up on this beginning.

NOTES

1. Even scholarship on the South's poor or working class (or the "plain folk"), which might be expected to cover social welfare topics, has been concerned with other issues, such as the relationships between planters and nonslaveholding whites or the culture of mill villages, and has left unexplored questions of what working-class southerners thought about the welfare state or other social welfare issues. See for example, Bill Cecil-Fronsman, *Common Whites: Class and Culture in Antebellum North Carolina* (Lexington: University Press of Kentucky, 1992); or I. A. Newby, *Plain Folk in the New South: Social Change and Cultural Persistence, 1880–1915* (Baton Rouge: Louisiana State University Press, 1989).

2. Clarke Chambers has made a similar observation about the field of social welfare history; articles in social welfare history are usually categorized as family, women's, immigration,

urban, black, or local history. "'Uphill All the Way': Reflections on the Course and Study of Welfare History," *Social Service Review* 66 (December 1992): 493.

3. Clarke A. Chambers, "Toward a Redefinition of Welfare History," *Journal of American History* 73 (September 1986): 407.

4. Gerald N. Grob, *Mental Institutions in America: Social Policy to 1875* (New York: Free Press, 1973); David J. Rothman, *The Discovery of the Asylum: Social Order and Disorder in the New Republic* (Boston: Little Brown, 1971); Allen F. Davis, *Spearheads for Reform: The Social Settlements and the Progressive Movement, 1890–1914* (New York: Oxford University Press, 1967); Herbert Gans, "Redefining the Settlement's Function for the War on Poverty," *Social Work* 9 (October 1964): 3–12.

5. Walter Trattner, *From Poor Law to Welfare State: A History of Social Welfare in America* (New York: Free Press, 1974); Philip Klein, *From Philanthropy to Social Welfare* (San Francisco: Jossey-Bass, 1971); Benjamin Klebaner, *Public Poor Relief in America, 1790–1960* (New York: Arno Press, 1976); Clarke A. Chambers, *Seedtime of Reform: American Social Service and Social Action, 1918–1933* (Minneapolis: University of Minnesota Press, 1963).

6. Roy Lubove, *The Professional Altruist: The Emergence of Social Work as a Career, 1880–1930* (Cambridge: Harvard University Press, 1965). As Chambers has noted, much early social welfare history was written by social workers and public policy practitioners. Their interests undoubtedly helped to fuel the concern with the professionalization of social work. Chambers, "Toward a Redefinition," 411–12.

7. Chambers, "Toward a Redefinition," 416.

8. See especially Frances Fox Piven and Richard A. Cloward, *Regulating the Poor: The Functions of Public Welfare* (New York: Random House, 1971); Walter I. Trattner, ed., *Social Welfare or Social Control? Some Historical Reflections on Regulating the Poor* (Knoxville: University of Tennessee Press, 1983); Marvin E. Gettleman, "Philanthropy as Social Control in Late Nineteenth-Century America: Some Hypotheses and Data on the Rise of Social Work," *Societas* 5 (Winter 1975): 49–59.

9. Such as Andrew Billingsley and Jeanne M. Giovannoni, *Children of the Storm: Black Children and American Child Welfare* (New York: Harcourt, Brace, Jovanovich, 1972); Edyth Ross, *The Black Heritage in Social Welfare* (Metuchen, N.J.: Scarecrow Press, 1978); Alvin Kogut, "The Negro and the Charity Organization Society in the Progressive Era," *Social Service Review* 44 (March 1970): 11–21; Sandra M. O'Donnell, "The Care of Dependent African-American Children in Chicago: The Struggle Between Black Self-Help and Professionalism," *Journal of Social History* 27 (Summer 1994): 763–76; Elisabeth Lasch-Quinn, *Black Neighbors: Race and the Limits of Reform in the American Settlement House Movement, 1890–1945* (Chapel Hill: University of North Carolina Press, 1993).

10. Important works include Mimi Abramovitz, *Regulating the Lives of Women: Social Welfare Policy from Colonial Times to the Present* (Boston: South End Press, 1988); Lori Ginzberg, *Women and the Work of Benevolence: Morality, Politics, and Class in the Nineteenth Century United States* (New Haven: Yale University Press, 1990); Linda Gordon, *Pitied But Not Entitled: Single Mothers and the History of Welfare* (New York: Free Press, 1994); Regina Kunzel, *Fallen Women, Problem Girls: Unmarried Mothers and the Professionalization of Social Work, 1890–1945* (New Haven: Yale University Press, 1993); Molly Ladd-Taylor, *Mother-*

Work: Women, Child Welfare, and the State, 1890–1930 (Urbana: University of Illinois Press, 1994); Marian Morton, And Sin No More: Social Policy and Unwed Mothers in Cleveland, 1855–1990 (Columbus: Ohio State University Press, 1993).

11. Including, for example, Priscilla Ferguson Clement, Welfare and the Poor in the Nineteenth-Century City: Philadelphia, 1800–1854 (Rutherford, N.J.: Associated University Presses, 1985); Ruth Crocker, Social Work and Social Order: The Settlement Movement in Two Industrial Cities, 1889–1930 (Urbana: University of Illinois Press, 1992); Rivka Lissak, Pluralism and Progressives: Hull House and the New Immigrants (Chicago: University of Chicago Press, 1989); Reena Sigman Friedman, These Are Our Children: Jewish Orphanages in the United States, 1880–1925 (Hanover, N.H.: University Press of New England, 1994).

12. Michael Katz, Poverty and Policy in American History (Philadelphia: Academic Press, 1983); Mary Odem, Delinquent Daughters: Protecting and Policing Adolescent Female Sexuality in the United States, 1885–1920 (Chapel Hill: University of North Carolina Press, 1995); Beverly Stadum, Poor Women and Their Families: Hard Working Charity Cases, 1900–1930 (Albany: State University of New York Press, 1992).

13. For example, Linda Gordon, Pitied But Not Entitled: Single Mothers and the History of Welfare (New York: Free Press, 1994); Theda Skocpol, Protecting Soldiers and Mothers: The Political Origins of Social Policy in the United States (Cambridge: Belknap Press, Harvard University Press, 1992); Seth Koven and Sonya Michel, "Gender and the Origins of the Welfare State," Radical History Review 43 (Winter 1989): 112–19; Seth Koven and Sonya Michel, eds., Mothers of a New World: Maternalist Politics and the Origins of Welfare States (New York: Routledge, 1993); and Ann Orloff, The Politics of Pensions: A Comparative Analysis of Britain, Canada, and the United States, 1880–1940 (Madison: University of Wisconsin Press, 1993).

14. The discussions in the 1990s about foster care versus orphanages, for example, were informed by such works as Marilyn Holt, The Orphan Trains: Placing Out in America (Lincoln: University of Nebraska Press, 1992); Hyman Bogen, The Luckiest Orphans: A History of the Hebrew Orphan Asylum of New York (Urbana: University of Illinois Press, 1992); Nurith Zmora, Orphanages Reconsidered: Child Care Institutions in Progressive Era Baltimore (Philadelphia: Temple University Press, 1994); Eric Schneider, In the Web of Class: Delinquents and Reformers in Boston, 1810s-1930s (New York: New York University Press, 1992); and Peter C. Holloran, Boston's Wayward Children: Social Services for Homeless Children, 1830–1930 (Rutherford, N.J.: Associated University Presses, 1989).

15. The closest thing to a general history of southern social welfare policy to date is Elizabeth Wisner's pioneering Social Welfare in the South from Colonial Times to World War I (Baton Rouge: Louisiana State University Press, 1970). As laudable as the book is, it has its limitations (as the author herself noted.) Not only does it lack coverage of the developments of the twentieth century, it also leaves out significant topics in social welfare, such as the care of dependent children.

16. Wisner, Social Welfare in the South, 11–12.

17. Virginia Bernhard, "Poverty and the Social Order in Seventeenth-Century Virginia," Virginia Magazine of History and Biography 85 (April 1977): 146, 149, 151.

18. Barbara Bellows, Benevolence among Slaveholders: Assisting the Poor in Charleston, 1670–1860 (Baton Rouge: Louisiana State University Press, 1993), 3. North Carolina passed

a general poor law in 1755, but later amendments to the act indicated that many settlements in the colony had failed to appoint vestries, thus providing no relief for the poor. Wisner, *Social Welfare in the South*, 14–15.

19. Although less common, the records nevertheless give testament to the practice. Wisner reports one instance in Arkansas as late as 1897. *Social Welfare in the South*, 40.

20. Michael Katz, *In the Shadow of the Poorhouse: A Social History of Welfare in America* (New York: Basic Books, 1986), 14.

21. Bellows, *Benevolence among Slaveholders*, 5.

22. Joseph Cepuran, *Public Assistance and Child Welfare: The Virginia Pattern, 1646 to 1964* (Charlottesville, Va.: Institute of Government, 1968), 10.

23. Bernhard, "Poverty and the Social Order," 153–55.

24. Wisner, *Social Welfare in the South*, 32–33.

25. Trattner, *From Poor Law to Welfare State*, 23.

26. For the later nineteenth century, see Peter J. Rachleff, *Black Labor in the South: Richmond, Virginia, 1865–1890* (Philadelphia: Temple University Press, 1984), 13–25.

27. Crandall A. Shifflett, *Patronage and Poverty in the Tobacco South, Louisa County, Virginia, 1860–1900* (Knoxville: University of Tennessee Press, 1982), 71.

28. Wisner, *Social Welfare in the South*, 22.

29. Wisner, *Social Welfare in the South*, 24.

30. Katz, *In the Shadow of the Poorhouse*, 15. Katz argues that rural counties closed their almshouses because most rural dependents were slaves who were to be cared for by their owners.

31. Bellows, *Benevolence among Slaveholders*, 136–37. Private orphanages predated the publicly funded ones. The first in the South appears to have been the Bethesda orphanage near Savannah, Georgia. Wisner, *Social Welfare in the South*, 19.

32. Cepuran, *Public Assistance*, 11.

33. Wisner, *Social Welfare in the South*, 55; Cepuran, *Public Assistance*, 11; Peter Wallenstein, *From Slave South to New South: Public Policy in Georgia in the Nineteenth Century* (Chapel Hill: University of North Carolina Press, 1987), 29.

34. Wallenstein, *Slave South to New South*, 24–26.

35. Wallenstein, *Slave South to New South*, 74.

36. Bellows, *Benevolence among Slaveholders*, 25.

37. Gail S. Murray, "Charity within the Bounds of Race and Class: Female Benevolence in the Old South," *South Carolina Historical Magazine* 96 (January 1995): 57.

38. Bellows, *Benevolence among Slaveholders*, 71–73.

39. Bellows, *Benevolence among Slaveholders*, 105.

40. Wallenstein, *Slave South to New South*, 77.

41. Bellows, *Benevolence among Slaveholders*, 36, 46.

42. Bellows, *Benevolence among Slaveholders*, 36, 178; Roy M. Brown, *Public Poor Relief in North Carolina* (Chapel Hill: University of North Carolina Press, 1928), 52.

43. Paul Escott, "'The Cry of the Sufferers': The Problem of Welfare in the Confederacy," *Civil War History* 23 (September 1977): 230–31; Wisner, *Social Welfare in the South*, 48.

44. Trattner, *From Poor Law to Welfare State*, 73.

45. Wayne Flynt, *Poor But Proud: Alabama's Poor Whites* (Tuscaloosa: University of Alabama Press, 1989), 40.

46. Wisner, *Social Welfare in the South*, 51.

47. Escott, "Cry of the Sufferers," 234–40.

48. Robert H. Bremner, *The Public Good: Philanthropy and Welfare in the Civil War Era* (New York: Knopf, 1980), 91.

49. Wisner, *Social Welfare in the South*, 78.

50. Flynt, *Poor But Proud*, 52–53; Wisner, *Social Welfare in the South*, 75.

51. John Hope Franklin, "Public Welfare in the South During Reconstruction, 1865–1880," *Social Service Review* 44 (December 1970): 383.

52. Wallenstein, *Slave South to New South*, 131–39.

53. Bremner, *The Public Good*, 150.

54. Franklin, "Public Welfare in the South," 383.

55. Wallenstein, *Slave South to New South*, 147; Bremner, *The Public Good*, 167.

56. Flynt, *Poor But Proud*, 184, 187.

57. Dewey Grantham, *Southern Progressivism: The Reconciliation of Progress and Tradition* (Knoxville: University of Tennessee Press, 1983), 217–18.

58. A few examples of this voluminous literature are Lasch-Quinn, *Black Neighbors;* John P. McDowell, *The Social Gospel Movement in the South: The Women's Home Mission Movement in the Methodist Episcopal Church, South 1886–1939* (Chapel Hill: University of North Carolina Press, 1982); Elsa Barkely Brown, "Womanist Consciousness: Maggie Lena Walker and the Independent Order of Saint Luke," *Signs* 14 (Spring 1989): 610–33; Dorothy Salem, *To Better Our World: Black Women in Organized Reform, 1890–1920* (Brooklyn: Carlson, 1990); Anastatia Sims, "'The Sword of the Spirit': The WCTU and Moral Reform in North Carolina, 1883–1933," *North Carolina Historical Review* 64 (October 1987): 395–414.

59. Wisner, *Social Welfare in the South*, 114–16.

60. Steven Noll, *Feeble-Minded in Our Midst: Institutions for the Mentally Retarded in the South, 1900–1940* (Chapel Hill: University of North Carolina Press, 1995), 9, 157.

61. Wisner, *Social Welfare in the South*, 9, 45.

62. John B. Boles and Evelyn Thomas Nolen, eds., *Interpreting Southern History: Historiographical Essays in Honor of Sanford W. Higginbotham* (Baton Rouge: Louisiana State University Press, 1987).

63. Wisner, *Social Welfare in the South*, vi.

64. Franklin, "Public Welfare in the South," 380.

PART ONE

State Policies

PART ONE

State Policies

Laissez Faire and the Lunatic Asylum

State Welfare Institutions in Georgia—

The First Half-Century, 1830s–1880s

PETER WALLENSTEIN

During the Age of Jackson, Americans formulated definitions of social problems and deployed state power to seek solutions to them. Through the remainder of the nineteenth century, American states developed various types of social welfare institutions. Georgia participated in those developments, even exemplified them, though its peculiarities as a slave society, its percentage of black residents, and its travails through Civil War and Reconstruction shaped developments there. In this essay, Georgia will bear the burden of representing the southern variant of that history.

Before the 1830s, Georgia had no mental hospital, nor had it any school tailored to the needs of blind or deaf residents. That situation greatly changed over the next two generations. By the 1850s Georgia had established all three kinds of institutions for whites, and by the 1880s it had done so for blacks, too. Thus the kinds of social welfare institutions that sprouted over the northern landscape came to be featured in the South as well. Though developments in the South tended to lag behind those in the North, the lag was brief, as the South adapted northern models in much the same way that the North had adapted Western European approaches in social welfare.

This essay will explore the background to Georgia's institutions for deaf, blind, or insane people. It will suggest answers to such questions as: How did broad social, economic, and political currents shape the history of Georgia's welfare institutions? What rationales, what objectives, characterized Georgia's facilities? To what extent were they public, and to what extent private? How did the state go about providing financial support for them? How did the state and the institutions go about incorporating black students and inmates into facilities that started out exclusively white? Along the way, this point of entry into public policy and social welfare in nineteenth-century America will suggest implications that go beyond the three institutions that are its focus.

American states undertook responsibilities in the nineteenth century that, almost everywhere and in every respect, far outreached anything that the colonies had attempted. Not until sometime after independence, indeed for the most part after the War of 1812, did the new departure develop. A constellation of changes had to emerge before it could. For one thing, nothing could be attempted without financial support, and only in the 1830s did states come into the kinds of funds that might facilitate a much more active role in social welfare.[1] For another, the broad changes often associated with the Age of Jackson brought a sense of optimism that social problems could effectively be addressed, coupled with a sense of urgency.

The liberty that so many Americans celebrated in the Age of Jackson brought with it responsibilities as well as privileges, vulnerability as well as empowerment. In Georgia only white men could vote, only they had full liberty of contract, and only they had full responsibility for their dependents as well as for themselves.

Most Americans would never be white men, and none started out that way. In terms of qualifying for full citizenship in antebellum America, deficiencies in age could be remedied, as boys became men, but deficiencies in race or gender could never be. White men deserved liberty, went the dominant belief, and they were alike empowered and compelled to compete in the land of liberty. All other people would dwell in a world of paternalism, where their needs would be looked after if they stayed in their designated places and played their assigned roles. Special environments must envelop all these exceptions. Plantations might harbor African Americans, for example; an Indian territory might hold America's other large racial minority.[2]

And other groups? The family would protect most white women and children. For various groups of whites—residents elsewhere than in the land of liberty—private philanthropy, user fees, and governmental support could combine to foster other settings. Common day schools might prepare most young citizens for the roles they must play as adults. Special live-in environments might assist some youngsters, in particular those bearing the burdens of blindness or deafness, to grow up as self-reliant citizens. Moreover, some adults would appear to lose their minds, and a special setting—through commitment or coerced participation, if necessary—might assist them in finding themselves again and returning to full responsibility. Thus, laissez faire could be squared with the lunatic asylum, liberty with paternalism, individual responsibility with social welfare.

Not all social welfare institutions functioned in identical ways. Crucial to their differences is the distinction between social welfare and social control, between benevolence and coercion. The new institutions stretched along a continuum between social welfare and social control. Each displayed both features, yet social welfare better characterized those whose clients were voluntary, social control those that involved force. The schools, whether for blind students or for deaf ones, represented more the social welfare side of these efforts, the mental institution the social control side. All, however, came equipped with an ideology that clients should emerge better able to support themselves, better able to run their own lives.

Georgia exemplified the southern variant of the new social welfare policies that flourished in the Age of Jackson and that continued to develop in the years that followed. By two measures—one chronological, the other financial—the Georgia experience suggested that social control outweighed social welfare in importance. The mental hospital took far more public dollars than did either of the special schools. Moreover, it developed before those schools did, whether for white Georgians before the Civil War or for black Georgians after Emancipation.

Ideas, Institutions, and Finances: Precursors and Preconditions

David J. Rothman's book, *Discovery of the Asylum*, launched modern historical studies of American social welfare policy.[3] Rothman emphasized the emergence of penitentiaries and insane asylums in Early National and Jacksonian America. He presented them as social factories designed to manufacture more-competent citizens and intended, like their products, to be self-supporting as much as possible. That is, the institutions should help pay their own way through inmate labor; when those inmates left the institutions to return to the wider world, as it was expected—or at least hoped—they would, they should be able to run their own affairs, support themselves, and do so in a socially acceptable manner.

Rothman's insights have wider application than the more urban, more industrial American Northeast from whose history he derived the bulk of his material. They apply to Georgia. Peter McCandless's book on the treatment of insanity in South Carolina is generally consistent with Rothman's approach.[4] And, while Rothman emphasized institutions of social control—the penitentiary and the mental institution—his approach also works when applied to schools for deaf or blind people.

Jacksonian reformers believed that the state should foster all those institutions, but the institutions should rely as little as possible on public funds. In asylums and schools alike, a client's stay should be temporary, not permanent, and should result in demonstrably changed behavior. Clients should emerge cured of their curable liabilities. Blind people, though still unable to see, might be able to read and to support themselves. Deaf people would not hear any better, but they, too, should emerge with the tools of self-sufficiency. Blind or deaf, they should emerge empowered to compete, and thrive, in the Jacksonian world. And inmates of the mental institution would, it was hoped, again find their full faculties.

Critical to the early development of all these institutions was the question of how to finance them. It is no historical accident that Georgia launched its new initiatives in the 1830s or that it substantially increased its spending in the late 1850s. And the Georgia story may prove instructive as historians explore developments in other southern states.

Americans have demonstrated little fondness for paying high taxes. That is, they have displayed a stronger desire to support a wide array of expenditures than they have a wish to pay the taxes that would fully fund those ventures. The 1830s brought Americans in every state, in the North and South alike, a nontax bonanza of public revenue that permitted them to have their fiscal cake and eat it too. The federal treasury ran a huge surplus, derived from revenues from the sale of western lands, but national politics led to decisions not to spend much of that money directly on education or transportation. Congress determined to apportion the surplus to the states according to federal representation.[5] Georgia therefore found itself able to hold its taxes down, even to reduce them, while investing unprecedented funds in a bank, a railroad, higher education, a fund for common schools—and a mental institution.

The 1850s brought a similar windfall and similar budgetary results. The railroad that had been launched in the late 1830s, the Western and Atlantic, took a long time to get completed, but then it began to generate huge profits for its investors, the taxpayers of Georgia, who chose to replicate the program of the 1830s. The state proved able to hold the line on taxes, even reduce rates, while launching major new initiatives—in railroad finance, once again, and in the support of common schools and higher education—and greatly increasing its spending on a mental institution and on schools for deaf or blind white Georgians.[6]

In 1852 Gov. Howell Cobb proposed that "one-third of the large revenue of the State Road shall be devoted to the maintenance of the three great objects of the State's charity: the Lunatic Asylum, [the school for] the Deaf and Dumb, and the school for the Blind."[7] And so it was. More than in the 1830s, in the late 1850s Georgia could and did increase its spending on institutions of social welfare and social control.

The development of Georgia's social welfare facilities demonstrated the diffusion of men, institutions, and ideas in the late-eighteenth and early-nineteenth centuries. Therapeutic institutions for deaf people, blind people, and those considered mentally ill had their genesis principally in France in the late eighteenth century, though pioneer efforts also occurred in England, Germany, and the United States. In 1775 Abbé Charles Michel de l'Epeé founded a school for the deaf, where he matured a system of sign language to enable his students to communicate. Ten years later, Valentin Hauy adapted some of de l'Epeé's ideas when he founded a school to render blind people both literate and self-supporting. Hauy gave public demonstrations to obtain first private donations and then public support. During the French Revolution, the national government took over both schools and opened them to the poor.[8]

Another French citizen, Philippe Pinel, had the greatest influence in Europe in propounding "moral treatment" for the mentally afflicted. His methods called for institutions that were therapeutic and not merely custodial. Sharing many ideas with Pinel, but more directly important in America than he, were a British Quaker, William Tuke, who established the York Retreat in 1796 and had many Quaker contacts in the United States, and Benjamin Rush, a leading physician in Jeffersonian America and for thirty years a professor of medicine at the University of Pennsylvania.[9]

European institutions and ideas called some Americans' attention to the needs of the mentally troubled and the physically handicapped; they also provided examples of what could be done for such people. Schools for the deaf and the blind, however, needed teachers and funds. Private citizens in New England paid to send Thomas Hopkins Gallaudet to Europe to study at the school founded by de l'Epeé; there he learned methods for teaching the deaf. Gallaudet's training, along with a five thousand dollar appropriation by the state of Connecticut, made possible the first permanent institution for teaching the deaf in America. The American Asylum at Hartford for the Education and Instruction of the Deaf and Dumb opened in 1817. By 1823 similar schools had opened with state support in New York, Pennsylvania, and Kentucky. By 1843—on the eve of Georgia's decision to inaugurate its own school—such schools also opened in Ohio, Virginia, and Indiana.[10]

Within a few years, the story was repeated with schools for the blind. Samuel Gridley Howe visited schools in Edinburgh, Paris, and Berlin in 1831, and the next year the New England Asylum for the Purpose of Educating the Blind opened in Boston. By 1833 similar institutions opened in New York City and Philadelphia. Like the schools for the deaf, all three depended on both private contributions and state appropriations.[11] These early northern institutions contributed to the founding, about a generation later, of their counterparts in Georgia.

The Beginnings in Georgia: The First Generation, 1830s–1850s

In the quarter-century before the Civil War, Georgia developed institutions for its insane, deaf, and blind citizens. Georgia's welfare expenditures began in the prosperous mid-1830s, when the state received much of its revenue from nontax sources. Then, dependent on tax revenue for a time, social spending held at a low level through the 1840s. While seeming to demonstrate a return toward laissez faire, the more restricted level of public activity is better understood as displaying a reduction in resources, not a retrenchment in attitudes.[12] In the 1850s, as the Western and Atlantic Railroad again made large amounts of nontax revenue available for public use, Georgia enlarged its welfare facilities and further extended their benefits. The institutions for the insane, deaf, and blind absorbed 10 percent of state spending in the 1850s, more than education did.

Until the 1830s, local governments provided the only public assistance available to Georgians who were insane, deaf, or blind. Some such people received support from county or town "pauper" funds, and the legislature authorized Gwinnett and Talbot counties, for example, each to establish an "asylum for the lunatic and invalid poor." But in 1833 a deaf man named John J. Flournoy petitioned the legislature to inaugurate schooling for the deaf, and at the same time Tomlinson Fort, who had attended Benjamin Rush's medical school, led an effort to launch a state mental institution. Gov. Wilson Lumpkin endorsed both causes in 1834, and social welfare in Georgia soon began to follow the lead set elsewhere in the country.[13]

The Georgia legislature appropriated forty-four thousand dollars between 1837 and 1841 to erect an asylum at Milledgeville, the state capitol at that time, for insane white residents. When the institution first opened, the legislature authorized the county courts to commit persons they deemed "dangerous," but inmates were to be supported either by the counties that sent them or by private funds. In 1842 the legislature authorized the state to support, for the duration of their sentences, any lunatics sent from the nearby state penitentiary. Finally, in 1843, the legislature declared that the state would pay up to fifty dollars per year for the support of each pauper patient. By 1850 the annual appropriation for the maintenance of indigent inmates was six thousand dollars, and annual salaries at the asylum cost another six thousand dollars.[14]

Revenue from the state railroad permitted much higher expenditures for the asylum in the 1850s. During that decade, Georgia spent about $280,000 for building improvements, and total spending on the institution amounted to 8 percent of all state spending in the years 1856–60. The legislature appropriated three thousand dollars to buy for the asylum several slaves, "individual servants . . . who have been long employed and found to possess such qualities as render them particularly valuable to the Institution."[15] Growing rapidly, by 1861 the asylum had 322 inmates—187 men and 135 women. By 1860 the state spent an annual $15,000 for pauper patients and $44,400 for salaries and help.

Despite increased appropriations, the state bore less than two-thirds of the costs of maintaining the asylum. The institution obtained more than one-third of its revenue in 1859, for example, from patients who paid all or part of the costs of their keep. Roughly one-fourth of all patients paid all or part of their costs, and one-third of the revenue from paying patients came from clients from states other than Georgia. In addition the asylum's inmates produced much of the soap, clothing, vegetables, poultry, eggs, and milk consumed at the institution.

Dorothea Dix was a major advocate, in the South as well as the North, both of insane asylums, which she called "my chief work," and of penitentiary reform, her "secondary one." She influenced developments in states from Massachusetts to Mississippi, although she had little specific impact in Georgia. Still, she visited the state briefly a few times and was warmly received. In 1846 she found the Georgia penitentiary "excellently ordered" but the mental institution "very bad."[16] Later, however, she discerned considerable improvement.

Unlike most northern reformers, Miss Dix shunned the antislavery movement and thus retained her legitimacy in the South. As she wrote in 1850 from Mississippi, where she found legislators distracted from her cause by sectional politics, "I have *no* patience and no sympathy either with Northern Abolitionists or Southern agitators." In January 1859, the Georgia insane asylum's superintendent, Dr. Thomas F. Green, wrote her that he kept a "Dix room" in the institution's Centre Building "in the sincere hope, that it might be often occupied by the lady, whom it will be our peculiar pleasure always to honor." The next month, she visited Milledgeville, and soon afterward she procured various materials in the North for the institution. Dr. Green reported happily to her in July that the asylum was prospering. The number of patients had continued to increase, he wrote, yet "we have sent fifteen home, well, since you were with us."[17]

In 1835 the state began to offer schooling to deaf white Georgians. At first it set aside funds to educate students for as long as four years each at the American Asylum in Connecticut, and it paid six hundred dollars a year for a commissioner to make all the arrangements for applicants' educations and to convey them to the Hartford school. Six Georgia students attended in 1835. By 1838 the legislature had established a standing annual appropriation of $4,500 for the education of deaf Georgians.

In the 1840s, the state prepared for deaf education. The state commissioner arranged for the Hearn Manual-Training School at Cave Spring in Floyd County to establish a department for deaf students. After one of the school's teachers, Oliver P. Fannin, attended the Hartford institution to learn its teaching methods, the legislature directed that a portion of the annual appropriation be used to establish a new institution near the Hearn School, appropriated an additional four thousand dollars to pay for new buildings there, and rescinded its authorization for students to attend out-of-state schools at state expense.

The Georgia Asylum for the Deaf and Dumb opened in 1849. The school sought higher appropriations by sending students to Milledgeville to demonstrate their "proficiency" in exhibitions before the legislature, and in 1852 the annual appropriation was increased from forty-five hundred dollars to eight thousand dollars. Additional appropriations enabled the school to increase the variety of its facilities; to extend, from four years to six, the maximum period of its support for each student; and to expand its enrollment from twenty-five students in 1851 to forty-four by 1856.

The Georgia Asylum for the Deaf and Dumb was intended not merely as a place to impound children unable to hear but as a place to educate them to self-sufficiency. On every day but Sunday, students spent six hours on academic studies and three hours at work—young men in shops, young women in a "domestic" department. To support a request for a two-thousand-dollar appropriation to provide additional workshops, the institution observed that its shoe shop more than paid for itself: "We do not ask for means to support the trades; set them afloat and they will sustain themselves."[18] It received the requested funds.

The school accepted both paying and state-supported students. Tuition for paying pupils was $175 a year; prospective state beneficiaries had to be unable to pay that amount. The school reportedly attempted to treat both nonpaying and paying students alike: "All who are admitted, those who pay their own way as well as beneficiaries, are to compose one family, and be placed on a level [of] equality as to attention, dress and labor."[19]

Though the 1850 census enumerated 224 blind white residents of Georgia, no institution existed at that time to help them. After a blind teacher's arrival in Macon from Philadelphia in early 1851 energized the local community, private citizens subscribed $802 to begin schooling four blind children, two of them indigent. The teacher, Walter S. Fortescue, had graduated from the Pennsylvania Institute for the Blind and the University of Pennsylvania.[20]

Organizers of the Academy for the Blind in Macon sought state support and, to impress legislators with the educability of blind youths, emulated the Asylum for the Deaf in sending students to Milledgeville to display their proficiency. The organizers' petition to the legislature reported that twenty-five states had appropriated public money for educating the blind. Noting that the more successful schools were "private corporations founded in the charity of a community, governed by elective trustees, and sustained by aid from the State," they requested that the academy be "placed on a permanent basis with liberal advantages as well for indigent as for paying pupils." The Macon press supported the effort: "Let Georgia then add to existing institutions for the Deaf and Dumb and the Insane, another for . . . the Blind, that her beneficence may be dispersed impartially to all her unfortunate children, according to their respective need."[21]

The legislature responded in 1852 by incorporating the Academy for the Blind and appropriating five thousand dollars for each of the next two years. So far as public funds permitted, the school selected and educated indigent blind youths aged twelve to thirty, and paying students also attended. Having assumed partial responsibility for the academy, the legislature continued its support. In addition, between 1854 and 1859, the state spent sixty-nine thousand dollars to build and furnish a new home for the school. Most of the music and trade teachers were graduates and former teachers at the Pennsylvania or New York institutes for the blind.

Before 1865 public policy never addressed the question of black Georgians who happened to be deaf or blind, but the question did arise with regard to insanity. County court could order any black person, slave or free, confined in jail if it considered him or her to be a public nuisance or a danger to the community. The owner of an insane slave could, if he wished, maintain custody by posting a five-hundred-dollar bond to guarantee proper control. In 1853 Gov. Howell Cobb suggested making space for blacks at the insane asylum. The institution offered to do so, if properly funded and on a segregated basis. Seeing no compelling need as long as slavery controlled black Georgians and provided for them, the legislature waited until after Emancipation to make space for them at the asylum.[22]

In sum, the quarter-century before the Civil War brought a small constellation of new social welfare institutions to Georgia. Quite aside from common schools as well as institutions of higher education, these included a school for deaf white youngsters, a school for their blind counterparts, and a mental institution. In the 1830s Georgia constructed a foundation for its emerging social welfare policy, and in the 1850s it built a much more elaborate structure. The future seemed secure, with institutions and finances alike in place. Then came secession, war, devastation, transformation.

Transition through Desolation: The 1860s

All three of Georgia's social welfare institutions faced great trials during the Civil War. The state could not continue to increase its contributions to their maintenance and growth, and all faced disruption—even the prospect of relocation or closure. Nor did the state's diminished financial capacity ease after the war. And then came questions of whether any of the institutions could remain exclusively white.

Thus the three institutions faced new questions. After Emancipation, who would their clients be, and how many? Would any, even among white clients, be able to pay their own way, or must the state bear the full costs? Moreover, from where would state financial support come now that the tax-free bonanzas of the prewar years had vanished, and, because of Emancipation, the tax base had so greatly shrunk?[23]

The largest of the institutions, the insane asylum, had a fiscal experience that proved representative. During the war years, beginning in 1861 and continuing on into 1865, appropriations failed to keep up with a terrible inflation. Patients at the asylum continued to produce three to six thousand dollars worth of garden produce, milk, meat, poultry, eggs, lard, soap, and clothing each year. Revenue from paying patients, fourteen thousand dollars in 1860, continued in similar amounts, but in depreciating Confederate currency. The 1850s building program ended, but the cost of provisions, the most expensive item in the institution's wartime budget, climbed rapidly. The number of inmates declined by 10 percent during the war, from 322 in 1861 to 290 in late 1864, but appropriations for the support of pauper patients surged from seventeen to ninety-two thousand dollars. The institution continued its operations throughout the war.

The school for the deaf received ten thousand dollars in 1861, its last full year of operations before Reconstruction. After the two principal teachers left to enter the Confederate military, the board of trustees sent most pupils home and closed the school in March 1862. As late as 1864, however, the legislature appropriated twelve hundred dollars to support two orphan girls "who are left there, and who have no homes nor relatives to take care of them." To look after the two girls and the institution's property, the trustees selected a family to occupy the premises.[24]

The Georgia Academy for the Blind had to struggle also, but, like the insane asylum, it maintained operations through the Civil War. In December 1863, when the Confederate army required suitable accommodations for a military hospital near Macon, the academy relinquished its home and moved thirty miles southwest to Fort Valley. Funds or no funds, educational and building materials became unavailable. Although the academy had to economize and change location, it remained open. The principal could write in late 1864 that, though "war, with all its horrors and desolating influences, afflicts the land, this Institution is quietly maintaining its way in the career of beneficence for which it was designed."[25]

The year 1865 was the hardest year of all for the academy and the asylum. Without negotiable currency after the death of the Confederacy, they depended on credit and the Federal Army for provisions. When the first postwar legislature met at the end of the year, it passed a resolution advancing twenty-five hundred dollars to the Academy for the Blind and twenty thousand dollars to the Lunatic Asylum.[26]

Georgia's welfare institutions began to rebuild, quickly returned to their prewar size, and then resumed the gradual expansion that had characterized their prewar history. For 1866 the legislature appropriated as much to support the schools for the deaf (eight thousand dollars) and the blind (seven thousand dollars) as it had for 1860. It authorized $14,500 for salaries and $50,000 (up from $15,000 before the war) to support pauper patients at the insane asylum. To repair and improve buildings and to replace furnishings and educational supplies, the state also spent twenty-five hundred dollars on the school for the deaf and seventy-five hundred dollars on that for the blind in 1866 and 1867.

Citing the state's "fiscal embarrassments," Gov. Charles J. Jenkins declined to approve expenditures to reopen the school for the deaf until February 1867.[27] The governor's decision to delay reopening, unique as it was, highlights how the state had grown committed to supporting its social welfare institutions, despite any "fiscal embarrassments." There was no going back to a more fully laissez-faire world, to a time, like the 1820s, without those institutions.

Though no legislature met in 1867 to make appropriations for 1868 (Congress had suspended civilian government and inaugurated Reconstruction), expenditures for all three institutions continued with hardly a ripple. In October 1867 Gen. John Pope, commanding the Third Military District, ordered the state treasurer to continue making quarterly payments to state officers, the penitentiary, and the three welfare institutions. In turn

Governor Jenkins, before he was removed from his post, ordered the Western and Atlantic Railroad's superintendent to supply the quarterly funds that each institution would have received if the 1867 session had met and roughly duplicated the 1866 appropriations act. When Provisional Governor Thomas H. Ruger took office, he perpetuated this plan. The Western and Atlantic's net earnings, about twenty-five thousand dollars per month, sufficed to support all three welfare institutions at their authorized spending levels.[28]

The 1860s brought a transformed fiscal environment to Americans. Fiscal bonanzas came in waves before the Civil War but vanished afterward. (The great exception was the chronic, tariff-driven, federal budgetary surplus of the 1880s, which was diverted to pensions for Union soldiers.)[29] Policy makers of the late nineteenth century had to look to tax revenues to fund social welfare. The fiscal luxuries that white Georgians had experienced in the 1830s and 1850s would not come again.

The South faced a far more serious crunch than did the North. Southern states, on average, saw their civil populations rise by half in the 1860s—Georgia's nearly doubled—as slaves that had been "property" became freed people and thus citizens. Many more people needed places in schools and welfare institutions. At the same time, Emancipation—together with wartime death, destruction, and disruption—slashed the tax base, the private wealth, and the public resources that might have been tapped to fund social welfare. The challenge was huge.

A Second Generation: Race and the Reconstruction of Georgia's Three Welfare Institutions

In the two decades after Emancipation, Georgia made provision for black clients at all three institutions. The prewar sequence, from social control to social welfare, was repeated. The state moved quickly, before the advent of Republican rule, to accommodate black inmates at the mental institution. Not until long after Republicans had vanished as a potent political force in Georgia did the state make provision for black clients at the schools for the deaf and blind.

At all three institutions, a postwar policy of segregated inclusion supplanted the prewar policy of black exclusion. This is entirely consistent with Howard Rabinowitz's formula in "From Exclusion to Segregation."[30] Yet

Georgia failed to manifest the linkages that Rabinowitz posits between this change and Republican rule. To the contrary, "Radical Reconstruction" in Georgia, which did nothing to provide facilities for black citizens who were deaf or blind, did little more than continue what was already being done with insane freedmen.

All three institutions, never having had black students or patients before Emancipation, had yet to face the question of meeting black Georgians' needs. The school for the deaf, in its 1868 report, noted a need for segregated state facilities for blacks, and it estimated that these would cost three or four thousand dollars to build and furnish. The school did not insist, however, and the legislature did not respond. The Academy for the Blind did not even raise the subject until its 1875 report. Not until the early 1880s did either school provide facilities for black Georgians.[31]

As early as 17 August 1865, by contrast, the insane asylum reluctantly received its first black patient, and the superintendent, Dr. Thomas F. Green, feared the arrival of many more. From a perspective that appears typical of men in his position after the war, Dr. Green observed in his 1865 report that, under slavery, blacks "enjoyed entire freedom from cares and anxieties, and in the rare instances in which an insane negro could be found, there was an owner who could and did take care of the poor creature. Now . . . they are undoubtedly under the influence of almost every exciting cause of disorder of the brain." The "dictates of humanity," as well as the "welfare of society," he concluded, required "proper arrangements" in "separate quarters." A joint legislative committee voiced similar premises when it reported in 1866 that, with the end of slavery but not of "unbridled lust," Georgia might anticipate "insanity in the negro much more common under this new dispensation than it was under the old and better code."[32]

The state felt compelled to provide adequate facilities for insane black men and women. The 1866 legislative committee's majority report suggested an appropriation of twenty thousand dollars, and the minority report ten thousand dollars, to provide accommodations for "the most unfortunate class of that unfortunate race."[33] Responding to the "dictates of humanity" and the "welfare of society," the legislature appropriated ten thousand dollars in 1866 to provide a building for about fifty black inmates.

Because the building became full within months of its completion in

August 1867, the institution sought a similar appropriation for a second building. In addition it urgently needed funds to supply black inmates with furniture, bedding, clothing, food, and medicine. In the absence of state money for these items in 1867 and 1868, the Freedmen's Bureau supplied monthly rations. The asylum ran short of space and funds alike for more residents, black or white. In October 1865, the institution held 275 inmates; by mid-1868, it held 336 whites and 52 blacks and could accept new applicants only as vacancies opened. Struggling with the cost of provisions and feeding more patients yet receiving less money from paying ones, the institution relied on the state for ever-larger appropriations. It also needed building funds to cope with overcrowding and a growing backlog of applications.

Completing the task begun in 1866, subsequent legislatures authorized funds for support and construction. For substantial spending on construction, the institution had to await actions by the last Republican legislature, which authorized $68,000—$50,000 for accommodations for 150 more white patients, and $18,000 for 50 more blacks—and the first Redeemer session, which appropriated $54,855. An 1877 act ended the policy of charging Georgia residents who could afford to pay for their own support. By the 1880s annual appropriations for support exceeded one hundred thousand dollars, far higher than the expenditures of either the antebellum years or Reconstruction.[34]

The Georgia Institution for the Education of the Deaf and Dumb reopened in February 1867, and by 1869 it had more than fifty students. In need of annual appropriations larger than those before the war, it had more students, all of them state-supported; it had to pay high salaries for qualified teachers and much higher prices for provisions; and it had to subsidize the mechanical department, which, with fewer advanced students and higher prices for materials, could no longer sustain itself.

Opening the school without charge to all qualified applicants, the legislature ended distinctions between paying and state-supported students in 1868. The institution supplied not only free tuition but shoes for all pupils as well as clothing for students whose parents were unable to pay for it. The school now depended entirely on the state for its revenue, and it suffered financial difficulties in 1869, when the more conservative legislature that year slashed its funding. But annual appropriations moved to higher levels in 1870 and never again dropped below $12,500. In 1880 a fifteen thousand dollar appropriation supported sixty-four white students, thirty-two of each sex.

Enrollment at the Academy for the Blind doubled to more than fifty by the mid-1870s. In 1866 the school inaugurated its mechanical department, for which it had waited a decade. In addition to teaching music and academic courses, the school could now teach its male students to make brooms and other items, while the young women continued their instruction "in plain sewing and other branches of domestic employment." Money was always tight. Some revenue continued to come from paying students, and, beginning in 1866, the legislature provided the academy eleven thousand dollars for annual support. By 1877 the academy's appropriation of $13,500 provided schooling for sixty-two white students, thirty-four male and twenty-eight female. As late as 1876 and 1877, two students from the black-belt counties of Wilkes and Houston paid tuition, but in 1883 the legislature established free tuition for all Georgia residents admitted to the school.[35]

In 1875, for the first time, the Academy for the Blind raised the question of accommodations for black citizens. Former owners and county authorities had notified the school of several blind freedmen, each of them "too old to derive benefit from the school department, but not too old to receive industrial training." Beginning in 1878 two young black men from Macon, who continued to live at home, received day-school instruction "in a room in the workshop."[36]

Finally, in 1880, the school began a campaign for funds to open a segregated branch and requested an appropriation of ten thousand dollars to obtain buildings and begin a program. The principal, W. D. Williams, reported statistics showing fully as many blind black children as whites and noted that he had had to reject applications by several on account of their race. Not only had North Carolina and Maryland supplied facilities for blind and deaf blacks, he observed, but Georgia had undertaken the responsibility of providing public funds for black citizens in common schools, a university, and a mental institution. Surely it was time to expand that responsibility.

The legislature responded favorably to this strong argument and specific request by authorizing the ten thousand dollars. By November 1882 the academy had bought a nearby site, erected a brick building to house perhaps forty students, and admitted the first black students. The next year, six black students attended classes in literature and music in addition to the industrial training workshop. Growing slowly, the "colored department" reported eleven students, all male, in 1885.[37]

The school for the deaf, like that for the blind, eventually turned its attention to the needs of black Georgians. After the first mention in its 1868 report, the school made no further reference to the question until 1873, when officers reported having turned away black applicants because state law prevented their being educated "in the same house together" with whites. Noting that "humanity, charity, and the Civil Rights bill" all favored action, the president of the school's board of trustees suggested that to ignore black citizens' undeniable needs much longer might be seen as "intentional neglect."[38] He requested four thousand dollars to erect a building and two thousand dollars as an annual support fund. Still, the legislature failed to act.

Repeating its request in 1875, the school sought an additional two thousand dollars to buy a suitable building three hundred yards from the school for whites, one thousand dollars to provide a separate dining room and kitchen, and five hundred dollars for furnishings. The legislature now gave the school the authority to admit blacks and granted an initial two-thousand-dollar appropriation. Requesting money for repairs and support, the school promised that the branches would be kept "as distinctly separate as though the two Institutions were in different towns." In 1882, the same year black students first enrolled at the school for the blind, twenty black students—twelve young men and eight young women—at last began classes at the school for deaf Georgians.[39]

Conclusion: From the 1830s to the 1880s

Beginning in the 1830s with no state policy and no institutions, Georgia launched major initiatives regarding white residents who were blind, deaf, or insane. Before 1860 the state had developed special institutions for all three groups. After the military, financial, and political disruption of the Civil War and Reconstruction, Georgia's state-supported institutions resumed their prewar growth. Operations in the 1880s, even for whites, greatly exceeded those of the 1850s. By 1883, moreover, the state had terminated the previous distinctions between paying and nonpaying patients and students at all three facilities. In a more dramatic change, by the end of 1882 blacks as well as whites were routinely admitted, on a segregated basis, to all three institutions. Through two generations of development, basic institutional arrangements had emerged that would endure well into the twentieth century.

The Georgia story suggests that North and South differed in three broad ways. First was the lag between Georgia's adoption of new policies and the earlier actions of the pioneer states of the Northeast. The pioneer states supplied models for other states throughout the nation; provided places to send students until other states inaugurated their own institutions; and opened facilities to train teachers for new schools. Second was the enormous disruption of the war and the postwar years—the military and financial disruption of the war, followed by the economic difficulties and political turmoil of the postwar years. Third was the far greater numbers of black residents in the South and the policy crisis that southern states faced in approaching the question of black inclusion, as black residents were transformed from slaves to freed people to citizens.

Georgia stands in this essay as the representative southern state, neither entirely like the North nor entirely different from it. Just how typical its experience was remains to be seen. Further research on other states, in both the South and the North, will demonstrate how typical Georgia was in these and other matters of social welfare policy—and how representative Georgia was of the South as well as how southern states compared with northern.

Various questions remain. How universal were these kinds of institutions for white southerners before the war? What was the timing and nature of the inclusion of black southerners, whether before Emancipation or afterward, and how closely did that inclusion correlate with Republican control of each southern state's postwar politics? What was the internal life of each institution like? How well did the two schools actually perform in preparing students for economic self-sufficiency? How did the prewar and postwar facilities compare, and how also did the typical experiences of black residents and white ones compare?

Other questions have to do with politics and finances. How well does the launching of prewar institutions correlate with the federal treasury distribution of 1836? At what point did public institutions become entirely public in their financing? How much less—in terms of population or per capita wealth—did southern states spend on social welfare than did those in the North? What ought to remain of the conventional understanding that Republicans spent far more on social welfare, and their Bourbon successors far less, than other dominant political groups in the nineteenth-century South?

Finally, for such facilities as these in Georgia (and other southern states as well), how true is it that we need look back only to the 1880s to find the patterns of the rest of the century pretty much in place? For that matter, did those patterns largely persist until the New Deal or even on until the Great Society? These are all issues that warrant further research.

NOTES

1. Some of the material in this essay originally appeared in Peter Wallenstein, *From Slave South to New South: Public Policy in Nineteenth-Century Georgia* (Chapel Hill: University of North Carolina Press, 1987), and is used by permission of the publisher. For a discussion of the primary sources for such a history as this one, see ibid., 215–18.

2. For a discussion of liberty, power, and paternalism in Jacksonian America, see ibid., 86–96. White men lived in a world of ordered liberty. A work by William J. Novak should lay to rest the notion that nineteenth-century American governments generally refrained from intervening in social and economic arrangements. Novak, *The People's Welfare: Law and Regulation in Nineteenth-Century America* (Chapel Hill: University of North Carolina Press, 1986), emphasizes regulations that required little public funding.

3. David J. Rothman, *The Discovery of the Asylum: Social Order and Disorder in the New Republic* (Boston: Little, Brown, 1971).

4. Peter McCandless, *Moonlight, Magnolias, and Madness: Insanity in South Carolina from the Colonial Period to the Progressive Era* (Chapel Hill: University of North Carolina Press, 1996).

5. Edward G. Bourne, *The History of the Surplus Revenue of 1837* (New York: G. P. Putnam's Sons, 1887); Wallenstein, *From Slave South*, 29.

6. A full discussion of Georgia's prewar finances, including the fiscal bonanzas that led to enhanced social spending in the 1830s and again in the 1850s, can be found in Wallenstein, *From Slave South*, 23–85.

7. John C. Butler, comp., *Origin and History of the Georgia Academy for the Blind* (Macon, Ga.: J. W. Burke, 1887), 15.

8. Harry Best, *Deafness and the Deaf in the United States* (New York: Macmillan, 1943), chap. 22; Harry Best, *Blindness and the Blind in the United States* (New York: Macmillan, 1934), chap. 21; Gabriel Farrell, *The Story of Blindness* (Cambridge, Mass.: Harvard University Press, 1956), 18–32.

9. Norman Dain, *Concepts of Insanity in the United States, 1789–1865* (New Brunswick, N.J.: Rutgers University Press, 1964), chap. 1; Gerald N. Grob, *Mental Institutions in America: Social Policy to 1875* (New York: Free Press, 1973), chaps. 1–3.

10. Best, *Deafness*, 385–432; John Vickrey Van Cleve and Barry A. Crouch, *A Place of Their Own: Creating the Deaf Community in America* (Washington, D.C.: Gallaudet University Press, 1989), 29–47.

11. Best, *Blindness*, 306–33; Farrell, *Blindness*, 41–52; Harold Schwartz, *Samuel Gridley Howe: Social Reformer, 1801–1876* (Cambridge, Mass.: Harvard University Press, 1956), 40–66.

12. Wallenstein, *From Slave South*, 26, 31; Milton Sydney Heath, *Constructive Liberalism: The Role of the State in Economic Development in Georgia to 1860* (Cambridge, Mass.: Harvard University Press, 1954), 336–50, 368–74.

13. Wallenstein, *From Slave South*, 76.

14. Ibid.; Hortense Cochrane, "Early Treatment of the Mentally Ill in Georgia," *Georgia Historical Quarterly* 32 (June 1948): 105–18.

15. Georgia *Acts of the General Assembly* (1853–54), 81.

16. Letter from Dorothea Dix to [?], March 16, 1850, in the Dorothea Dix Papers, Houghton Library, Harvard University, as quoted in Wallenstein, *From Slave South*, 76.

17. Dix to [?], February 18, 1850, and Green to Dix, January 25 and July 25, 1859, in Dix Papers, as quoted in Wallenstein, *From Slave South*, 77.

18. Georgia Asylum for the Deaf and Dumb, *Sixth Annual Report* (1855), 7, 17; *Seventh Annual Report* (1856), 6.

19. Georgia Asylum for the Deaf and Dumb, *Second Annual Report* (1851), 21.

20. Wallenstein, *From Slave South*, 78; Butler, *Georgia Academy for the Blind*, 5–9.

21. Butler, *Georgia Academy for the Blind*, 5–14, 44.

22. Wallenstein, *From Slave South*, 89.

23. Ibid., 183–95.

24. Ibid., 108; Georgia *Acts of the General Assembly* (1863–64), 123.

25. Butler, *Georgia Academy for the Blind*, 132–98.

26. Ibid., 192–94; Georgia *Acts of the General Assembly* (1865–66), 56.

27. Georgia *Journal of the Senate* (1866), 22.

28. Wallenstein, *From Slave South*, 147.

29. Ibid., 212; Theda Skocpol, *Protecting Soldiers and Mothers: The Political Origins of Social Policy in the United States* (Cambridge, Mass.: Harvard University Press, 1992), chap. 2.

30. Howard N. Rabinowitz, "From Exclusion to Segregation: Health and Welfare Services for Southern Blacks, 1865–1890," *Social Service Review* 48 (November 1974): 327–54, and *Race Relations in the Urban South, 1865–1890* (New York: Oxford University Press, 1978), chap. 6.

31. Wallenstein, *From Slave South*, 147.

32. Lunatic Asylum, *Report* (1867), 8, 23; (1865), 8–9; "Report of the Majority and Minority of the Committee on the Lunatic Asylum" (1866), 7 (Georgia State Library, Atlanta, Ga.). A regional context is supplied in John S. Hughes, "Labeling and Treating Black Mental Illness in Alabama, 1861–1910," *Journal of Southern History* 58 (August 1993): 435–45.

33. "Report of the Majority and Minority of the Committee on the Lunatic Asylum" (1866), 8, 12.

34. Peter Wallenstein, "Prelude to Southern Progressivism: Social Policy in Bourbon Georgia," in Winfred B. Moore Jr. et al., eds., *Developing Dixie: Modernization in a Traditional Society* (New York: Greenwood Press, 1988), 137–48.

35. Butler, *Georgia Academy for the Blind*, 191–264.

36. Georgia Academy for the Blind, *Twenty-fourth Annual Report* (1875), 6–7; *Twenty-ninth Annual Report* (1880), 17.

37. Wallenstein, *From Slave South*, 149–50; Georgia Academy for the Blind, *Thirty-Fourth Annual Report* (1885), 8.

38. Asylum for the Deaf and Dumb, *Sixteenth Report* (1873), 8–9.

39. Wallenstein, *From Slave South*, 150; Asylum for the Deaf and Dumb, *Nineteenth Report* (1876), 6.

Confederate Pensions as Southern Social Welfare

KATHLEEN GORMAN

Sitting outside the county courthouse, still in the remnants of a tattered butternut uniform with an empty sleeve, an aged Confederate veteran entertains an audience of children with war stories. This image is the one most commonly associated with Confederate veterans in the decades following the war. However the reality was not nearly so romantic. As the decades passed southern veterans not only grew older but also increasingly grew impoverished and desperate. To care for them required an extraordinarily extensive and expensive southern social welfare system. Almost one million men had served in the Confederate military, and as they aged, they presented a new problem in American history: how to provide for veterans on the losing side of a war (and not only were these men on the losing side, but they were men who many northerners viewed as traitors). Well into the twentieth century the South cared for these veterans, and it chose to care for them in a way consistent with its values. Only those veterans who presented themselves as having been participants in a glorious Lost Crusade would share fully in the Confederate pension system.

This study will examine the development of this system based on the experience of Georgia. The actual operation of the system in one typical Georgia county will be considered, and the fates of two veterans, James J. Garrett and Rolly Needham, will illustrate the system's subjectivity. Despite the similarity of their wartime experiences, these two men were treated very differently by the pension system.

Despite the Confederate pension system's importance, it has not been the subject of much study. Most of the information about the pensions comes from the work of William Glasson, who wrote a series of articles for scholarly journals early in the twentieth century. Glasson was a southerner upset by the disparity between federal and Confederate pension payments.

Table 1. Estimated Numbers of Confederate Veterans at Selected Dates

Year	Total	In Georgia
During war	900,000	100,000
1865	650,000	74,000
1890	432,020	47,080
1900	300,000	32,500
1910	190,000	20,000
1922	75,000	9,105
1928	25,000	3,070

Source: During-war estimates based on enlistment figures from Roger Ransom, *Conflict and Compromise* (Cambridge: Cambridge University Press, 1989), 190–92. The 1890 figures are from the 1890 Census. The 1900 and 1910 estimates are based on survival rates from John Ruoff's "Southern Womanhood, 1865–1920: An Intellectual and Cultural Study," (Ph.D. diss., University of Illinois at Urbana-Champaign, 1976), 98. The figures for 1922 and 1928 are from surveys contained in R. B. Rosenburg, *Living Monuments: Confederate Soldiers' Homes in the New South* (Chapel Hill: University of North Carolina Press, 1993), 163–64.

More recent discussion about Civil War pensions has focused instead on Union pensions. Theda Skocpol's *Protecting Soldiers and Mothers* examines the huge federal Civil War pension system and explains why it did not grow into a national social welfare system. Megan McClintock's article, "Civil War Pensions and the Reconstruction of Union Families," discusses how Union pensions were crucial in increasing enlistment during the war and in helping families survive and stay together in later years.[1]

The extensive Confederate pension system clearly requires more study. The sheer numbers of Confederate veterans meant that caring for them placed a strain on each individual state's resources. Georgia, which provided a substantial number of men for the war effort, demonstrates this most clearly. Table 1 estimates the total numbers of Confederate veterans and those living in Georgia at selected dates. Approximately 650,000 men survived their Confederate military service. In 1890 there were about 432,020 Confederate veterans still living. More than 10 percent (47,080) of these men lived in Georgia.[2]

As losers of the war, Confederate veterans were not eligible to participate in the federal system. Therefore any support had to come from the southern states themselves. With the demise in 1865 of the national Confederate government there was no single, central agency available to distribute pensions. Nor did the victorious North allow southern states to start their pension systems immediately after the war. Reconstruction governments, under Republican regimes, controlled each state's budget and were able to prevent spending that honored anything connected to the Confederate cause. Highly organized, expensive systems were on hold until after Radical Reconstruction was over. But after "Redemption" southern states rapidly moved in to help their heroes. A Texas comptroller's report provides an overview of how much Confederate states were paying their veterans in 1908. Of the eleven former Confederate states, Florida and Georgia expended the most ($900,000), while South Carolina spent just $250,000 on its veterans.[3] This dramatic difference in expenditures is due partially to the size of the states involved, but is also a result of the different amount of discretionary revenue available in each state.

Comprehensive pension systems began in both the North and South in the 1890s, as it became increasingly necessary to take care of the aging veterans. But in the South, this was also the decade where "New South" rhetoric was at its height. An intrinsic part of that rhetoric was to honor the old heroes: the New South creed explicitly called for remembering the Old South and the Lost Cause. Therefore pensions served a dual purpose in the 1890s South: a practical one in caring for the aging veterans and an intangible one in connecting the rhetoric of the New South with the assumed reality of the Old South.[4]

Each state had specific eligibility requirements for its own pensions. Unlike the federal system, none of these states recognized the mere attainment of a specific age as entree into the pension system, although indigent veterans were provided for in most southern states. The development of the Georgia pension system is similar to that of most other Confederate states. It began as a limited social welfare system in 1871 by supplying artificial limbs to the many veteran amputees. By 1889 otherwise disabled veterans were made eligible for benefits as well. Pensions were then extended to "disabled and diseased" veterans with the amounts determined by their specific disability. In 1896 the state made indigent veterans eligible to receive benefits. That same year the governor appointed the state's first Commissioner of Pensions whose job it was to review every application. For the next twenty-four years varying income restrictions were applied to determine eligibility until, in 1920, veterans who had been honorably discharged from the Confederate Army were eligible for pensions regardless of income or assets.[5]

Widows of veterans were also eligible for state assistance. In 1893 widows who had not remarried and whose husbands died during the war became eligible for pensions. The year in which the marriage took place often became a point of contention. In 1933 a widow who had married the veteran by 1881 was eligible, but four years later the couple only had to have married by 1920. During this period, to remain eligible for the pension the widow could not have remarried since the death of her veteran husband. It was not until 1944 that widows who had remarried became eligible for Confederate pensions. The result of this change was that widows were still being added to the rolls as late as 1960. When the last surviving veteran died in 1952, there were still 401 widows on the rolls.[6]

Georgia veterans and widows did not get rich from their pensions. In fact, the amount they received was considerably less than that paid to their federal counterparts. The amount varied depending on the type and extent of disability. It ranged from $150 annually for a completely disabled veteran to $5 per finger or toe lost. Indigent veterans received sixty dollars a year. Table 2 provides a complete comparison of the amounts. Georgia pensions were first paid annually, then quarterly, and finally, in 1929, increased amounts were paid monthly. The small amounts paid to some disabled veterans forced many to try to get themselves reclassified as indigent to receive increased benefits. With the removal of income restrictions, pay was standardized for all veterans (who were always paid more than widows). Even with increases in payments, veterans living well into old age did not receive much money. In 1937 veterans received thirty dollars a month, seven years later that amount had increased to fifty dollars, and by 1949 it was up to seventy-five dollars. Veterans living in the state's Confederate home received only five dollars monthly.[7]

Although the amount paid to each veteran was small, the total expenditures were a significant proportion of Georgia's annual budget. The *Annual Reports* of the comptroller general show pension expenditures were consistently the second-largest expense (trailing only education) for the state. Between 1892 and 1921 the percentage of state expenditures spent on pensions never dipped below 10 percent. The number of veterans reached its

Table 2. Annual Pension Amounts Based on Disability Type

Disability	Georgia Pension	Federal Pension
Total Loss Sight	150	1,200
Loss Sight 1 Eye	30	144
Total Loss Hearing	30	480
Loss 1 Hand	100	360
Loss Both Hands/Feet	150	1,200
Total Disability 1 Arm	50	432
Incapacity Manual Labor	50	360
Loss 1 Finger or Toe	5	24

Source: Theda Skocpol, *Protecting Soldiers and Mothers: The Political Origins of Social Policy in the United States* (Cambridge, Mass.: Belknap Press of Harvard University Press, 1992), 140.

peak in 1912 when there were 19,972 on the rolls. By July 1, 1937, Georgia had spent a total of about $49 million on pensions.[8]

During the Great Depression the state found it increasingly difficult to meet its monthly obligations, even occasionally missing payments. The tone of correspondence to the Pension Office reflects the increasing desperation of the times. Children and grandchildren of veterans flooded the Pension Office with letters claiming they had inherited pensions from their parents or grandparents. The commissioner routinely sent letters to those people informing them that pensions could not be given to anyone other than veterans or their widows.[9]

Because of the large amount of money involved, the state was forced to turn to alternative methods to finance pensions. Much of the needed revenue came from cigarette taxes. The state, believing the pension rolls would continue to decrease rapidly, reduced the tax on cigarettes from 20 to 10 percent in 1931, believing that amount would completely cover the costs of the pensions.[10] However this plan failed to account for the increasing numbers of widows who became eligible for pensions each year; nor did the plan consider the declining state revenues caused by the depression. The result was a temporary inability of the state to meet its obligations, leaving destitute, elderly veterans and widows even more desperate.

The vast amounts expended by Georgia and its southern brethren meant those states, among the poorest in the nation, did not have money to spend in other areas. Veterans certainly contributed a portion of their pension money right back into their communities but not as much as if the state had taken that money and invested in the construction of roads, bridges, or more schools. The desire to pay homage to and take care of the aging heroes carried with it a high price to the state and its other citizens. However it was a price southern states were eager to pay.

Pension systems did not operate in a vacuum. Within each state pensions were distributed and used at the local level. In Georgia most day-to-day pension issues were handled at the county level. And, while regulations might be established at state levels, those regulations were interpreted and enforced by county officials who often wielded the real power of deciding which veterans would receive a pension. It was in the actual distribution of pension payments that the distinct regional characteristics of this social welfare system become most apparent.

The operation of this regimented and complicated pension system can best be illustrated by examining how it functioned in Walton County, Georgia. Walton County was in many ways a typical southern county during Reconstruction. One way to illustrate the typicality of Walton is to take a brief look at its development through Reconstruction. Located just east of Atlanta in the Georgia upcountry, Walton had just begun to be engulfed by the black belt's economy when the war erupted. After the war the economy of Walton dramatically changed. Sharecropping and tenancy of small farms replaced ownership of larger farms. The production of cotton dramatically increased while the production of food crops decreased just as dramatically. Previously self-sufficient yeoman farmers found themselves suddenly dependent on landlords, the marketplace, and other outside assistance. The picture that emerges of Walton is the same one that emerged throughout the agricultural South: numerous individuals were displaced by the changing economy.[11]

In Walton County, as elsewhere in the state, the pension process began when the applicant and two witnesses arrived at the county ordinary's office to fill out an application form. The witnesses were required to answer questions concerning the applicant's war service and current economic situation. It was strongly preferred that the witnesses had served in the same unit as the applicant and that they could answer specific questions about his wartime service. One reason for this is that Confederate military records were incomplete and disorganized for decades after the war. The state records department would attempt to verify an applicant's service, but it was not always able to do so.

The applicant then had to be examined by two doctors who would testify as to his ability to work at his chosen occupation. The doctors often used extremely vague language, preferring the phrase "broken down" to giving a specific medical diagnosis.[12] Because most of the applicants were farmers, the doctors were most interested in establishing the inability of the applicant to support himself through manual labor. Because the pension system only became available to nonwounded men in the late 1890s, most of the applicants were already in their fifties or sixties, and it was easy to state truthfully they could no longer farm. In the last local step of the application process the county ordinary checked the tax digest for the preceding three years to make sure the applicant met the financial restrictions currently in effect.

The application was then sent by the ordinary to the Georgia commissioner of pensions who had final approval. If the application was disapproved, the commissioner would send it back with some indication of why it had not been approved. This response was often written on the original application form that would then be returned to the ordinary. If the application was approved, the check would be sent (first quarterly and later monthly) to the ordinary who would pass it on to the veteran. Pensions were renewed annually and each renewal required the applicant to again present himself to the ordinary; requests for change in the type of pension required the applicant go through the process as if he were applying for the first time. Each change in the pension laws also required the applicant to reapply to ensure he met the revised requirements.[13]

At each step of the way there were problems with this system. The longer a veteran waited to apply the less chance there was that there would be witnesses to his service available to testify. If a man was not particularly well-liked, others might (and did) refuse to help him get his pension. If a veteran moved into the county from elsewhere there was often no way for him to get such witnesses. If he had not received a pension from his previous county, he was unlikely to be approved in his new county of residence. If he had previously received a pension from another county, the pension was routinely transferred to the new county. Pensions were paid by the state, so the county really did not have much of an incentive to enforce pension requirements stringently. However other, unwritten criteria often guided local officials. The applicant's reputation for loyalty to the Lost Cause could be as big a factor in the final decision as the legal criteria.[14]

A disproportionate amount of power was put into the hands of one elected official, the county ordinary, and into the hands of the examining doctors. For much of the time under discussion in this essay, the county ordinary of Walton was either G. A. Garrett or R. C. Knight, and both were extremely powerful men in Walton. Both Garrett and Knight held other elected offices prior to their becoming ordinary. Garrett was tax collector for nine years while Knight had served two terms as sheriff. They were already important men when they took office, but their power increased as ordinary. The state pension commissioner was J. W. Lindsey for almost the entire forty years under discussion. At any step of the way, these officials could either greatly help or hinder a veteran's chance of getting a pension by their choice of words on the application. This system illustrates how deeply the system of patronage remained ingrained in the New South just as it had been in the Old South. It was not enough to have served the Confederacy honorably; the veteran also needed to be an "honored" member of the community with others willing to swear to his worthiness. Being accepted by the community was as important as being able to prove honorable service. Honor was defined by the community in the New South just as it had been in the Old South. Even the questions on the applications emphasized the concept of honor. Witnesses were asked about the character of the applicant and the quality of his military service. There was a great emphasis on being present with one's unit when it surrendered. More problems occurred when the applicant had not surrendered with his unit (whatever the reason) than with any other part of the application, with the commissioner demanding to know the exact reason for his absence.[15]

Most Walton County pensioners were in dire straits by the time they first applied for their pensions. At the time of their first pension application almost 78 percent of those responding to the question said they had no income; only 17 of 299 respondents reported annual incomes of more than $50; and almost 88 percent claimed to have no assets. These factors explain why more than 81 percent indicate they relied on their families for their support. These figures also provide another explanation for the widespread support for Confederate pensions: families caring for these men needed the money as much as the veterans themselves.[16]

More than 90 percent of the pensioners reported their occupation since

Table 3. Income of Walton County Pensioners Reported at Time of Application

Income	Number	Percentage
$ 0	232	77.6
$ 1– 49	47	15.7
$ 50– 99	7	2.3
$100–199	7	2.3
$200–299	1	0.3
$300–399	1	0.3
$400–499	0	0
$500+	1	0.3
Total	296	98.8

Source: Pension applications from Walton County in Georgia Department of Archives and History microfilm collection.

1865 was farming, and about half said they still considered themselves farmers. The lack of assets would suggest they were tenants or renters rather than owners of the property they worked. Tables describing the status of veterans are presented here. The average Walton veteran remained on a pension for about eight years with one veteran receiving a service pension (one not related to a disability) for thirty-eight years.[17]

However not every eligible Confederate veteran in Walton found it easy to receive the full pension to which he was entitled. The system operated in such a way as to ensure that only "worthy" veterans received full pensions. The case histories of two veterans from the county will illustrate this point quite clearly. James J. Garrett served in the Walton County infantry during most of the war. He was injured in battle but returned from his injury to finish out the war with his unit. He was honored repeatedly by the county for his service and, despite being relatively poor, often socialized with the elite of the county. The local newspaper often referred to Garrett as the oldest living Confederate veteran in the county although he was not. He was the oldest living veteran in the county who was a Walton native but not the actual oldest living veteran residing there.[18] For the last forty-three years of his life, Garrett received a Confederate pension. He received a disability pension beginning in 1893 with the amount fixed at fifty dollars annually through at least 1907.

Table 4. Assets of Walton County Pensioners
Reported at Time of Application

Assets	Number	Percentage
$ 0	280	87.8
$ 1– 99	2	0.6
$ 100– 249	2	0.6
$ 250– 499	2	0.6
$ 500– 749	6	1.9
$ 750– 999	6	1.9
$1,000–1,999	18	5.6
$2,000+	2	0.6
Total	318	99.6

Source: Pension applications from Walton County in Georgia Department of Archives and History microfilm collection.

Table 5. Means of Support of Walton County
Pensioners Reported at Time of Application

	Number	Percentage
Self	19	7.9
Family	194	81.2
State	5	2.1
Other	20	8.4
Total	238	99.6

Source: Pension applications from Walton County in Georgia Department of Archives and History microfilm collection.

The commissioner of pensions had been reluctant to accept his initial application and had sent back the form with specific questions for the witnesses about Garrett's service. Among the questions he wanted answered were several concerning the state of Garrett's health during and since the war and whether the present state of his health could have been caused by something other than the war. Garrett responded by submitting new witness statements that answered the questions. Among his new witnesses was a former governor, Henry D. McDaniel. McDaniel, Georgia governor during the mid-1880s, made the following statement: "I know that J. J. Garrett was a member of Co. H 11th Ga. Regiment and . . . that he was wounded as described in the affidavits hereto attached. I know that he has complained of that wound and its consequences ever since the close of the war between the states. And recently I looked at his leg and saw that it was inflamed as described by witness N. J. Garrett. As I remember meeting him for several years he constantly used a stick and now uses one. I am satisfied it is necessary." Undoubtedly the support from such a powerful man (who obviously was well acquainted with Garrett) helped J. J. get his pension application approved. The examining doctors also agreed with McDaniel's statement. They noted he had never really healed from the gunshot wound in the left thigh suffered in 1864 and therefore was unable to perform manual labor.

In 1924 Garrett applied to change from a disability to a service pension. The pension commissioner was again not particularly impressed with his first application to change. His initial witness, F. S. Kent, was not with the Walton infantry when it surrendered, having been discharged earlier because of chronic disease. The commissioner asked G. A. Garrett, county ordinary, to inquire as to whether J. J. had actually been with the company when it surrendered. Apparently Garrett's answer satisfied him, and the commissioner approved the request for the following year. What the Pension Commissioner may not have realized is that George A. Garrett was the younger half-brother of J. J. and would have been extremely unlikely to do anything to damage his older brother's chances for a pension. Both pension applications were ultimately successful only after J. J. called on some of his connections. His half-brother made it possible for him to upgrade his disability pay. He only received his disability pension with the help of his powerful friends—people he knew well because of their shared war experience.

But not all veterans found powerful people willing to help them get their pensions, and the differing results are striking. Rolly Needham also served in the Walton infantry and was also injured during the war. However, unlike Garrett, he was unable to return to his unit. The war had been a painful experience to Needham in many ways: he suffered an injury that would trouble him throughout his life, and his older (and only) brother was killed in action. He did not see the war as a glorious experience and appeared to refuse to use it as a way to increase his social status. He did move from being a yeoman farmer to a relatively well-off farmer after the war, but he remained isolated from his community. And this isolation cost him more than just social status. Rolly Needham started drawing a disability pension in 1890. He received twenty-five dollars annually for his disabled foot. The 1897 renewal form (which is almost as complete as a new application) was witnessed by an impressive group: Lt. C. P. Blasingame, J. E. Nunnally (the Blasingame and Nunnally families were among the most respected in Walton and led the local Farmer's Alliance and veterans' organizations), and Henry McDaniel (again, the former governor). Blasingame reported he was a witness to Needham's wounding. All three vouched for his actually being wounded in battle. However none of his witnesses could or would vouch for its effects on him: "I Henry McDaniel can say from my own knowledge that the applicant Rolly Needham was a private in Co. H 11th Ga. Regiment & was wounded at Second Battle of Manassas Aug. 30th 1862 but I cannot state the character and extent [of the wound's effect on him]. . . . He was a good soldier and is known as a reliable citizen in his community." This statement is not exactly a glowing endorsement of the civilian Needham and is much less helpful than the statement McDaniel wrote for Garrett. Nunnally and McDaniel both claimed Needham lived too far away for them to know anything about his present condition or even much about him since the war. However, Needham lived in the same general area as Garrett. Blasingame did not directly comment on Needham's current situation, merely saying he agreed with Nunnally. Fortunately for Needham, his doctors were much more forthcoming. The two doctors fully explained the consequences of the wound: "Muscular contractions around ankle joint which tightens inter-osseous muscle rendering walking difficult and painful—said condition—owing to length of time—is *incurable*." This 1897 application also includes an overview of Needham's health and physical capabilities at the time as seen by County Ordinary R. C. Knight. Knight reported Needham experienced pain while "walking or doing any manual labor while on his feet rendering him unable to do manual labor on the farm which is his only occupation. Applicant can do nothing except see to the work of his children having to use the [*sic*] most of the time a crutch or stick in walking." The pension applications reveal that Rolly was illiterate and his application forms were filled out by the ordinary.

In 1915 Rolly attempted to switch from a disability pension to a service pension, which would pay more. In this application Needham reported he owned two hundred acres worth fourteen hundred dollars and supported himself with a small income from the farm. J. W. Thompson was witness as to his service and apparently had been wounded at Manassas with Needham. The two men made the trip back from Virginia together after surrender. J. W. Lindsey, Commissioner of Pensions, was still not impressed. Lindsey replied that the value of Needham's property was worth more than the fifteen hundred dollars allowed by law. The county ordinary, then E. M. Williams, said Needham's property was worth $1,865 and disqualified automatically. Apparently Williams did not bother to inform Needham that he did not qualify. And it is not completely clear from the tax digest who was correct in determining Needham's assets. He owned two hundred acres after selling off some land in 1913. The value of the land was given as fourteen hundred dollars for the tax year of 1914, but sixteen hundred dollars for 1915. If Needham was more popular or more powerful, clearly Williams would have given him the benefit of the doubt and allowed him to claim the higher pension. Lindsey disapproved the application and sent it back to Williams noting the problems with the reported assets. It was not until 1919 and the removal of income restrictions that Needham was able to receive a full pension. He received this pension for only a short time prior to his death in 1920. By that time his disability pension had grown to forty dollars annually from the twenty-five dollars it had been since 1890. The unwillingness of Needham's peers from the Walton infantry to testify strongly in his behalf suggests they were displeased with him for some reason, either with the quality of his war service or his unwillingness to play the hero's role after the war.[19] This displeasure was more important than just being ignored at social events; it could seriously influence such tangible issues as receiving pensions.

The pension system in the South, unlike that of the North, was not simply payment for successful services rendered. It would be possible to suggest Confederate pensions were paid merely to acknowledge the effort of veterans if the price involved was not so high and the eligibility requirements not so dependent on patronage. The veterans had to be "honorable" to make it through the application process. The other part of the reason for paying pensions to the losers is that they were needed. Southern veterans were aging right along with their northern counterparts, and they and their families needed the same assistance as Union veterans. Pension benefits served this dual purpose, honoring the mythic heroes and providing for their economic support. These purposes cannot be separated, and they are what clearly mark this as a southern social welfare system. Aging veterans were cared for in a consciously "southern" way. It was necessary to provide for this aging population, but if caring for the veterans was the only aim, it would have been unnecessary to place restrictions on receiving that support. Restricting which veterans would receive pensions meant many elderly veterans who needed help did not get it. The South wanted to care for its heroes, but it also wanted to decide which heroes were worthy of its care.

NOTES

I would like to thank Jan Walmsley for her invaluable assistance, Roger Ransom for his help, and the Social Science History Association (SSHA) panel for comments on a work in progress.

1. Some of William H. Glasson's work includes "Federal and Confederate Pensions in the South," *South Atlantic Quarterly* 9 (1910): 280–85; "The South's Care for Her Confederate Veterans," *The American Monthly Review of Reviews* 36 (1907): 40–47; and "The State Military Pension System of Tennessee," *Annals of the American Academy of Political and Social Science* 18(1901): 485–88. Megan McClintock's work is "Civil War Pensions and the Reconstruction of Union Families," *Journal of American History* 83 (September 1996): 456–80. One aspect of the lives of Confederate veterans that has received treatment is R. B. Rosenburg, *Living Monuments: Confederate Soldiers' Homes in the New South* (Chapel Hill: University of North Carolina Press, 1993). Theda Skocpol's *Protecting Soldiers and Mothers: The Political Origins of Social Policy in the United States* (Cambridge, Mass.: Belknap Press of Harvard University Press, 1992) also provides a good comparative look at the development of social welfare systems in the United States and Western Europe.

2. 1890 Census Special Section on Civil War veterans. Most veterans were involved in some form of agricultural work.

3. Information on Confederate pension systems is from Texas, Comptroller's Office, *Special Report on the Confederate Pension Law* (Austin: Comptroller's Office, 1908), 3–4.

4. Kathleen Lynn Gorman, "When Johnny Came Marching Home: Confederate Veterans in the New South" (Ph.D. diss., University of California, Riverside, 1994), chap. 2.

5. Information on Georgia pensions is from Georgia, Georgia Confederate Pensions and Records Department (hereafter referred to as GCPRD), *1943–44 Annual Report*. The *1960 Annual Report* indicated three widows were added to the rolls that year. Glasson, "The South's Care," 45.

6. GCPRD, *1943–44 Annual Report*. Glasson, "The South's Care," 45.

7. GCPRD, *Report of Commissioners of Pensions 1900–17, Correspondence with Governor*, July 1949, *1937 Annual Report, 1943–44 Annual Report*. Skocpol, *Protecting Soldiers*, 109.

8. As late as the mid-1950s the state was still spending more than four hundred thousand dollars on Confederate pensions. Information in the preceding paragraph is from GCPRD,

Report of Commissioners, Correspondence with Governor, July 1949, *1937 Annual Report, 1943–44 Annual Report,* and Peter Wallenstein, *From Slave South to New South: Public Policy in Nineteenth-Century Georgia* (Chapel Hill: University of North Carolina Press, 1987), 138–92.

9. Information in the two preceding paragraphs is from GCPRD, *General Correspondence, 1937 Annual Report,* and *Correspondence with Governor's Office.*

10. GCPRD, *General Correspondence.* Georgia, *Journal of the House of Representatives of the State of Georgia at the Extraordinary Session of the General Assembly* (Atlanta: State Printing Office, 1931), 672–85.

11. Discussion of Walton's place in the postwar world is taken from David Weiman, "The Economic Emancipation of the Non-Slaveholding Class" *Journal of Economic History* 45 (March 1985): 74–77; Steven Hahn, "The 'Unmaking' of the Southern Yeomanry: The Transformation of the Georgia Upcountry, 1860–1890," in Steven Hahn and Jonathan Prude, eds., *The Countryside in the Age of Capitalist Transformation: Essays in the Social History of Rural America* (Chapel Hill: University of North Carolina Press, 1985), 180–84; Robert Preston Brooks, *The Agrarian Revolution in Georgia, 1865–1912* (Madison: University of Wisconsin, 1914; reprint, Westport, Conn.: Negro Universities Press, 1970), 71, 127; Steven Hahn, *The Roots of Southern Populism: Yeoman Farmers and the Transformation of the Georgia Upcountry, 1850–1890* (New York: Oxford University Press, 1983); and appropriate federal agricultural censuses.

The primary source of information about Walton County itself is Anita Sams, *Wayfarers in Walton: A History of Walton County, Georgia, 1818–1967* (Monroe, Ga.: Genera Charitable Foundation of Monroe, Georgia, Inc., 1967). This work is much like an almanac in that it is a collection of information about the county. However Sams includes almost no information about African Americans or about anything that reflects negatively on the county or any of its leading residents.

12. In fact, 153 of 255 (60 percent) county applicants were classified as "broken down" by the doctors.

13. The information in the preceding paragraphs was gathered by analyzing the pension applications from Walton and reading the pension commissioner's correspondence.

14. Skocpol notes a similar phenomenon with Union pensions. "In short, individual gumption, social connections, and a good deal of outreach by party politicians shaped the specific destinations, timing, and generosity of Civil War pensions." *Protecting Soldiers,* 148.

15. There is at least one case in the Walton applications of an applicant noting no one he had served with would come with him to testify in his behalf. J. T. Tuck indicated on his application that because he had refused to serve as a witness for others (believing pensions were not needed), no one would stand up for him. The ordinary filled out the forms for many illiterate veterans, further increasing their dependence on him. The doctors noted more than once that an applicant was an honorable old man for whom the state had a responsibility to care. Biographical information on Garrett and Knight is from Sams, *Wayfarers,* 508–18.

At the same time the Confederate pension system was developing and focusing attention on the concept of honor, definitions of manhood were being challenged and refined. Glenda

Elizabeth Gilmore's *Gender and Jim Crow: Women and the Politics of White Supremacy in North Carolina, 1896–1920* (Chapel Hill: University of North Carolina Press, 1996) discusses the development of the "New White Man" who had to remove African Americans from any position of power and replace his Confederate veteran father as the elite in the region.

16. McClintock's "Civil War Pensions" notes the same need among Union soldiers' families and the pressure put on the federal government to take care of the families.

17. Information on the status of Walton veterans is based on reviewing 350 pension applications from Walton County contained in the Georgia Department of Archives and History's microfilm collection. Men who only received disability pensions were not included because of the lack of information included on those applications. Many veterans' applications do not include any kind of closing record so it was not possible to determine the amount of time they spent on the rolls, making the figures for years on pension much too low.

18. There are numerous indications of the respect Garrett was given in his community. He was chosen repeatedly to serve on the grand jury, an honor given to selected county residents by a committee consisting of the justices of the inferior court, sheriff, and clerk of the superior court. He also was chosen in 1900 "to care for and support" Mrs. Henrietta Hustin, "an unmarried wealthy woman," for the rest of her life. It is clear his peers considered Garrett to be an honorable man and worthy of whatever benefits they could provide for him. Walton County, County Court, *Grand Jury List,* 1881–1905, and *Deed Book F,* 376–77.

19. Walton County, *Tax Digest.* All information on the pension applications of Garrett and Needham is from the appropriate pension application. Both men were featured in articles in their local papers. Rolly Needham's interview with the Loganville *Record* on February 15, 1918, focused on the then-current crisis of World War I, while Garrett's interview with the Walton *Tribune* on March 25, 1932, dwelled on the past, particularly the Civil War. Determining the specific cause of friction with Needham is not easy, although it is possible he either actually did or was thought to have shot himself in the foot to escape the war, but there is no indication of that in his records. Even the mere hint of such an allegation would be enough to cause others to ostracize him. His ostracization is also clear in that he was not chosen for such things as grand jury service when he was clearly qualified.

It is nearly impossible to determine how many pension applications were denied, although simply scanning the applications indicates the commissioner had problems with many and required them to be resubmitted. The same applicant might (and did) reapply annually for years hoping for approval. Denials were written right on the actual application form, and there is no centralized list of denials; the only way to determine the percentage of disapproved applications is to go through each and every application.

Regulating the Poor in Alabama

The Jefferson County Poor Farm, 1885–1945

JAMES H. TUTEN

"The word 'poorhouse' has become the threatening symbol of one of humanity's great degradations," wrote Harry Evans in 1923. Evans, who made one of the earliest surveys of this institution, found in the very name a "sound like the crack of doom. It is a word of hate and loathing, for it includes the composite horrors of poverty, disgrace, loneliness, humiliation, abandonment, and degradation."[1] From 1773 until the mid-twentieth century, institutions for the poor served as clearinghouses for society's outcasts. In the North, towns and cities operated such institutions, while in the South county governments were responsible for the poor. By the 1880s Americans had made the poor farm system the primary means of poor relief. But by the 1920s, when Harry Evans wrote his book, the poor farm as an institution was losing credibility because it was both expensive to operate and inhumane to the inmates. Evans's progressive criticism paved the way for the New Deal programs for poor relief, which began in the 1930s.

This essay will examine the records of Alabama's Jefferson County Poor Farm, a good example of a poor farm with substantial surviving records that illustrate the nature of poor relief and the ways in which it changed between 1885 and 1945, paralleling national and regional changes. The narrative will explore how progressive reformers sought to lessen the stigma attached to being a pauper and to ease the conditions at the farm. The efforts of reformers led to the construction of a new, safer, and more serviceable facility in 1930. Having a slightly better understanding of public health factors, they also removed children, the insane, and the tubercular to separate specialized facilities elsewhere in the state. However, despite their good intentions, the constraints reformers placed on racial and gender segregation and the increasing age and ill health of the inmate population prevented them from achieving their goals.

Alabama, like the rest of the nation, viewed the care of the poor as a local issue during the nineteenth century. This viewpoint was rooted in the traditions of English common law and in the Elizabethan Poor Law of 1601. These laws made local governments responsible for the poor, and they distinguished between the "deserving" and "undeserving" poor. In keeping with the spirit of reform in America in the late nineteenth century, Alabamians viewed poor farms as beneficial for the indigent. The only serious statewide reform movement focusing on poor farms was aimed at increasing efficiency instead of creating a new system. In the mid-1880s a few reformers, such as Sen. Ira Foster, pushed for a consolidation of county poor farms into regional centers serving several counties. Foster and his supporters recognized that considerable waste and inefficiency resulted from the decentralized system, in which rural counties maintained a poor farm for one or two persons while such populous areas as Jefferson County housed numerous poor people. Their movement did not succeed, however, because of localist sentiment and an apparent lack of interest among legislators.[2]

Jefferson County, established in 1819, became a plantation agricultural area during the antebellum period. In the 1870s, Col. James R. Powell and several other men formed the Elyton Land Company to finance and build an industrial city in the county and to exploit the prodigious veins of iron ore and coal there. Birmingham became known as the "Magic City," as it grew into not only the largest city in the state but also became the model of the New South's commitment to industry and boosterism.[3]

With this growth in population came significant problems with poor relief. Early poor relief in Jefferson County, however, belied the county's urban image; county commissioners used methods more common in rural areas of the nation. The county commissioners engaged in the pauper lease system, which was used by many rural counties in the South. Pauper leasing involved collecting bids for the care of the poor and awarding the contract to the lowest bidder. In 1883, for example, John Foster leased some Jefferson County paupers for $4.05 each per month. Foster was responsible for their food and clothing, while the county provided shelter. In return Foster earned a sum from the county. Essentially he won the contract to be the supervisor of the poor farm. In contemporary terms this system was privatized poor relief.[4] The county also used outdoor relief, making payments to the poor, but the Jefferson County Poor Farm filled the growing need for institutionalized aid in the area.

Jefferson County maintained the poor farm in Woodlawn, which in the late nineteenth century was a suburb of Birmingham. It was designed with work in mind. Convicts, paupers, and other able-bodied residents worked on the poor farm in an effort to provide food for themselves and other inmates. The varieties of vegetables and the methods of farming and animal husbandry employed on the poor farm were the same used on the small sharecropper or tenant plots from which many of the poor had come. However poor farms did not succeed in becoming self-sufficient in their agricultural efforts.[5]

It has been suggested that one function of poor relief is to discipline the poor.[6] The history of the Jefferson County Poor Farm certainly supports this conclusion. The county commissioners established rules of conduct for the inmates in 1885. These rules included admonitions to eschew profanity and maintain cleanliness and also required frequent sanitizing of bedding, requiring that "new straw [be] put into the beds" monthly. More important, though, were the rules requiring the appointing of some inmates as cooks for the institution, and those requiring all inmates to comply with the work duties assigned to them. The thirteenth rule established by the commissioners clarified the importance of discipline, providing that inmates "failing to comply with any of the provisions . . . shall be subject to having [their] rations reduced, or otherwise punished in such ways as shall be presented by the inspector."[7]

The extant records for the poor farm begin in 1885, when the superintendent started keeping a detailed account of each inmate, recording the dates of and reasons for admission and departure, along with such demographic characteristics as age, sex, and race. The inmates themselves, like many people on the bottom socioeconomic rungs of American society, left behind few records. However the records of the Jefferson County Poor Farm provide key information about the inmates and reveal how they, and the institution itself, changed over time. This study will examine a sample by using the records for 1885, 1915, and 1930, which will provide a framework for understanding the way the poor farm operated.[8] The institution was far from ideal for solving the problems of poor relief in Jefferson county, but as needs and problems changed, the institution also showed changes in its demography and its organization.

The records from 1885 explain the conditions that brought people to the poor farm. In the nineteenth century, poor farms and almshouses were not strictly institutions for the destitute, but rather served rural areas as combined orphanage, sanitarium, old age home, and insane asylum. Thus, paupers, or persons present strictly due to financial condition, only constituted one quarter of Jefferson County's inmate population. The factor forcing people to the poor farm most frequently was chronic or serious illness.[9]

Nationally it was common for children to reside in this type of institution, which contributed to a surprising demographic trait of the Jefferson County Poor Farm in 1885: the overall youth of the population. The data from 1885 strongly suggest that in the 1880s old age could not have been a severely limiting factor upon the agricultural capability of the poor farm. The mean age of residents was 33.8.[10] Even in the late nineteenth century, thirty-three years old was far from elderly. The mortality rate for inmates admitted to the poor farm in 1885 was only 44 percent of the total, a relatively low rate considering the high incidence of illness among the population. However the relatively low rate of mortality may be explained by the youthfulness of the population. The average age of 33.8 among 1885 inmates counters the claims that poor farms were full of elderly people.[11] Although the county claimed throughout the 1890s to be burdened by the expense of coffins and burials for paupers, on the Jefferson County Poor Farm in 1885, most inmates were near the prime age of their working lives.[12] Therefore other causes must have brought about the failure of the farm's agricultural enterprises at the Jefferson County Poor Farm.

The demographic breakdown of the poor farm in 1885 reveals other important characteristics of the inmate population. Immediately apparent is the nearly equal distribution among race and sex categories. It is generally true that populations tend toward equilibrium between male and female; therefore it is not surprising that men made up 56 percent of the inmates and women 43 percent. On the other hand, the farm's near parity along racial lines reveals that race played a vital role in determining who was impoverished and who entered the poor farm. The 1880 Census reported that blacks constituted only 21 percent of the county population, but they made up 43 percent of the inmate population.[13]

The Jefferson County Poor Farm records also explain how inmates

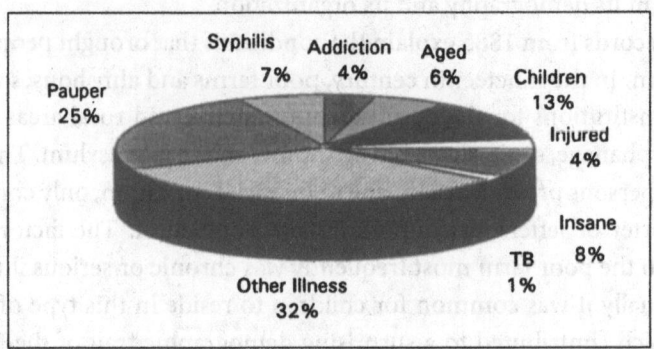

Figure 1. Reasons for Entry 1885

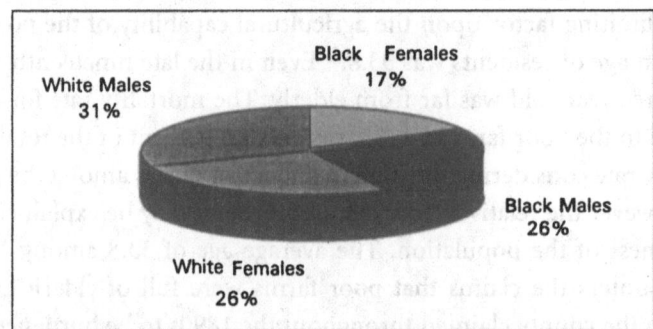

Figure 2. Race and Sex 1885

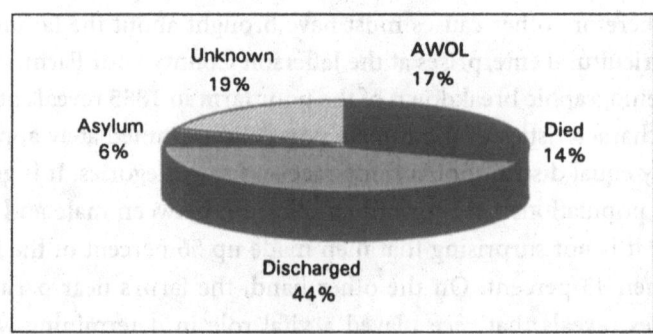

Figure 3. Means of Departure 1885

departed. One reason for taking someone away from the poor farm was serious mental illness. In 1885 the insane made up 8 percent of the population of the poor farm, but the superintendent eventually transferred many of these inmates to the state asylum in Tuscaloosa. It is not always clear what was meant by the term "insane" as used in the records. The poor farm's bookkeeper used several different terms to describe the insane: "simple," "idiot," "insane," and in one extreme case "raving maniac." Those considered "simple," or who suffered from some form of mild mental disability, did not require treatment in the asylum; this would account for the fact that some inmates were never transferred there.

Aside from transfer, there were many reasons for discharge. Most of the inmates regained their health or improved their circumstances enough to leave. The superintendent discharged 44 percent of the 1885 inmates after they recovered or some family member undertook custody and care of them. Another 17 percent left the institution without leave from the administrators, which suggests that some patients were anxious to escape the poor farm. The escapees of the Jefferson County Poor Farm may have decided that poverty outside the institution was preferable to the misery within.[14]

In 1885 the county commissioners allowed relief in both the form of the poor farm and in the form of outdoor payments. Outdoor payments were designed to help poor families without recourse to an institution. However, in 1897, paralleling a nationwide trend to end outdoor payments, Jefferson County ceased giving them altogether, which increased pressure on the farm. Two years later, as the county recovered from a severe smallpox epidemic, the county commissioners turned their attention to the poor farm again. They hired a matron for the institution who was responsible for custodial staff, food service, and nursing care for the inmates. Simultaneously the county hired a staff physician for the inmates' health needs. A new bureaucracy for county poor relief was now in place, made up of the county commissioners, the overseer for the poor, the poor farm superintendent, the physician, and the matron. Poor relief became centralized, bureaucratized, and increasingly controlled. This trend would continue into the next century.[15]

Progressivism in Alabama gained momentum during the first decade of the twentieth century, but it was not until the second decade that the poor enjoyed any helpful change. The 1897 reforms had done little to improve conditions. The county commissioners, responding to public criticism, authorized inspections of the farm in 1911 and 1912. The health officer's report noted good conditions but severe overcrowding. The report called for newer, larger facilities that were better equipped to serve the incurably ill inmates that constituted most of the population. Many insane inmates could not be transferred to Tuscaloosa because of overcrowding at the state asylum. As a result the poor farm now contained insane wards, which were separate from the other poor farm buildings. In 1912 the county constructed a new brick building for the insane inmates. The remaining facilities included wooden buildings segregated by sex and race, two wards each for white men and women, but only one each for black men and women. The county segregated inmates with tuberculosis in their own dormitory. The staff reportedly cleaned and disinfected the buildings, but they were already in bad condition in 1912 and would deteriorate further until the county provided new facilities.[16]

By 1915 the records showed significant changes in the age, race, and sex of the population on the poor farm. The mean age of inmates for 1915 was forty-three, exactly ten years older than the mean for 1885.[17] We must ask why the mean shifted ten years during this thirty-year period. One explanation may be in the much larger population within the poor farm itself. The number of admissions grew from 76 in 1885 to more than 370 in 1915. This larger group might be expected to represent a somewhat older general population. More important, children were now excluded from the poor farm rolls. By this time children were not admitted with parents entering the poor farm, as they had been in past years. Progressive reformers' growing concern for the well-being of children led to reforms in child labor laws and to separate care and housing for poor children. One reason for this was to protect them from the conditions on county poor farms.[18]

Unlike the 1885 data, the demographic breakdown of the Jefferson County Poor Farm in 1915 did not reflect general characteristics in the county's population. The ratio of male to female citizens in the county population was 52 percent male and 48 percent female, but 67 percent of the poor farm was male. The racial demography of the poor farm was more surprising. Nearly three-quarters, or 74 percent, of the inmates were black in 1915, while the county population was only 43 percent black. These figures underscore the fact that the average poor farm inmate was a black male and that white women were least likely to be found in the poor farm. It is

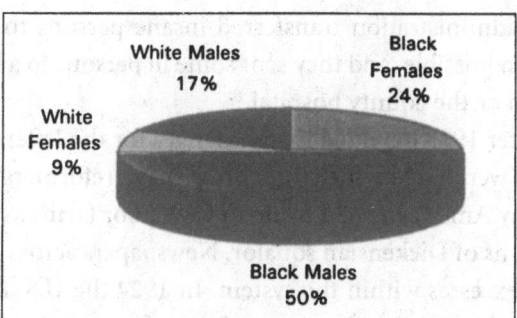

Figure 4. Race and Sex 1915

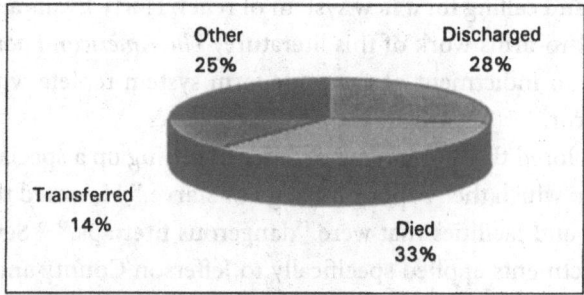

Figure 5. Means of Departure 1915

not surprising that white women were found least often, considering the symbolic place awarded them in southern culture. The conditions of tenancy and sharecropping and the prevailing black codes all placed economic and social pressures on black men, which resulted in widespread poverty in Alabama.[19]

The statistics on means of departure for 1915 also reveal significant changes from 1885. Most notable was the sharp rise in mortality among inmates, which accounted for a third of the departures. This can be explained mostly by the rise in mean age among inmates, the increased length of stay, and the transformation of the institution into a place of residence for chronically ill persons. Conversely the number of inmates discharged back into the community dropped to 28 percent, underscoring the institution's changed role from a temporary shelter, or a place to begin life anew, to a place for those who were dying or or who needed long-term care. Finally the number of inmates transferred to other institutions rose to

14 percent. The administration transferred insane persons to the Tuscaloosa asylum when possible, and they sent some ill persons to a local tuberculosis sanitarium or the county hospital.[20]

The decades after 1915 heralded many changes for the Jefferson County Poor Farm. They were largely fueled by progressive reformers' criticisms. By the 1920s many Americans had come to view poor farms as inhumane, wasteful institutions of Dickensian squalor. Newspapers across the country had exposed the excesses within the system. In 1924 the U.S. Department of Labor conducted a nationwide survey of poor farms, in part to demonstrate how miserably they served the poor. Throughout the decade intellectuals, social workers, and reformers generated literature denouncing the poor farms and calling for a new system of relief. Harry Evans authored the scathing call-to-arms work of this literature, *The American Poor Farm and Its Inmates*, an indictment of the poor farm system replete with descriptions of horror.[21]

Evans deplored the "inhumane practice of setting up a special place and labeling it, to which the . . . poor must go or starve." He noted the "neglect of inmates" and facilities that were "dangerous firetraps."[22] Several of his general indictments applied specifically to Jefferson County and Alabama. Jefferson County was guilty of holding "hospital cases, the feeble-minded, the insane, the deaf and dumb, the blind," and children in the institution. Alabama certainly fell under one part of the indictment, by "maintaining scores of poorfarms . . . when one [institution] would render more efficient, more economical, more scientific service." In several categories, however, Jefferson County did not sink as low as other counties. Evans also decried the general failure of good bookkeeping on inmates and crops, but Jefferson County kept excellent records. Jefferson County also no longer contracted out paupers after the 1880s, and they did not "sentence criminals to poorfarms."[23] Though it was neither the best nor the worst example of its kind, the Jefferson County Poor Farm had the dubious distinction of being the largest in Alabama for many years. At the time the surveyors produced their report in 1924, the inmate population was 144 with 32 acres under cultivation.[24] The U.S. Labor Department report generated little notice in Jefferson County. One newspaper writer commented that "[i]t costs Alabama less per inmate to maintain her almshouses than any other state in the union," but he did not specify whether he wished to praise the state's thriftiness or to chastise its callousness.[25]

Such ambivalent attitudes toward the poor in Jefferson County were about to change. In the 1930s the Great Depression crippled the nation and compounded economic difficulties in Alabama. Many people lost their means of caring for themselves and turned in desperation to the poor farm. Residents of Jefferson County had already begun to notice problems with the poor farm even before the stock market crash. In a speech to the Birmingham Kiwanis Club in February of 1929, the president of the Jefferson County Board of Revenue called the poor farm "a disgrace, a fire-trap [which] should be replaced."[26] The following day, both major newspapers in the city carried reports on the poor farm because of the report of the Jefferson County Grand Jury, which met quarterly to try cases and make decisions on local policy. The grand jury roundly condemned the facilities and called for the construction of a new building. The jury's action came as no surprise, since it was the twentieth consecutive jury to take such action. The jury reported that "the detention house is badly ventilated and should not be used for the housing of human beings."[27]

The stir created by the grand jury and the board of revenue's motion to build a new facility gathered steam throughout the year. The county commissioners decided to relocate the poor farm from Woodlawn to an out-of-town location at Ketona, the site of the county farm and pesthouse. By 1929 the commissioners recognized two reasons to abandon the Woodlawn real estate. The property had escalated in value, giving the county an unexpected source of potential revenue. As one paper reported, "The property is valuable and will bring a neat sum."[28] It was also thoroughly inadequate for the poor relief needs of the county. By May of 1929, the commissioners had decided to sell the Woodlawn site. In July the county finally authorized the construction of a new poor farm.[29]

Many economic changes occurred during the remainder of 1929, including the stock market crash and the full onset of economic depression; yet the planning for the new poor farm went forward. While expensive public works projects were questioned in many places, the Great Depression increased the importance of a new facility for the poor. In March of 1930 the commissioners allocated $150,000 for the new construction and commissioned the architect George P. Turner to draw up plans. Turner's commission from the county required that "the building will be fireproof, modern in every respect, with accommodations for approximately 225 persons."[30] The plans actually produced by Turner provided for 335 inmates, and the contractor's bids totaled $250,000. Despite the higher-than-predicted cost, plans for "the most modern structure of its type in the South" continued.[31]

Turner's plans were elaborate in some ways, resulting from his survey of almshouses across the region. The new poor farm utilized a southern colonial style with white columns for the main building. Certainly this architectural style had been popular in the region for many years; still, the choice of a plantation-style big house suggested some remnants of symbolic paternalism. This two-story building served as administrative offices and housed a hospital with an elevator. The dormitories connected with the main building and with each other to form a campus for the poor. Turner designed eight primary dorms, segregated by race and sex, and two smaller secondary dorms, one for the insane and the other for black convicts. Apparently the county returned to the use of convict labor to aid with the poor farm, and race influenced the decision to locate only black convicts there.

Despite the racism inherent in this decision, the commission made some progressive steps. The buildings were nearly all single story to ease the egress for feeble inmates in case of fire. The institution no longer advocated farming labor for its inmates. In a feature inspired by "sentiment," according to the *Birmingham News*, administrators decided to discontinue the policy of separating married couples and designated some space within the dormitories for them. The central building held a physical plant on the lower floor that provided steam heat to the campus and to a shoe shop and barber. The second story, at ground level for ease of access, housed a central kitchen that cooked for the four segregated dining rooms. Finally for the spiritual care of the inmates, two chapels—one for each race—stood at the end of the two courtyards.[32]

In July of 1931 the county commissioners held an open house to show off their new poor farm, which they renamed the Jefferson County Home. The board of revenue thought that "home" sounded more pleasant and carried less stigma than "almshouse" or "poor farm." This approach, designed to lessen or eliminate the stigmas associated with poor relief, denoted a change in attitude that was occurring not only in Jefferson County but throughout the nation. Jefferson County was proud of its new facility and of the progressivism and humanitarian concern for the poor that it demonstrated. The *Birmingham News* boasted, "A visit to the home will be likely to send one away with a desire ... to congratulate Jefferson County upon having such a home with . . . so fine a staff, and then upon having a commission which shows so fine an understanding of the value of social work that it has made this institution a social agency in the community."[33]

Not all progressive voices agreed that a new facility was the best solution. In an editorial of June 31, 1930, the *News* pondered the intelligence of building a new facility for indoor relief while communities in Europe, South America, and some eleven U.S. states were creating old-age pension systems. The editorialist candidly called this movement "not only illuminating—it is arresting. One is . . . constrained to wonder if Alabama . . . will decide to abandon the almshouse system with all its dismal horrors and enormous expense and substitute direct relief instead."[34]

The movement against poor farms led by fraternal organizations and the Department of Labor contributed to this open debate over improved indoor relief versus outdoor relief. In August 1930, Thomas Huey, a progressive businessman and past board member, went before the board of revenue and urged that plans for the new poor farm be replaced by a pension system. He stated that the new facility would be "as obsolete in Jefferson County as a horse and buggy is today."[35] Huey marshaled the report of the Department of Labor to demonstrate how much spending on indoor relief in Alabama actually went into salaries, suggesting that the same money would be better used as a direct grant to the poor and old. He may also have influenced the change in name of the facility, because he brought up the stigma associated with living in an institution for the poor. He echoed the arguments and statistics of *The American Poor Farm and Its Inmates*.[36] The progressive advocates for the new site at Ketona, however, won the day. W. E. Corning, a member of the board of revenue, argued that "old age pensions would not only be impartial, but would open a way for graft." He argued further that the cost of pensions would be much higher than that of the poor farm and that inmates received health care in the institution, which they could not receive elsewhere. While the advocates for pensions lost that case, they proved to be in accord with national sentiments, which would lead to the creation of Social Security in the coming years.[37]

Meanwhile, the nature of the poor farm itself had also been changing as the institution adjusted to new social and economic demands. Analysis of the inmates present in the poor farm in 1930 reveals a further shift in population from that of 1915. The mean age had continued to rise, reaching 57.4 in 1930. By this time, therefore, the average age of inmates had risen beyond what was considered to be middle-aged during this preantibiotic era of medicine. The three different figures for age distribution clearly indicate that the largest age cohorts moved to older age groups across these forty-five years. In 1885 there were no inmates over eighty-five, and there were nearly fifteen under the age of ten. But by 1930 the overall population was located entirely in the older cohorts, with children having disappeared altogether. The population had completed a shift, from a hodgepodge of races and ages to a largely older group, who were unable to care for themselves because of poverty, senility, or disability, and were likewise unable to contribute to the corporate good through labor on the farm.[38]

The calculations for race and sex demonstrate further the high presence of males among inmates and a slightly lower presence of blacks. Jefferson County possessed a 50/50 ratio along gender lines in 1930, yet males continued to make up more than two-thirds of the poor farm population, 70 percent. The racial composition had moved nearer to parity since 1915, with blacks accounting for 52 percent and whites 47 percent of admissions in 1930. The county's racial composition was 61 percent white and 38 percent black in 1930, so the disproportionate representation of blacks, and especially black males, continued throughout the period of this study.[39]

The changes in the statistics for means of departure from the institution also reflected the trend toward older inmates in the poor farm. The most striking change was the near reversal in the percentages for inmates that were released and those who died in the home. In 1885 44 percent had departed of their own ability, but that figure had declined to 28 percent by 1915. The figures from 1930 showed only a negligible further decline in the number of people discharged, falling to 27 percent. Inmates continued to run away from the poor farm; they were 17 percent of the population in 1885 and 14 percent in 1930. The poor farm remained an unpleasant place to be and many exercised any opportunity to leave.

A rise in mortality figures coincided with the drop in discharges as the population aged and their risk for illness grew. In 1915 a third of the inmates perished within the institution; that figure had increased to 41 percent by 1930. Since inmates in the poor farm tended to be older as a group over the course of this period, mortality and length of stay are worth considering. Though it is not possible to construct a useful index of mortality, raw figures help illuminate this primary demographic feature.[40] Of the seventy-six inmates admitted in 1885, eleven died in the poor farm. The

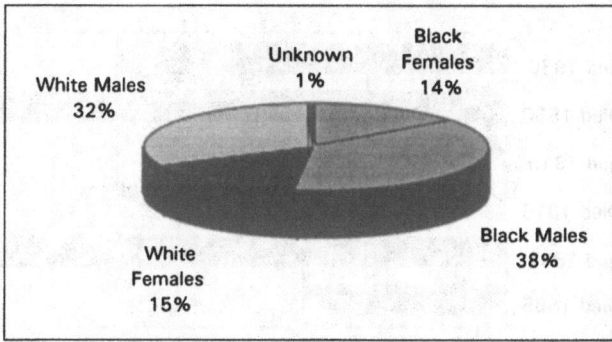

Figure 6. Race and Sex 1930

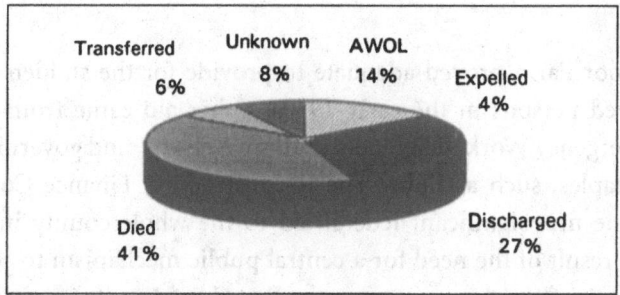

Figure 7. Means of Departure 1930

admissions of 1915 totaled 371, of which 129 died, and the 1930 admissions numbered 214, of which 86 died. Percentages illustrate the change even more clearly: for 1885 the percentage of admissions that died in residence was 14.5 percent, while the percentage for 1915 was 34.8 percent, and the percentage for 1930 was 38.3 percent. In 1885 most inmates left the institution alive, while in 1930 most of the inmates died in residence (most of this change occurred between 1885 and 1915).[41] Since inmates were in residence for a greater duration, and were at the same time older than previous populations, it would be reasonable to expect a rise in mortality in keeping with the changes. Other factors, especially the age and poor physical condition of the poor farm population, had a greater impact upon mortality.[42]

The early 1930s were years of great change for poor relief in Jefferson County and the nation. The Jefferson County Community Chest and the Red Cross had provided some outdoor relief in the late 1920s and the early years of the Great Depression, but neither these groups nor the Jefferson

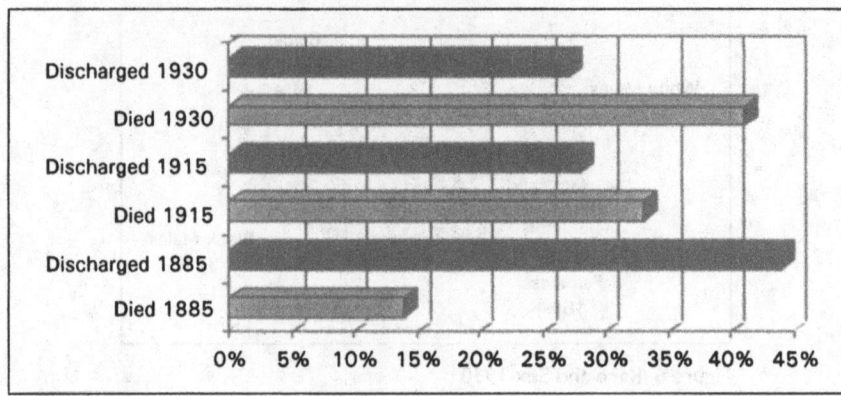

Figure 8. Cumulative Means of Departure

County Poor Farm proved adequate to provide for the sudden deluge of unemployed persons in the early 1930s. Other aid came from Birmingham's Emergency Work Relief, new charitable efforts, and government gifts of food staples, such as flour. The Reconstruction Finance Corporation brought the first significant federal aid to the whole county in 1932. In 1933, as a result of the need for a central public mechanism to administer relief from the federal government, the Red Cross Family Service of Jefferson County became a government entity, the Jefferson County Department of Public Welfare.[43]

Unparalleled federal intervention followed during Franklin Roosevelt's New Deal. The Civilian Conservation Corps, the Agricultural Adjustment Act, and other New Deal programs subsidized farmers, banks, and other businesses, helping some remain employed. But no piece of New Deal legislation had a bigger impact on the institutionalized poor than the Social Security Act of 1935. Social Security was precisely the type of outdoor relief that some reformers in Jefferson County had anticipated in 1930 when they argued against the new poor farm. The act stipulated that persons over age sixty-five and disabled persons would be eligible for pensions. In short Social Security was designed to help the types of persons then populating most of the poor farms in the nation.[44]

The following year, the transformation in poor relief began in earnest as the Alabama Department for Social Welfare organized and set to work deinstitutionalizing the poor. The seventh issue of *Alabama Social Welfare*, the department's newsletter, focused on the almshouses of the state and argued, as had others since Harry Evans, that all of them should be closed:

"The Social Security Act has made possible this advancement in the care and treatment of aged individuals." By the middle of 1936 Alabama counties had closed thirty-three such institutions, but the Jefferson County Poor Farm remained. The editors of the journal argued that counties saved money by closing their doors, and that the poor enjoyed both a better quality of life and an absence of stigma when pensioned and living in a family home. As for the poor under sixty-five years of age, the state contributed money in the form of matching grants to the counties for their care outside the institution.[45]

The rush to close poor farms continued throughout the remainder of the decade. In 1935 Alabama counties operated sixty-three poor farms and almshouses in the state, but by February of 1938 only thirteen remained open. Writers in *Alabama Social Welfare* trumpeted the quick progress that they felt had been made, especially in the realm of public opinion: "[T]raditions about the care of dependents began to go as enlightened public opinion grasped the principles . . . underlying public welfare methods."[46] Despite the enthusiasm for deinstitutionalization, Jefferson County and several other counties resisted this initial wave of closings. The county commission declared that it would not close the home at Ketona because the majority of its inmates required constant health care. Furthermore, they considered such action to be "neither economical nor practical for Jefferson County."[47]

The closings continued at a slower pace after 1938, largely because the remaining institutions, such as Ketona, served more populated counties with greater need for long-term institutional care. In 1941 only nine were still operating. Half of all inmates in the state by that time lived in Ketona. Even as late as 1947 Jefferson, Mobile, and Blount Counties maintained almshouses. As the *Birmingham Post-Herald* noted, however, "The poorhouses . . . are nothing like the old institutions. Today they are more like public nursing homes where public funds are used to take care of chronically ill persons for whom no other provisions have been made."[48]

As usually occurred in Jefferson County, the cycle of neglect and inhumane care returned to the county despite the new facilities.[49] In 1945 the county grand jury found fault with the staff and medical care and deplored the persistent problem of housing a large number of insane people. This time, the county commissioners sought to correct the problem by changing the institution's mission. They attempted to get Ketona named as a state nursing home, as the state was considering creating regional nursing homes at the time. The county commissioners hoped to turn over the responsibility for the home to the state, but ultimately these plans were not accomplished. Instead the county continued to operate the Jefferson County Home at Ketona as a nursing care facility, as it does to this day. It is impossible to say when the Jefferson County Home ceased to be a poor farm and became a nursing home because it had been moving gradually toward full-time care for the elderly as the inmate population aged.[50]

The Jefferson County Poor Farm can teach us much about the character and development of many aspects of southern society in the late nineteenth and early twentieth centuries. Race has been, and continues to be, an important consideration when examining poverty in the United States, and especially in the South. The calculations from 1885, 1915, and 1930 demonstrate, when compared to the county population at large, that the black population of Jefferson County was disproportionately represented in the poor farm. The reasons for this were many, but throughout this period most stemmed from the system of racial segregation that cut blacks out of avenues to education and economic opportunity. Not only did blacks suffer a higher rate of poverty, but they also endured further stigma through the segregation system within the poor farm itself. Although there are no records to indicate the quality of care, it is worth remembering that whites received preferential treatment in all other areas of southern society and presumably received it in the poor farm as well. Historian Wayne Flynt has marveled that "[a]mazingly, a white society that tolerated no race mixing . . . placed black and white indigents into the same facilities."[51] While it is true that separate institutions did not exist for the two races, they certainly remained thoroughly segregated within the institution, maintaining the southern caste system even in the debased environment of the county poor farm.

The demographic patterns of the Jefferson County Poor Farm demonstrate the declining health of the population. The rates of mortality were increasing despite the advances in medicine during the period. Although at the start of the study the average age of inmates was surprisingly young, the population tended to shift toward a more elderly group of inmates. Inmates were remaining within the institution for a year on average by the time of the Great Depression, but had very brief periods of institutionalization between 1885 and 1915. These findings raise some questions for further research. What was the effect of the Great Depression on the poor farm?

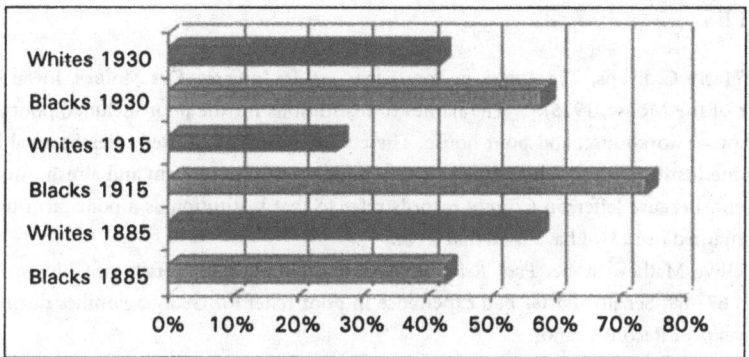
Figure 9. Cumulative Race Figures

What causes brought the younger poor farm inmates to the institution in 1885 and 1915? Further demographic study and research informed by the discipline of public health may shed more light on this part of the American past.

Public poor relief in Jefferson County sought simultaneously to reproach the poor and to keep them alive. The example of Jefferson County shows that progressive administrators made some genuine advances for the poor farm inmates. The best examples were the change in name to lessen the stigma of being a pauper and the significant expense and care given to constructing a new, safer, and more serviceable facility in 1930. However, despite some progressive strides, a cycle of recrimination over poor farm conditions persisted. The history of the poor farm of Jefferson County shared a common pattern with poor farms nationally, beginning as a small institution in the 1880s and reaching a peak during the years of the Great Depression before stabilizing as a result of New Deal relief policies. Jefferson County was unique for Alabama in that its poor farm did not close as did most in the 1930s, but instead like many institutions in the nation it formally changed function to care for the elderly. The statistics from the poor farm indicate that this change to elder care was in fact a natural outgrowth of the aging inmate demographic pattern. Ultimately we must remember that institutional care for the poor, insane, and indigent has been beset with problems of racial discrimination, incompetent care, and high mortality that recurred despite repeated efforts to correct them. These historical facts are worth remembering as we contemplate the future of poor relief in our day.

NOTES

1. Harry C. Evans, *The American Poor Farm and Its Inmates* (Des Moines, Iowa: Loyal Order of the Moose, 1926), 5. The names of institutions for the poor included poor farm, almshouse, workhouse, and poor house. These names were often used interchangeably for the same institution even though the strict connotations of poor farm and almshouse were different. Because Jefferson County records refer to that institution as a poor farm until it was renamed in 1931, I have used that term.

2. Olive Mathew Stone, *Poor Relief in Alabama* (Chicago: University of Chicago Press, 1929), 67–69. Senator Foster had experience in poor relief for Georgia families during the early years of Reconstruction.

3. Florence H. W. Moss, *Building Birmingham and Jefferson County* (Birmingham, Ala.: Birmingham Printing Company, 1947), 12–23, 106–13; William W. Rogers, Robert David Ward, Leah R. Atkins, and Wayne Flynt, *Alabama, The History of a Deep South State* (Tuscaloosa: University of Alabama Press, 1994), 280–85.

4. Anita Van de Voort, *Public Welfare Administration in Jefferson County, Alabama* (M.A. thesis, Tulane University, 1934), 7–10. The county spent $1,250 for the care of paupers during the first six months of 1884.

5. Records of the Jefferson County Alms House, Birmingham Public Library, Department of Archives and Manuscripts, Records of Poor Farm 1885–1909, 197–235. All citations of the poor farm records are from this collection unless otherwise stated. The extant records of the agricultural enterprises indicate that the inmates raised crops and animals that were common all over the rural South: vegetables, greens, pork, poultry, and beef. The poor farm stood on North Old Fiftieth Street, Woodlawn. *Birmingham News,* May 12, 1929; Van de Voort, 19.

6. Francis Fox Piven and Richard A. Cloward, *Regulating the Poor* (New York: Vintage Books, 1993), introduction.

7. Van de Voort, *Public Welfare,* 10–12. The records of the commissioners are not available, but pertinent sections were quoted at length in this work.

8. These three years of poor farm records were chosen because 1885 is the first year of extant records. The last year chosen, 1930, was the final year the poor farm was in its Woodlawn location. In addition the county was in the throes of the Great Depression in 1930, but the New Deal was not yet under way. The third year, 1915, was halfway between the two extremes and can provide an idea of the development of the institution in the early part of the century. The data from 1910 was incomplete though closer to the exact midpoint between the two extremes.

9. Poor farm records, 1–2. Tuberculosis and syphilis were designated because of the prominence of those diseases during the time. Addictions, though considered a disease today, were not considered so then and because of the frequency of appearance warranted special recognition.

10. The standard deviation for the 1885 data set was 22.7, the mode 42 out of a range from 0 to 85 and with 76 cases.

11. Steven R. Hoffbeck, "'Remember the Poor' (Galatians 2:10): Poor Farms in Vermont," *Vermont History* 57 (1989): 231–33.

12. Van de Voort, *Public Welfare*, 12–15. Granted that the deviation from the mean of 22.7 points out the likely presence of elderly inmates and also of children too young to work, most inmates should still have been capable of considerable labor.

13. U.S. Department of Interior, Census Office, *The Tenth Census of the United States: 1880*, vol. 1, 380.

14. Piven and Cloward, *Regulating the Poor*, 3, 33.

15. Alabama, and Birmingham in particular, experienced a rigorous period of progressive reforms during the first decade of the century. See Dewey W. Grantham, *Southern Progressivism* (Knoxville: University of Tennessee Press, 1983), 46–47, 218–20, 222; Van de Voort, *Public Welfare*, 15–18; Elizabeth Wisner, *Social Welfare in the South: From Colonial Times to World War I* (Baton Rouge: Louisiana State University Press, 1970), 45–47.

16. Van de Voort, *Public Welfare*, 17–20; Wayne J. Flynt, *Poor but Proud: Alabama's Poor Whites* (Tuscaloosa: University of Alabama Press, 1989), 183–85.

17. The standard deviation was 18, the mode 40, out of a range from 0 to 103 and 371 cases.

18. Stone, *Poor Relief in Alabama*, 68–69.

19. U.S. Department of Commerce, Bureau of the Census, *The Thirteenth Census of the United States: 1910*, vol. 2, 53.

20. The other category accounted for the remaining 25 percent of the inmates. Their means of departure was not known. Undoubtedly many of them fall into the categories of "died," "AWOL," or "transferred."

21. Evans, *American Poor Farm*, 1–3. Note that "fraternal" is meant inclusively here, as several women's organizations participated in addition to the Loyal Order of the Moose, Woodmen of the World, Beavers National Mutual Benefit, the Macabees, the Supreme Tribe of Ben Hur, the Degree of Honor, and the American Legion.

22. Evans, *American Poor Farm*, 3.

23. Ibid., 3. The final portion of Evans's work was essentially a reprint of the Bureau for Labor Statistics' *Cost of American Almshouses*.

24. Ibid., 101, 108–18. The 32 acres is a ratio of .22 acres per inmate.

25. *Birmingham News*, September 6, 1925.

26. Ibid., February 27, 1929.

27. Ibid., February 28, 1929, and *Birmingham Post*, February 28, 1929.

28. *Birmingham News*, May 11, 1929, and April 28, 1930.

29. Ibid., June 2, 1929.

30. Ibid., April 4, 1930.

31. *Birmingham News*, July 16, 1930, and *Birmingham Post*, July 16, 1930. Day and Sachs was the lowest-bidding general contractor at $197,000.

32. *Birmingham News*, July 24, 1930. The segregating of married couples served several purposes, but primarily it is a punishment for being poor.

33. Quote from the *Birmingham News*, October 1931 and July 14, 1931; see also *Birmingham Post*, March 3, 1931. Woodlawn had become even more overcrowded during the interim of the construction, providing for 220 inmates.

34. *Birmingham News*, July 31, 1930.

35. Ibid., August 6, 1930.

36. Evans, *American Poor Farm*, 5.

37. Ibid., 5.

38. The standard deviation for 1930 was 17.17, the mode 60, out of a range from 16 to 100 and with 214 cases.

39. U.S. Department of Commerce, Bureau of the Census, *The Fifteenth Census of the United States: 1930*, vol. 3, 101.

40. I used the following method for computation: deaths were counted only if the inmate died while residing in the institution, with no difference between an inmate who died on the second day in residence or in the sixth year. In 1885 the mean number of days that inmates spent in the institution was 108.9. The 1915 inmates had a mean length of stay of 74.4 days, a drop from the previous figure. At the same time, the number of inmates who died in residence rose significantly. While the length of stay had decreased, more people were dying and fewer were leaving or recovering. But the reduced tenure did not last, for in 1930 the mean had risen to 361.1 days.

41. The standard deviation for 1885 was 117.9, the median was 68, and the mode 136. The range was 393 out of a count of 76. For 1915 the standard deviation was 173.5, the median was 20, and the mode 1. The range was 1890 out of a count of 384. The figures for 1930 were a standard deviation of 928.7, a median of 56.5, and a mode of 17 with a range of 6,387 and a count of 156.

42. Bruce Smith, "Poor Relief at the St. Joseph County Poor Asylum, 1877–1891," *Indiana Magazine of History* 86 (June 1990): 187–95. Smith provides figures for means of departure, sex ratios, mean age, and length of stay. Although his study is of an earlier period, the figures provide useful material for comparison.

43. Van de Voort, *Public Welfare*, 62–73. The first head of the Department of Public Welfare was Roberta Morgan. The new department also took over some of the responsibilities of the Federation of Jewish Charities. The officials of the county and the city divided funding responsibility 60 percent to 40 percent, with Birmingham responsible for the larger portion.

44. Walter I. Trattner, *From Poor Law to Welfare State* (New York: Free Press, 1984), 271–77.

45. *Alabama Social Welfare*, vol. 1, no. 12, 1–4. See also *Birmingham News*, June 15, 1937, June 16, 1937, and February 15, 1938. Some relatives took in inmates because the pension no longer made them a liability upon family financial resources.

46. *Alabama Social Welfare* 3, no. 5 (May 1938): 14–15.

47. *Birmingham Post*, September 7, 1938.

48. *Birmingham Post-Herald*, November 3, 1947. See also *Alabama Social Welfare* 6, no. 4 (April 1941): 4.

49. *Birmingham Post Herald*, June 21, 1945. These cycles evident on the local level would seem to support the suggestions of Piven and Cloward on the cyclical patterns of relief.

50. *Birmingham News*, October 10, 1945.

51. Flynt, *Poor But Proud*, 184.

We Take Care of Our Womenfolk

The Home for Needy Confederate Women in Richmond, Virginia, 1898–1990

SUSAN HAMBURGER

Concern for the welfare of Civil War veterans and their dependents manifested itself in pensions and group homes for former soldiers and their widows. However the North and South approached such assistance differently. Theda Skocpol states that federal pensions were viewed politically and morally as a just repayment for sacrifice rather than as the European socioeconomic conception of old-age pensions benefiting those with diminished finances. Preventing a veteran who had honorably served the Union from experiencing the shame and degradation of becoming an almshouse inmate or charity case justified pensions, soldiers' relief, and veterans' homes.[1] Megan J. McClintock argues that the promise of federal veterans' pensions not only encouraged enlistment during the war but also controlled the private lives of pensioners and widows by passing judgment on their worthiness to collect by investigating living arrangements and familial relationships.[2] Southerners, on the other hand, could not partake of federal pensions or veterans' homes and relied instead on each state to allocate pension funds and on state governments and private organizations to operate homes. The fate of widows, mothers, and daughters rested in the hands of the social welfare administrators who decided the worthiness of these women to be accepted into the old-age homes.

As southern women had found an acceptable public outlet through nursing and writing during the Civil War, they applied their managerial and caregiving talents to alleviating social welfare problems in the late nineteenth and early twentieth centuries. As Sandra Gioia Treadway notes,

"Both black and white women worked through traditional church societies and ladies' guilds but also established new vehicles for their efforts: associations to aid the poor, the sick, and the veterans, widows, and orphans of the war; reform organizations; self-help and recreation societies for working women; and pioneering day-care programs for the children of working mothers."[3]

The Home for Needy Confederate Women in Richmond, Virginia, an early "old-age home," served to assist the women whose lives the Civil War disrupted through the death of their male providers. It also provided an opportunity for socially conscious women to contribute to their community at a time when "a passion for the Lost Cause became the vogue for white residents."[4] The soldiers' relief and ladies' aid societies during the war predated the Confederate memorial associations that brought women together to work toward a common goal as mourners and cultural guardians at the grassroots level during a time when they "struggled with the desire of many men to forget" the war.[5] The history of the Home for Needy Confederate Women exemplifies the determination of a group of Virginia women not only to provide comfortable housing for a specific class of "deserving," destitute white women but also to make the building a permanent memorial to their sacrifices.

By the 1880s both the North and the South recognized the need to care for poor, disabled, and unemployable elderly soldiers, their wives, widows, and orphans. Some states constructed facilities only for men, some allowed men to bring their wives, others specialized in caring for widows and/or orphans. Homes that restricted themselves to veterans and/or widows closed when the last residents died; others changed their mission to accommodate the needs of different retirees, such as when the Indiana Veterans' Home included veterans of other wars in 1976. The Widow's Home for women with children in Augusta, Georgia, became a way-station for the industrial working class and no longer housed permanent residents.[6]

In Richmond, Virginia, on February 22, 1885, the Lee Camp Soldiers' Home, a community of buildings located on the thirty-six acre former farm and homestead of Channing Robinson, opened its doors to Confederate veterans to much fanfare.[7] The needy and indigent women of Virginia would have their own champions and supporters a decade later.

The Ladies' Auxiliary of George E. Pickett Camp, Confederate Veterans, Richmond, concerned about the dire straits of numerous female relatives of dead and disabled Confederate soldiers, sought to relieve their suffering. In a March 29, 1897, broadside, the auxiliary appealed to the people of the Commonwealth of Virginia for practical aid in founding a home for aged, feeble, and dependent women of the Confederacy. Led by Pres. Mrs. Robert N. Northen and committee chair Mrs. M. A. Burgess, the auxiliary organized a Confederate Festival from May 19 to 29 at the regimental armory to raise money for a home.[8] With the one-thousand-dollar profit the auxiliary planned to buy the house at Ninth and Leigh Streets where several nearly destitute Confederate women lived.[9]

Before the auxiliary could legally purchase property or receive public funds for the project, the Commonwealth required them to organize formally and obtain a charter from the Virginia General Assembly. On March 3, 1898, the legislature approved "[a]n act to incorporate the Home for Needy Confederate Women" to allow the corporation to establish and conduct a home for the needy widows, wives, sisters, and daughters of Confederate soldiers.[10] The directors, headed by LaSalle Corbell Pickett, the wife of Confederate general George E. Pickett, as honorary president, consisted of prominent middle-class Richmond women including Alice A. (Mrs. Augustus J.) Pyle and Sarah J. (Mrs. Peyton) Carrington.[11]

While the day-to-day management of the home resided with an executive committee of the all-female board of directors, a five-member advisory board, a treasurer, and three trustees (all men) handled the business affairs and held "the legal title to all bonds, stocks, and securities, donated to or purchased by the Home."[12] Richmond mayor Carleton McCarthy, three ex-military men, two judges, and two civilians constituted the initial members of the advisory board and trustees.[13]

Selecting a suitable location became a primary concern. In 1900 new officers of the auxiliary collected five hundred dollars at a second fundraising bazaar. With the fifteen hundred dollars plus one thousand dollars appropriated by the state legislature, the board of directors bought a house for seventy-five hundred dollars at 1726 Grove Avenue.[14] The board designated October 15 as the first of many "Donation Days" established to collect merchandise and furnishings to outfit the home; they received many contributions of various kinds and requested a Confederate flag.[15] Northern as well as southern supporters sent checks for the new charity.[16]

Ten inmates moved into the home on October 15, 1900.[17] The establishment and opening of the home brought support and encouragement from

Gov. James Hoge Tyler, former governor Fitzhugh Lee, the Rev. Dr. Moses Drury Hoge, and other prominent Richmonders. At the formal ceremony on October 30, Mayor McCarthy, who spoke on behalf of the women board members, presented the home to the Commonwealth. Governor Tyler accepted the institution and returned it to McCarthy for the board to manage. When news of the home spread, even before it opened, letters of application for admittance arrived from all over the state.[18]

The home prospered until the 1902 depression reduced donations and financial support; the inmates sought employment to support themselves. Board member Alice Pyle, a local businesswoman, visited the markets after hours in her carriage to ask for the bruised and damaged produce to feed the women.[19] On the verge of bankruptcy, the board turned to Elizabeth "Betsie" Lyne Hoskins Montague. She had moved from Danville to Richmond in 1898 with her husband, Andrew Jackson Montague, the newly elected attorney general for the Commonwealth. Jack Montague, the son of the secessionist Civil War lieutenant governor of Virginia, developed into a moralistic, idealistic progressive reformer who, as governor (1902–6) supported judicial streamlining, strengthening education, and improving mental hospitals, but he also appealed for a "return to the ideals of other days."[20] Because of her husband's political positions, Mrs. Montague had access to a wide variety of influential people. Betsie Montague fit Anne Firor Scott's description of the new southern woman who "maintained the graciousness and charm which had been the sound part of the chivalric ideal and, without losing her femininity or abandoning her responsibility for the propagation of the species, became an important force in public as well as in private life."[21] Approached by the board of directors to become a member in 1899, Betsie Montague considered the request. Her husband agreed that the home represented one of the outstanding needs of the time, and she accepted.[22] The board then offered her the presidency, but she declined in favor of giving the position to Miss Mary Custis Lee, daughter of Confederate general Robert E. Lee. The two worked out an agreement whereby Montague would be the acting president when Lee traveled out of town. This arrangement lasted until Lee died in November 1918, and Montague assumed the presidency until her own death thirty-three years later. While raising three children, this daughter of a Civil War veteran single-mindedly devoted her life's work to one cause—providing a home for needy Confederate women.[23]

Betsie Montague realized that the home needed to establish a stable financial policy and counter the indifference and apathy of potential supporters whom she hoped to enlist in her cause. The board members made house-to-house visits to solicit money, food, furniture, and clothing for the home; they regularly visited the bakery and market to collect donations of unsold fruits, vegetables, and bread to feed the inmates. They spoke before women's organizations and church groups to make them aware of the home and its needs and sought their support.[24]

Montague gave speeches to chapters of the United Daughters of the Confederacy throughout Virginia and at the national convention. She reminded them of past generosity and noted that "our reliance on the public, already greatly burdened, makes our income precarious and uncertain. We are debarred from State help by the new Constitution [of 1902]; therefore, you see the necessity of my begging that you will each take to your respective chapters the message from these helpless women." The chapters responded with barrels of fruits and vegetables, furniture, clothing, and money. She spoke to Richmond schoolchildren who donated their lunches to feed the inmates.[25] Other fund-raising techniques included Flag Days, Button Days, Tag Days, card parties, and dramatic presentations to provide money for the upkeep of the home.[26] Before enacting the new constitution, the legislature appropriated five thousand dollars in 1902, in addition to one thousand dollars previously allocated, for the home. The city of Richmond donated a burial lot in Riverview Cemetery and included $150 in its 1901 budget and $300 in its 1902 budget for the home's operating expenses.[27]

The small home on Grove Avenue did not contain enough room for all the applicants and soon sheltered thirty-two women in space designed to accommodate ten. Sarah Frances (Mrs. William) Grady, one of the first women to move into the home and its first superintendent at age sixty-five, recalled that "there were five small beds crowded into one small chamber, hardly space enough to get between them. In those days all of us women did the work of the home, took care of it and even had to take our market baskets and go out and get our own food supplies."[28] Montague, realizing they needed to move to more expansive quarters, began planning a large fund-raising bazaar. As the first lady of Virginia, Montague could broadcast the home's needs beyond state lines. She received support and contributions from Madame Shen of the Chinese legation in Washington, President Theodore Roosevelt's daughter Alice, and from forty-one chapters of the

United Daughters of the Confederacy and fourteen Confederate camps.[29] The Confederate fair, held March 16–26, 1903, raised between $7,000 and $10,000 for the home; although considerable, it was still insufficient to meet the $16,500 asking price of the house Montague planned to buy.[30]

Montague traveled to New York to solicit the aid of Richmond native Arabella Yarrington Huntington, widow of railroad magnate Collis Potter Huntington, and other sympathetic philanthropists to secure the balance of the purchase price plus additional renovation money.[31] She complained that, while "in a small way several had responded to our appeal," the various chapters of the United Daughters of the Confederacy in the Commonwealth failed to give their hearty cooperation to raising money for the home because they had pledged themselves to build the Jefferson Davis monument (erected in 1907) in Richmond. More concerned with the living than the dead, Montague, also president of the Lee Chapter of the U.D.C., pointedly commented, "We would not under-estimate the noble work of the Daughters of the Confederacy in preserving our history in tablets of marble, but we would direct their attention to the perfecting of this Home for the wives, sisters, and daughters of our valiant dead. We must help them now or not at all." She asked each U.D.C. chapter and veteran's camp to pledge ten dollars annually to the home.[32]

On April 25, 1904, the board completed the purchase of the new home at 3 East Grace Street from the estate of Robert S. Bosher and opened the doors on June 27. One resident, a cousin of Chief Justice John Marshall, described the new home as "a nice boarding-house for ladies." Capt. Sallie Tompkins, who became a resident in 1906, expressed her gratitude for the home the next year, writing that she felt "not only perfectly comfortable but entirely satisfied with my surroundings." For meals three times a day, the inmates who could go up and down the stairs dined together at the family-sized tables in the basement; those unable to negotiate the three flights of stairs ate in their rooms. The new facility could house forty to fifty inmates. To buy an elevator for the home in 1921, Montague recruited Mrs. James A. Ridgely, president of the women's Democratic organization of Hamilton County, Ohio, to organize Pencil Day. In September one hundred Richmond women captained teams of ten to sell pencils to raise the money.[33]

The two most prominent and visible organizations devoted to the memory of the Confederacy, the United Daughters of the Confederacy and the

Confederate veterans' camps, took different approaches toward the Home. The U.D.C. members came from the middle and upper classes. They championed the Lost Cause in newspapers and schools and before the legislature. In shaping public opinion throughout the South for many years, they successfully kept the Confederacy's presence alive. While the Richmond chapters actively donated their time, energy, and funds to help the Home for Needy Confederate Women, the primary focus of the organization concentrated on propaganda, education, and building monuments. The sole relief fund in which the general organization participated benefited women who lived in states without a U.D.C. chapter and who did not receive a Confederate pension.[34] They looked backward rather than forward.

By way of contrast, the Confederate veterans involved themselves directly with the home. The Lee Camp Soldiers' Home provided an annual appropriation to the home for years until 1914 when they could no longer afford it, and the organization also furnished a room specifically for widows of Lee Camp members.[35] Controversy arose in 1911 over the expulsion of a Lee Camp widow, Mrs. Minerva L. Hutchins, for "insubordination." The camp resolved in 1909 that the quartermaster would be in charge of the endowed room, and two members of the auxiliary would serve on the Home's board of directors.[36] Contrary to the rules of the board in which all furnishings become the property of the home, the camp believed it retained ownership.[37] However they failed to negotiate these conditions with the board, nor did they notify the board of the resolutions until 1911 when the furor over Mrs. Hutchins' behavior erupted.[38] Hutchins believed herself exempt from the home's authority and beholden only to the camp; she refused to perform her assigned duties and in so doing encouraged other inmates to rebel. Not simply a local matter, the power struggle between the two organizations for control and autonomy involved the state attorney general who served as chairman of the Lee Camp committee. The women held their ground and passed a resolution requesting the Lee Camp to withdraw Hutchins and to secure the resignations of their two representatives on the board.[39] The relationship eventually improved between the board and the camp, and they again worked together amicably.

Betsie Montague dreamed of building a permanent memorial to the women of the Confederacy and set out to accomplish this formidable task with all the resources she could command. She gathered letters of endorsement from Carlton McCarthy, former Richmond mayor and now Virginia's state accountant, and Gov. William Hodges Mann in 1910. In 1912 the board of directors proposed deeding the home to the United Daughters of the Confederacy. On behalf of the Committee on the Home for Needy Confederate Women Proposition, Miss Mildred Rutherford visited the home and prepared her report and assessment. She agreed with Montague's argument that a living monument for the needy women would most benefit the memory of slain Confederate soldiers: "When their needs cry out to us for bread, shall we give them a stone?" While she recommended accepting the offer, the final report to the annual convention did not include Rutherford's recommendation and left it up to the chapters to decide, which apparently they did unfavorably. Montague appealed to the General Assembly in 1914 for a state appropriation to meet operating costs, and the legislature responded by passing an act appropriating five thousand dollars for 1914 and 1915 for the home; regular state aid then continued until 1982. The State Corporation Commission also amended the charter in 1916 to allow the home to include female descendants of Confederate soldiers.[40] Commonwealth financial, executive, and legislative support during the progressive era almost guaranteed the success of Montague's cause.

As if proving that the home needed a new building, a fire burned much of the roof and gutted most of the interior on December 24, 1916, of the home's current location. Montague, now living in Washington, D.C., where her husband served as U.S. Representative for the Third District of Virginia from 1913 to 1937, returned to restore order and find temporary homes for the inmates during the two months the building underwent repairs. The catastrophe only strengthened her resolve to build a fireproof home for the Confederate women.[41] While most of the social welfare accomplishments in Virginia's progressive period occurred between 1900 and 1910, the 1920s saw the emphasis on special interest projects, exemplified by the success of Montague's lobbying efforts for the home.[42]

Montague decided the most appropriate location for a permanent home should be on the Lee Camp Soldiers' Home property owned by the Commonwealth, and she worked diligently with camp and state officials to obtain the property. The Lee Camp, on November 21, 1924, designated a two-and-one-half-acre tract facing North Sheppard Street for the home. While state senator William Wickham sponsored a bill to give the site to the home, Gov. Elbert Lee Trinkle vetoed it. In a January 26, 1926, letter to the senate, Trinkle opposed certain provisions in the bill, which included expanding eligibility to "lineal female descendants and collateral female kindred" and making the home a "perpetual" memorial. Trinkle stipulated that the building must cost at least $250,000, and if the board failed to build it within eight years from the date of the deed, the property would revert to the state. On March 4, 1926, the General Assembly ratified a compromise with Senate Bill No. 19 that included Trinkle's changes.[43]

Montague immediately organized a fund-raising committee of influential citizens to meet the conditions of the bill. She used her personal contacts to the home's advantage as well. Residents of Atlanta and Washington, D.C., pledged money. In Washington, Montague sponsored a costume event entitled "Ball of the Sixties," netting fifteen hundred dollars for the home. Through her solicitations, financiers and philanthropists George Foster Peabody and Robert Fulton Cutting donated money, and John Barton Payne, American Red Cross president, gave ten thousand dollars. Montague's friend Jessie Ball (Mrs. Alfred I.) duPont and Mary Custis Lee contributed generously throughout their lives. First Lady Grace Coolidge sold a counterpane pattern Montague had taught her to *McCall's* magazine and donated the $250 to the home fund. Montague also enlisted the assistance of Jewish citizens of Richmond.[44] The board received $250,000 from the estate of Dr. Alexander Spiers George, a Richmond physician, which it used as the nucleus for a $1 million endowment.[45]

Construction began on February 15 and was completed by October 1, 1931. Lee, Smith & Vandervoort, architects and engineers in Richmond, modeled the building after the White House; it contained eighty-two bedrooms and an infirmary with ten beds. The matron, nurses, and employees occupied six bedrooms. Inmates, friends, and benefactors donated the furnishings. Forty-two residents moved into their new home at 301 North Sheppard Street on May 23, 1932.[46]

The Virginia General Assembly increased the state appropriation to twenty-five thousand dollars per year. Despite Gov. John Garland Pollard's hearty endorsement of the new building in 1931, in December 1932 he notified Montague of the regrettable but necessary 10 percent reduction in general fund appropriations. Although Virginia was less hard hit than most states during the depression because of its diversified economy, Pollard responded to the crisis by reducing expenditures.[47] The home lost a critical $1,250 for the first half of 1933 because the state sustained revenue shortfalls and higher costs for prisons.[48]

The Commonwealth did not fund the home without opposition. The board received criticism for its handling of finances and admission procedures. A vocal minority persistently complained that the board relied on the state appropriations for operating expenses rather than using inmates' initial contributions and other monetary donations. Montague wanted to build the endowment to make the home self-supporting and to free it from state funding.

Critics questioned the admission procedures, which appeared to favor candidates with five thousand dollars to add to the endowment over those who were truly indigent. The admission criteria did not specify a dollar amount but required an inmate to turn over all of her real and personal property upon entry.[49] A 1943 audit of the previous six years revealed that 54 percent of the inmates contributed various amounts ranging from $100 to $7,550 (from one woman) while the remaining 46 percent contributed nothing.[50] In 1946 a seven-member statewide study commission headed by delegate Ceylon Grey Quesenbery investigated the allegations, visited the home, and inspected the accounts. A public meeting on October 18, 1946, heard complaints from several witnesses about priority admittance for the five-thousand-dollar donors. Mrs. W. G. Tyler, chair of the applications committee, denied preferential treatment, claiming that they balanced paying and nonpaying admissions. Montague testified that "[w]e want to build our endowment as fast as we can and we want to relieve the State before the State relieves us."[51] "Faced with the possibility of the withdrawal of State aid for our running expenses," she appealed to Bernard M. Baruch in 1947 for assistance "to become independent of State politics." She complained that "the public feels less responsibility for its former good citizens than for its criminals, insane persons, and chronically 'indigent.'"[52]

The Quesenbery Commission report in 1947 recommended limiting the home's operation to the lifetime of the daughters as originally specified, thereby nullifying the "and female descendants" emendation. It also recommended limiting the appropriation to a per diem for the genuinely needy and to the closest kin of Confederate soldiers but not their descendants.[53]

These limitations rang the death knell for the home. With the decline in the number of the original class of inmates specified in the charter, the home would no longer receive state funding for lineal female descendants and would have to rely on income from endowments and donations. Governor Trinkle's removal of "permanent" memorial from the act granting the Soldiers' Home land to build the new home also predicted a time when the few remaining Confederate daughters would make operation of the eighty-two-bedroom home economically unfeasible.

The limitations also indicate the prevailing attitude toward charity. The Quesenbery Commission recognized the state's obligation to "continue its support of those in the original group in the institution," but "other than the duty the State owes to its citizens generally it owes no obligation to [later female descendants]. . . . So long as the human race exists there will undoubtedly be persons in the enlarged class eligible to enter the Home. Aside from the question of policy, the continuance of State support for those in this enlarged class would lead to never-ending conflict and dispute."[54] While lawmakers and funding agencies felt a responsibility to those directly affected by the Civil War, they did not see it as the state's obligation to provide this kind of social service ad infinitum, adhering to the long-held belief that charity is a matter for private agencies. The home as a permanent institution would satisfy the desires of U.D.C. women to erect a "monument" to the Confederacy and also, in practical terms, provide an ongoing old-age home for a select group of women. As recently as 1928, Richmond had no state institutions for aged and infirm women, and it had only five other places that cared for aged women, three sectarian and two public poorhouses.[55] Pragmatic choices by men generations removed from the war—men whose interests lay in the economic impact on Virginia at the end of World War II—overruled the concerns for a dwindling number of living reminders of another time.

When Betsie Montague wrote that "it is a sacred duty of the United Daughters of the Confederacy to care for these women" and "it should be an honor for the Sons of the Confederacy to do their manly part in this great work," she relied on the nineteenth-century notion of charity, which included relieving "the suffering of the deserving poor."[56] The bylaws of the home included as one of the criteria for admittance a judgment of the candidate's worthiness. Class, never explicitly written in the guidelines, determined a woman's worthiness from lineage (part of the documentation accompanying the application to prove a relationship to a deceased soldier) and recommendations from and interviews with character references. The application committee contacted an applicant's pastor and friends "regarding her worthiness," behavior, health, and demeanor.[57] While there were women of color whose male relatives died serving the Confederacy, the home implicitly excluded them.[58]

The home continued to accept applicants without, and with, money to add to the endowment and to seek financial contributions. In 1951 the board passed a resolution to sell for fifty thousand dollars the Grace Street property still owned by the home. The board attempted in 1956 to convince the legislature to amend the charter to include granddaughters, with no success.[59]

On April 13, 1989, the board reluctantly voted to close the facility. Janet R. (Mrs. Robert D.) Burhans, elected to the board in 1959 and the third generation of Montague women to preside over the home, succeeded her mother, Janet Roy Montague (Mrs. William Josiah) Nunnally, whom the board voted in as president at the meeting following Betsie Montague's death in 1951. Burhans said, "[E]conomics was the sole reason for closing the building . . . our money plain ran out. All the times we asked for donations, they were never forthcoming. We found that too many wars had intervened since the Civil War for people to take an overwhelming interest." She recognized that "this type of charity is more of a nineteenth century concept than twentieth century. These days you just don't have purely charitable things."[60]

Of the hundreds of women cared for in the home, seven remained in 1989. The building needed a new roof, new plumbing, and a new heating system, which would cost an estimated $1.5 million. Rather than deplete the endowment, the board in July 1989 moved the seven daughters of Confederate soldiers to the Brandermill Woods Active Retirement Center south of the Richmond city limits, despite protests from some of the inmates and irate supporters in the U.D.C. The Commonwealth agreed to support financially the last seven women if they vacated the home. The building reverted to the Commonwealth for the use of the Virginia Museum of Fine Arts.[61]

The vision of a handful of women doggedly brought to fruition by one woman, Betsie Montague, the building provided a home for needy Confederate women for almost eighty-nine years. Using her considerable political acumen, Montague convinced state government to appropriate funds at a time when the dominant male power base in Virginia politics was committed to "spending as little as possible on social programs."[62] The idea of the home and the building itself became anachronistic reminders of the

Lost Cause. A tangible reminder of Virginia's loss, a reverential monument to women's sacrifices, a place to honor and care for the daughters of the Confederacy, a physical manifestation of stubborn refusal to forget the war, a social residence for the right class of deserving white women, and a means to express the duty to take care of the womenfolk were embodied in the Home for Needy Confederate Women.

NOTES

1. Theda Skocpol, *Protecting Soldiers and Mothers; The Political Origins of Social Policy in the United States* (Cambridge, Mass.: Belknap Press of Harvard University Press, 1992), 139–41 and 150.

2. Megan J. McClintock, "Civil War Pensions and the Reconstruction of Union Families," *Journal of American History* 83 (September 1996): 456–80.

3. Sandra Gioia Treadway, "New Directions in Virginia Women's History," *The Virginia Magazine of History and Biography* 100 (January 1992): 18.

4. Michael B. Chesson, *Richmond after the War, 1865–1890* (Richmond: Virginia State Library, 1981), 171.

5. Anne Firor Scott, *The Southern Lady: From Pedestal to Politics, 1830–1930* (Chicago: University of Chicago Press, 1970), 155; H. E. Gulley, "Women and the Lost Cause: Preserving a Confederate Identity in the American Deep South," *Journal of Historical Geography* 19 (April 1993): 126; Suzanne Lebsock, *Virginia Women, 1600–1945: "A Share of Honour"* (Richmond: Virginia State Library, 1987), 103.

6. *Confederate Veteran* 24 (1916): 53, and *Confederate Veteran* 12 (1904): 150; Mattie McAdory Huey, *History of the Alabama Division United Daughters of the Confederacy* (Opelika, Ala.: Post Publishing Company, 1937), 81–86; *Minutes of the Eleventh Annual Reunion of the United Sons of Confederate Veterans in the City of New Orleans, La. April 25, 26, 27, 1906* (Nashville: Brandon Printing Co., 1907), 128; United Daughters of the Confederacy, *Minutes of the Annual Convention*, 1905–1916; Tommy G. Lashley, "Oklahoma's Confederate Veterans Home," *Chronicles of Oklahoma* 55, 1 (1977): 34–45. Electronic mail correspondence from archivists confirmed the existence and closing of homes in Kentucky, Louisiana, Maryland, Mississippi, Missouri, North Carolina, South Carolina, and Texas.

7. Virginia Harrington, "82 Women of the Confederacy Live in Richmond Memorial," *The Virginian-Pilot*, September 28, 1958; R. B. Rosenburg, *Living Monuments: Confederate Soldiers' Homes in the New South* (Chapel Hill: University of North Carolina Press, 1995), 27–28; George C. Rable, *Civil Wars: Women and the Crisis of Southern Nationalism* (Chicago: University of Illinois Press, 1989), 241–42 and 283.

8. "Will Build a Home," broadside, March 29, 1897, in the Home for Needy Confederate Women Records (hereinafter HNCW), Accession 34092, Archives Division, Library of Virginia, Richmond, Virginia; "Home for Confederate Women," *Confederate Veteran* 5 (1897): 207.

9. "The Story of the First Permanent Memorial to the Women of the Confederacy," 1–2, typescript, history folder, box 12, HNCW.

10. Ibid., 2; 1898 Va. Acts ch. 851; *History of the Home for Needy Confederate Women, 1900–1904* (Richmond, Va.: J. L. Hill Printing Company, c. 1904, 1905), 63.

11. Janet Burhans, "A Brief History of Home for Needy Confederate Women," 1, carbon typescript, HNCW; Margaret Nell Price, "The Development of Leadership by Southern Women through Clubs and Organizations," (M.A. thesis, University of North Carolina, 1945), 59. Additional participants included Mrs. Nelson Powell, Mrs. James B. Pace, Mrs. C. C. Roberts, Mrs. George Schlieser, Mrs. John O'Brien, Mrs. Alice Ready, and Mrs. A. C. Becker.

12. *Charter, By-Laws, Rules and Regulations Governing the Home for Needy Confederate Women* (Richmond, Va.: Whittet & Shepperson, 1910), 11.

13. Burhans, "A Brief History," 2. In addition to McCarthy, the members were Colonel Cutshaw, Gen. A. L. Phillips, Mr. S. H. Hawes, Mr. A. Ball, Maj. Robert Stiles, Judge George L. Christian, and Judge Clopton.

14. Capt. Carleton McCarthy, "An Historical Sketch," *History of the Home for Needy Confederate Women, 1900–1904* (Richmond, Va.: J. H. Hill Printing Co., c. 1904, 1905), 39.

15. Burhans, "A Brief History," 2; "Home for Needy Women," *Richmond Dispatch,* October 16, 1900, 4.

16. Burhans, "A Brief History," 2; "Home for Confederate Women," *Richmond Dispatch,* October 30, 1900, 5; Mary Custis Lee printed postcard to Robert Beverly, November 28, 1911, Beverly Family Papers, Virginia Historical Society, Richmond, Virginia (hereinafter VHS).

17. McCarthy, "An Historical Sketch," 41; "Home for Needy Women," 4. The first residents consisted of Mrs. Maria L. Brooks, Mrs. E. M. Cook, Mrs. Amelia S. Eubank, Sarah Frances "Fanny" (Mrs. W. F.) Grady, Mrs. Lucy F. Hurt, Mrs. Martha F. Johnson, Mrs. Mary Johnson, Mrs. Fielding B. Lewis, Miss Sallie Monroe, and Mrs. Lizzie (Mrs. A. E.) Omahundro who was elected matron.

18. Burhans, "A Brief History," 2; *Richmond Dispatch,* "To-Night—Society Notes," October 13, 1900, p. 6; "Home for Confederate Women," October 31, 1900, p. 3.

19. Burhans, "A Brief History," 2–3.

20. William Larsen, *Montague of Virginia; The Making of a Southern Progressive* (Baton Rouge: Louisiana State University Press, 1965), 71, 84, and 286; Raymond H. Pulley, *Old Virginia Restored: An Interpretation of the Progressive Impulse, 1870–1930* (Charlottesville: University Press of Virginia, 1968), 121.

21. Anne Firor Scott, *Making the Invisible Woman Visible* (Chicago: University of Illinois Press, 1984), 220.

22. "The Home for Confederate Women in Richmond," typescript, HNCW.

23. "The Home for Confederate Women in Richmond"; "The Story of the First Permanent Memorial to the Women of the Confederacy," 3, typescript, HNCW; "General Lee's Daughter Dead," *Richmond Times-Dispatch,* November 23, 1918, 1; "Mrs. Elizabeth Montague, Widow of Ex-Governor, Dies," *Richmond Times-Dispatch,* April 26, 1951, 5.

24. "The Story of the First Permanent Memorial," 4; Burhans, "A Brief History," 2.

25. Elizabeth Montague, Speech to U.D.C. Convention, 3, undated, HNCW; "The Story of the First Permanent Memorial," 4; Burhans, "A Brief History," 2; Ralph Clipman Mc-

Daniel, *The Virginia Constitutional Convention of 1901–1902* (New York: DaCapo Press, 1972), 95–96. The constitution prohibited the General Assembly or authorities of any city, town, county, or district from appropriating money to any charitable institution not owned or controlled by the state or locality.

26. Harry Kollatz Jr., "The Last Confederate Daughter," *Richmond: The Metropolitan Monthly* (October 1994): 31; "The Story of the First Permanent Memorial," 4.

27. McCarthy, "An Historical Sketch," 40–41.

28. Jack Burgess, "The Southland's 'House of Memories'," *Sunday Magazine,* undated clipping (c. January 1935), HNCW.

29. Kollatz, "The Last Confederate Daughter," 31; "The Story of the First Permanent Memorial," 4–5; McCarthy, "An Historical Sketch," 40; Burhans, "A Brief History," 3–4; *Richmond Times-Dispatch,* March 5, 11, and 13, 1903; "Widow of Noted Soldier is Century Old Today," *Richmond Times-Dispatch,* April 30, 1935, 1. Andrew Jackson Montague served as governor from 1902 to 1906.

30. Kollatz, "The Last Confederate Daughter," 31; "The Story of the First Permanent Memorial," 4–5; McCarthy, "An Historical Sketch," 40; Burhans, "A Brief History," 3–4; *Richmond Times-Dispatch,* "Confederate Fair," March 1, 1903, p. 6, "The Home Bazaar," March 8, 1903, p. 8, "To Open in Four Weeks," March 19, 1903, p. 12, "The Close Brilliant," March 27, 1903, p. 9, "Opening of the Bazaar," April 15, 1903, p. 1; Gaines M. Foster, *Ghosts of the Confederacy: Defeat, the Lost Cause, and the Emergence of the New South, 1865 to 1913* (New York: Oxford University Press, 1987), 158.

31. Kollatz, "The Last Confederate Daughter," 31; "The Story of the First Permanent Memorial," 4–5; McCarthy, "An Historical Sketch," 40; Burhans, "A Brief History," 3–4.

32. Mrs. Andrew Jackson Montague, President's Report, *History of the Home for Needy Confederate Women, 1900–1904,* 45–59.

33. Deed, May 6, 1904, HNCW; "The Story of the First Permanent Memorial," 5; Robert Stiles to Mrs. A. J. Montague, November 7, 1904; Montague, *History of the Home for Needy Confederate Women,* 43; Frieda Dietz Pollard, "Many Happy Reminiscences Enliven Lives of Confederate Home Folk," *Richmond Times-Dispatch,* April 22, 1928; Sallie L. Tompkins to Mrs. Montague, March 23, 1907, HNCW; "Elevator for Needy Women," *Richmond News Leader,* September 7, 1921.

34. Angie Parrott, "'Love Makes Memory Eternal': The United Daughters of the Confederacy in Richmond, Virginia, 1897–1920," in *The Edge of the South: Life in Nineteenth-Century Virginia,* Edward L. Ayers and John C. Willis, eds., (Charlottesville: University Press of Virginia, 1991), 220–22 and 228; *The History of the United Daughters of the Confederacy,* vol. 1 (Raleigh, N.C.: Edwards & Broughton Co., 1956), 199.

35. Resolution, July 17, 1914, copied from Minute Book 9, p. 35, R. E. Lee Camp, No. 1, VHS. The camp was rapidly losing its membership because of death of its members, experienced a decrease in its income, and its own expenses were increasing as members aged and became infirm.

36. D. A. Brown Jr., Resolution, March 19, 1909, Grand Camp Confederate Veterans, Dept. of Virginia, R. E. Lee Camp, No. 1 Records, 1883–1936, VHS.

37. D. A. Brown Jr., Report, January 1, 1910, R. E. Lee Camp, No. 1 Records, VHS.

38. Mrs. Andrew Jackson Montague to Col. John W. Gordon, May 5, 1911, R. E. Lee Camp, No. 1 Records, VHS.

39. Executive Committee, Home for Needy Confederate Women to Hon. Samuel W. Williams, April 19, 1911; Office of the Attorney General letter, undated carbon reply; Resolutions Passed by the Board of Directors of the Home for Needy Confederate Women at Their Monthly Meeting on May 4, 1911, R. E. Lee Camp, No. 1 Records, VHS.

40. "The Story of the First Permanent Memorial," 5, 6; Kollatz, "The Last Confederate Daughter," 31; Carlton McCarthy to Mrs. A. J. Montague, May 18, 1910, and William Hodges Mann to Mrs. A. J. Montague, May 19, 1910, Montague letters received, HNCW; "Report of the Committee on the Home for Needy Confederate Women Proposition," typescript, c. November 1913, HNCW; "Report of the Committee on the Home for Needy Confederate Women," United Daughters of the Confederacy, *Minutes of the Twentieth Annual Convention* (Nashville, Tenn., 1914), 361–64; 1914 Va. Acts ch. 40; *Home for Needy Confederate Women; Report of the Commission to the Governor and the General Assembly of Virginia. House Document No. 11* (Richmond: Virginia Division of Purchase and Printing, 1947), 4–5.

41. "The Story of the First Permanent Memorial," 6; Kollatz, "The Last Confederate Daughter," 31; "Plan Early Rebuilding of Confederate Home," *Richmond Times-Dispatch*, December 25, 1916, 10.

42. Pulley, *Old Virginia Restored*, 150–51.

43. "The Story of the First Permanent Memorial," 7; Kollatz, "The Last Confederate Daughter," 31; 1926 Va. Acts ch. 3; 1926 Va. Acts ch. 91; "Vets Would Give Home for Women," *Richmond Times-Dispatch*, November 22, 1924, 1; *Journal of the Senate of the Commonwealth of Virginia Begun and Held at the Capitol in the City of Richmond on Wednesday, January 9, 1924* (Richmond: Davis Bottom, Superintendent of Public Printing, 1924), 738; *Journal of the Senate, 1926*, 81–82.

44. "The Home for Confederate Women in Richmond," unpaginated typescript, history file, HNCW; Burhans, "A Brief History," 5; *History of the Home for Needy Confederate Women*, 4, 6; "Mrs. Coolidge Earns $250 and Gives It Away," *New York Times*, December 30, 1926; "Donates $250 Check to Home for Women," *Richmond Times-Dispatch*, December 30, 1926; "Large Donations for Women's Home," undated clipping (c. 1929), HNCW; Jessie Ball duPont to Mrs. A. J. Montague, October 11, 1943, HNCW; Elizabeth L. H. Montague to Mrs. Alfred I. duPont, December 15, 1947, HNCW; Richard Greening Hewlett, *Jessie Ball duPont* (Gainesville: University Press of Florida, 1992), 230–31. The trustees were requested, but not directed, to include thirteen specified institutions, including the home, among the beneficiaries.

45. "The Story of the First Permanent Memorial," 8; Kollatz, "The Last Confederate Daughter," 31; Mrs. William Lyne of Virginia, "The Culture of the Old South," *Confederate Veteran* 36 (January 1928): 13, and *Confederate Veteran* 37 (July 1931): 261–62; Jack Burgess, "The Southland's 'House of Memories,'" Sunday magazine section, January 1935, pp. 3, 10, from an unidentified newspaper clipping, HNCW records, Library of Virginia.

46. Burhans, "A Brief History," 6; architect's drawing, HNCW.

47. Virginius Dabney, *Virginia, the New Dominion* (Garden City, N.Y.: Doubleday & Co., 1971), 488, 491.

48. Burhans, "A Brief History," 6; John Garland Pollard to Mrs. Andrew Jackson Montague, January 10, 1931, and December 17, 1932, HNCW.

49. *Charter, By-Laws, Rules and Regulations Governing the Home for Needy Confederate Women*, 22.

50. Margaret Elliott, "Confederate Home Asks Turnover of Property," *Richmond Times-Dispatch*, undated clipping (c. 1946), HNCW.

51. "$5,000 Endowment Held Factor in Applicants' Bid to Enter Home for Confederate Women," *Richmond Times-Dispatch*, October 19, 1946, 2; *Journal of the House of Delegates of the Commonwealth of Virginia Held at the Capitol in the City of Richmond, Beginning Wednesday, January 9, 1946, Ending Wednesday, March 20, 1946* (Richmond: Virginia Division of Purchase and Printing, 1946), 165–66; *Home for Needy Confederate Women; Report of the Commission*, 4.

52. Mrs. A. J. Montague to Bernard M. Baruch, December 12, 1947, carbon typescript, HNCW.

53. "The Story of the First Permanent Memorial," 9; Elizabeth L. H. Montague to Mrs. Alfred I. duPont, December 15, 1947, HNCW; "'Strictly Limited' Financial Aid From State Suggested for Confederate Women's Home," *Richmond Times-Dispatch*, November 18, 1947, 1; *Home for Needy Confederate Women; Report of the Commission*, 6–9.

54. *Home for Needy Confederate Women; Report of the Commission*, 8–9.

55. "Data on the Various Homes for Aged Women in Richmond," report accompanying April 26, 1928, letter from John Kemble, HNCW.

56. Elizabeth L. H. Montague, typescript speech, c. 1915, HNCW.

57. *Charter, By-Laws, Rules and Regulations Governing the Home for Needy Confederate Women*, 15.

58. Ervin L. Jordan Jr., *Black Confederates and Afro-Yankees in Civil War Virginia* (Charlottesville: University Press of Virginia, 1995), 197–99.

59. Home for Needy Confederate Women Board Meeting Minutes, November 5, 1951, and June 7, 1956, HNCW.

60. HNCW Board Meeting Minutes, December 3, 1959, HNCW; "The Story of the First Permanent Memorial to the Women of the Confederacy," 11; Christopher Phillips, "The Removal of the Confederate Daughters—A Happy Band of Sisters with Many Memories," *Virginia Country* 13 (1990): 33; Gerald Mattineau, "Confederate Spirit Lives in Richmond," *Washington Post*, July 26, 1980, B1.

61. Jim Naughton, "The Last Home of the Lost Cause," *Washington Post*, April 14, 1989, C1 and C4; Christopher Phillips, "The Removal of the Confederate Daughters," 32–34.

62. Lebsock, *Virginia Women, 1600–1945*, 125.

PART TWO

Local Case Studies

National Trends, Regional Differences, Local Circumstances

Social Welfare in New Orleans, 1870s–1920s

ELNA C. GREEN

First-time visitors to New Orleans are often struck by the "patchwork quilt" of neighborhoods in the city. New Orleans has long been a city divided not only by race and class but also by religion and ethnicity. "The Irish Channel," "little Jerusalem," "the French Quarter": such neighborhoods reflected the cultural diversity of the city at the same time that they separated people into these discrete categories.

Throughout the nineteenth century, these categories also shaped the distribution of private philanthropy. Within each ethnic and religious group, the middle class and the wealthy of the city established charitable institutions to aid the poor who were most like themselves. Thus Kingsley House (the famous settlement house directed by Eleanor McMain) was proudly Irish. Touro Infirmary and the Hebrew Benevolent Society cared for the poor and aged of the German Jewish community, while the German Protestant Home assisted other German immigrants, and so on. By the end of the nineteenth century, New Orleans hosted a bewildering array of charitable organizations. Dozens of different orphanages, aid societies, and benevolent associations dotted the cityscape, each serving the needs of one particular group of the urban poor. The German community alone had established more than twenty-five different benevolent associations by 1897.[1] This multiplicity of organizations competed with one another for the charitable contributions of the city's wealthy citizenry, as well as for small annual subsidies from the city and state governments, as public welfare accepted and reinforced the distribution of relief by race and ethnicity.

Layered on top of this philanthropic matrix were the restrictions of gender ideology current at the turn of the century. The prescriptions of gender dictated that women's roles in benevolency would be different from those of men. Not only would many charitable activities be sex-segregated, women's "natural" understanding of "delicate" matters would also mean that whatever provisions the city made for unwed mothers, for one example, would be handled by women. But gender played an even more pervasive role in the disposition of charity in New Orleans in the Progressive Era. This essay will examine the evolving contours of gender and charity in the period from the 1870s through the 1920s.[2] It will demonstrate that concepts of gender helped to define poverty and charity, that gender permeated charitable institutions, and that gender, as an analytic device, can help us to unravel the complexities of class relations and urban reform movements.

Moreover, this essay is concerned with the development of social welfare thought in the postbellum South. Social welfare reformers found their activities circumscribed not only by southern race and class relations but also by powerful social and intellectual trends coming from outside the region. This essay will argue that the charity organization movement and the emergence and professionalization of the field of social work both provided further restraints on the progressive aspirations of southern reformers. Southern progressivism was limited by both its southern origins and by its national context.

A study, such as this one, that focuses on one city in particular offers both advantages and limitations. It can establish a local setting for looking at both national trends and regional variations. And, while New Orleans is undoubtedly not representative of the South as a whole, it nevertheless has much to tell us about the urban South. Historically one of the South's largest and most cosmopolitan cities, New Orleans often experienced changes and trends earlier than other southern cities. An examination of events in New Orleans, therefore, can help detect patterns occurring later in the rest of the urban South.

Although poverty was not a new phenomenon in the nineteenth century, it was not until the middle of the century that New Orleans first came to experience the kind of poverty, homelessness, and destitution that accompanied modern urban, industrial conditions. The relatively lower levels of pauperism of the past had been handled by private benevolent societies and individual almsgiving; New Orleans demonstrated long-standing reluctance to accept public responsibility for the poor.[3] Women's religious organizations in particular conducted charities and almsgiving, as nearly every church and synagogue in the city had its own women's benevolent society. Unlike many other southern cities, New Orleans had not developed a municipal system of public relief and was utterly unprepared to handle the increasing needs of the urban poor caused by foreign immigration, war, reconstruction, and recurrent industrial depressions.[4]

In the 1840s and 1850s, responding to the rise of immigration-linked poverty as well as to recurrent yellow fever outbreaks, religious groups began establishing charitable institutions to care for orphans, widows, and the elderly.[5] The city government began giving annual subsidies to these private charitable institutions.[6] During the Civil War, after New Orleans fell under federal control, military authorities also made contributions to many of these charitable institutions.[7] But these charities, numerous as they grew to be in the ensuing generation, were incapable of handling the devastation of the depression of 1873–78. For the victims of this industrial depression were not only orphans and the elderly, they were strong, healthy wage earners. Five thousand families in New Orleans faced starvation in 1874 and 1875; fifteen thousand workers remained unemployed as late as summer 1878. Thousands of homeless men and women slept in the city's jails at night free of charge, one of the few municipal concessions to poor relief.[8] Indeed, the city's response to the depression was draconian: it rebuilt its burned workhouse and reinstituted chain gangs that were used to deal with the problem of "tramps."[9]

Both the city of New Orleans and the state of Louisiana refused to alter established policies during the crisis. While both governments continued the precedent of giving small subsidies to private institutions, neither government would provide direct relief to the poor. In fact the state government was beginning to dismantle the social services machinery established by the Republican-dominated Reconstruction regime and was interested in retrenchment, not expansion of those services. The state was closing public institutions when it could, transferring responsibility to private institutions or local governments.[10] Legislative opposition to the state policy of subsidies to private, often sectarian, charities grew stronger with each year.[11] A new state constitution of 1879 (written by the Redeemers) prohibited further state appropriations for private charitable organizations. In 1880 the legislature passed the first state poor law, charging each parish with caring for its own poor and thereby relieving the state of the duty.[12]

In New Orleans, that obligation was discharged in two ways: through the "indoor" care available in the Touro-Shakspeare home, a privately endowed almshouse that had been given to the city in 1882, and through an increase in city subsidies to private institutions.[13] The number of private charities increased rapidly in the 1880s and 1890s, and the number that received municipal support also grew apace. The city gave annual stipends to twelve institutions in 1870; that number grew to fifty by 1933. As Elizabeth Wisner has noted, the fact that every important institution in the city was already receiving an annual subsidy made it all the more difficult to refuse requests from new organizations.[14]

Thus, by the 1880s, charity in New Orleans was predominately private, sectarian, and underfunded. Increasingly the charitable community in New Orleans bristled with tensions. Each society criticized the others for being "sectarian" while loudly proclaiming its own nonsectarian nature. In order to prove they did not discriminate according to religion, most of the charitable organizations faithfully reported the religious affiliations of their clients each year in their annual reports. So for example, the 1910 report of St. Anna's Asylum recorded that twenty-one of the eighty-five inmates that year were Catholic, sixteen were Presbyterian, and so on, down to the one Lutheran inmate.[15] Likewise the Home for Homeless Men, established in 1896, affirmed its nonsectarian nature while confirming its religious orientation: "Religiously the Home is non-sectarian, and all denominations are cordially invited to assist in the spiritual work of the institution."[16]

While they all claimed to serve the poor regardless of religion, few of the city's charities made the same assertion regarding race. Private charitable institutions nearly always specified their intentions to serve one race only. Thus, the Home for Homeless Young Women, established in 1886, admitted only destitute white women and girls.[17] The Employment Bureau of the Christian Woman's Exchange accepted job applications only from white women.[18] One of the few private charities in the city that did not segregate in this period was the St. Joseph's Home for the elderly. Run by the Little Sisters of the Poor, St. Joseph's home admitted African Americans beginning in 1883.[19]

Poor and working-class blacks in the city often had no recourse but to turn to their own mutual aid associations for assistance. John Blassingame has described the operation of several of these societies, some of which operated as life insurance companies or burial plans. Black benevolent associations also supported several important relief institutions in the city, including a home for the aged opened in 1875, and an orphanage opened in 1880.[20] Black middle-class clubwomen also helped to fill the gap left by segregated services: the New Orleans Phyllis Wheatley Club founded a black hospital in 1897, and it began receiving city appropriations the following year.[21]

This proliferation of charitable societies made for overlap of (and significant gaps in) services. The city's subsidy policy only made it worse. In its attempt to make "a fair division of the funds between the various sectarian groups" in the city, the municipal government distributed money with an eye to politics, not to rationality. Giving equal grants to the Protestant orphans' home and the Catholic orphans' home, without regard for the number of children actually in each facility, may have made good political sense but it also made for uneven distribution of services.[22]

Therefore in the 1880s (the lull between the depressions) some New Orleanians urged the local charitable community to join in the nationwide "charity organization" movement. Charity organization meant streamlining the distribution of charity and attempting to eliminate fraud by investigating all applications for aid thoroughly before referring them to the appropriate charitable institution. Charity organization societies in fact were pioneers in what would later come to be called casework by social workers. As a local worker put it, "We are gradually preparing complete records of the undeserving cases, so as to be always able to give good reason for refusing them aid. If any resident mendicants allege that the Conference of Charities will do nothing for them, the people to whom they apply can be pretty sure that these are undeserving."[23] The charity organization movement expressed special hostility to "outdoor relief," which it claimed pauperized its recipients by reducing the incentive to work. The movement believed that human beings were naturally inclined to laziness, and any temptation such as outdoor relief was irresistible.[24]

Representatives of the national charity organizing movement spoke in cities throughout the South in the 1880s and 1890s, attempting to spread the word about their "scientific charity." Although southerners tended to be generally suspicious of "outside" ideas that might serve to undermine white supremacy and Democratic party hegemony, charity organization was one concept that could easily be reconciled with southern mores. Charity organization, although arising in northeastern and midwestern urban centers during the 1870s, did not challenge the system of segregation emerging in the South in the 1880s. One defender of the charity organization movement explained that the Charity Organization Society (COS) did little work in African American neighborhoods because few blacks applied to their local COS for assistance.[25] But in fact, COS leaders accepted segregation both north and south, even if such a system was not "efficient" or "scientific."

Nor did the charity organization movement conflict with the other major ideological trend of the late nineteenth-century South: the New South Creed.[26] The South's post-Reconstruction leadership had decided that the best hope for the South was to remake it in the image of the North. In effect that meant unrestrained industrial and commercial development. The New South would engage in capitalism with a vengeance. Charity organizers found they could easily accommodate the New South–builders. Rather than challenging a system that paid low wages to women and children, charity organization workers instead "encourage[d] the employer to pay a fair wage, agents of the society not infrequently calling upon the employers of under-paid widows and children, and, failing to secure better pay for them, helping their clients to secure other jobs."[27] Thus the COS movement could coexist comfortably with the New South's industrialization, attempting to ameliorate suffering but not attacking the origins of that suffering. The South's political and economic leadership had little to fear from charity organizing.

The charity organization movement exerted powerful influence in the social thought of the Progressive Era, soon making significant impact south of the Mason-Dixon line. New Orleans's Conference of Charities was chartered in 1883, possibly the first such conference in the South.[28] Its stated goals were to protect the community from the imposture of mendicants, to reduce vagrancy and pauperism, to prevent indiscriminate and duplicate giving, to make employment the basis of relief, and to elevate the home life, health, and habits of the poor.[29] Like the national movement, local COS leaders in New Orleans believed that charity should be divorced from sentimentality and that scientific evaluation and rational planning be substituted.[30] This reform carried an implicit indictment of nineteenth-century female benevolency, as "sentimentality" was one of the quintessentially female characteristics of the Victorian era and of the benevolency that women exercised in the period.

The constitution and bylaws of the New Orleans COS specified that "[n]o question of religious belief, politics, or nationality was ever to enter into the work of the Corporation, and no person was to use his position in the Society for the purpose of proselytism."[31] But if the COS discouraged proselytizing for a particular sect, it nevertheless had a clear set of religious values that its supporters did indeed attempt to impose upon those poor neighbors who came to them for help. As Roy Lubove noted, charity organization was the creation of the Protestant middle class, which denounced rigid sectarianism but nevertheless was guided by an evangelical sense of mission.[32]

The charity organizers held individuals responsible for their own poverty. As one early observer noted, the COS movement rarely worked to eradicate the social causes of poverty, and instead it blamed the individual "mendicants" for their problems.[33] The purpose of their scientific investigations was to ferret out the particular cause: drunkenness, imbecility, immorality, etc. Perhaps the central principle to which charity organizations adhered was the conviction that work should be the condition for relief. The COS movement was firmly opposed to direct relief, or so-called outdoor relief, and worked to abolish such programs throughout the country. New Orleans had no formal program of outdoor relief to abolish.[34] So the COS presented the needy with one choice: either work or be institutionalized. The COS leaders believed that the "undeserving" poor, the "lazy, vicious paupers" could be transformed into "self-respecting, industrious, honest citizens" by compelling them to work.[35]

The willingness to work often served as the litmus test that distinguished between the "deserving" and the "undeserving" poor. Like many other charity organizations, the New Orleans COS set up a wood yard where new applicants were tested for their willingness to work. Although the elderly and the clearly infirm were excused from this test, almost no other man escaped the wood yard. Bricklayers, day laborers, skilled carpenters, and teachers all found themselves evaluated by whether or not they were willing to cut wood. Any man who refused to cut wood was then deemed a "mere tramp" and was refused assistance.[36]

Women who came to the COS for assistance were not subjected to the wood yard test, but they too were expected to work for their charitable support whenever possible. The Provident Sewing Association served as the "distinct woman's feature of our Charity Organization Society. The means so far used for the alleviation and advancement of our poor, has been the opening of a Sewing Room, and this work has progressed very favorably. We endeavor to train in the use of the needle.... We have opened one avenue of employment for our sisters, but many remain to be opened."[37] Women unwilling (or unable) to sew or do some other work would generally be refused further assistance from the COS.[38]

In fact work was "the bottom line" for the New Orleans COS, and the insistence on putting the poor to work often went beyond a reasonable limit, as a couple of examples from case records will illustrate. The following is from a case reported in 1885. A young French couple arrived in the city the previous year and became destitute. He was a gardener, she was a laundress. The man went to work on a plantation far from the city but could not support himself and have enough money to send to his wife. "She was too proud to beg, and, after being without food for two days, she was found on the floor of her room in a faint. A visitor who speaks French was sent to provide for her, and work was soon found, so that she became self-supporting." The COS did not simply send her to her husband, who could have supported them both. Instead she was made to go to work first.[39] A second example also was reported in 1885. An elderly widow who had spent several years in the Touro-Shakspeare Almshouse for the Aged applied to the COS for assistance. She was turned down because the COS decided that she could have supported herself by washing and ironing if she had tried.[40]

As the indirect result with this obsessive "work ethic," some women applicants to the COS were vulnerable to having their children removed from them. In case number 1596, a poor young woman who was deserted by her family was found in the streets "in a terrible condition" with a young infant (although shrouded by euphemism, this was probably a case of an unmarried mother). Her "exposure and sickness resulted in partial insanity." The COS helped arrange for her commitment to an asylum, and her child was removed from her custody. Although it is possible that this poor woman truly was insane, other such women were not. For example, in case 1611, another young woman with a child was found deserted. "A good position" was found for her, but it was in Alabama. The COS "placed" the child in an asylum in New Orleans.[41]

Unlike the homes for unwed mothers run by women's benevolent associations in the late nineteenth century, which struggled to keep mothers and babies together even when the mother was unmarried, the COS had no qualms about separating babies from their mothers.[42] For the workers of the COS, the "bottom line" was that these mothers needed to work to support themselves. Since few jobs were available to women that would allow them to keep their children with them, the obvious, rational, scientific answer was to place the child in an orphanage so that the mother could become self-supporting.[43] The orphanages in the city were filled with children who were neither orphaned nor abandoned, but rather those who had been separated from their mothers as the condition for assistance.[44]

The day-to-day operations of the COS reflected more traditional nineteenth-century values regarding gender roles. The Charity Organization Society employed male paid administrators and agents, while asking for female volunteers to serve as "friendly visitors." Friendly visitors served as the contact point between the needy and the benevolent. They were to be a source of information, sympathy, advice, and good cheer—a "kind friend" who reported back to the Society on the conditions she found.[45] "[B]y leaving investigation mostly in the hands of gentle and kind women, who often see clearer than men in cases of great need," charity organizations felt that they took best advantage of women's "natural" talents.[46] Such an arrangement also maintained the sexual division of labor of the middle classes: men worked for salaries, women did benevolent volunteering.

Like much other organizational activity in the nineteenth century, the charity organization movement in New Orleans had a "ladies auxiliary." The COS worked in cooperation with the awkwardly named Ladies' Unsectarian Aid Society, established in 1884. The Ladies Unsectarian Aid Society raised money for distribution to the worthy poor, while the male agents of the COS determined which among the poor were worthy.[47] Men therefore held the policy-making positions, while unpaid women did much of the work.

By creating a central, efficient, "scientific" investigatory agency to evaluate need, charity organization could have meant the end of racial, ethnic, and religious discrimination in philanthropy. Instead charity organization in New Orleans served to reinforce rather than challenge existing assumptions about racial, religious, and ethnic relations. By sending applicants to the "appropriate" religious institution, the COS effectively bolstered the preexisting system. "We must also remind the churches and charitable societies," announced the COS, "that our Aid Society proposed to help only those deserving and resident poor who are outside of all churches and other societies. The churches should take care of their own poor."[48] The

COS never questioned whether such sectarian arrangements ought to be changed.

As for racial mores, the COS had no intention of overturning the unscientific, inefficient delivery of services according to race. For, as one later student wrote, "The feeling that the colored people should care for their own unfortunates is popular among some of their very best friends of other groups."[49] Like most southern cities, the New Orleans COS ignored the African American community; recognizing the futility, black New Orleanians seldom applied to this white agency for help.[50] Instead blacks continued to develop their parallel social welfare system of mutual societies, religious charities, and separate institutions.

The philosophy of charity organization flowed out beyond the COS, as other benevolent organizations in the city were influenced by the methods and the philosophy of the charity organization movement. New charity organizing societies emerged; older groups adopted the methods and the assumptions of the COS. The Christian Woman's Exchange, for example, reported in 1886 that its "quiet but effective work" was "not a charity in the sense of alms-giving, for while to the helpless, the aged, the afflicted, in all sympathy we would give of our abundance, yet to those who cannot or will not accept alms, we give the truer charity, an opportunity for self support."[51] This charity organization philosophy was making slow headway, however, for the Woman's Exchange hinted that it had difficulty convincing some of the benevolent women of the city to support this program.[52]

The adoption of charity organization movement values did not go unchallenged. The COS itself noted its difficulty in finding "enough ladies to serve on the District Committees and examine carefully the results of the investigations." The charity organizers also complained of the lack of "cooperation on the part of the churches, benevolent societies and benevolent people of this city." Few people reported beggars to the conference, few checked with the conference first to see whether information already existed on someone they wished to help. "Even ministers, who know that the greatest possible injury that we can do to the mendicants is to give them money and thus encourage them in idleness, deception and vice, will give their half-dollar to every one who rings the door-bell."[53]

Women's groups in particular continued to express disagreement with the some of the basic precepts of charity organization. Like middle-class women throughout the country in the nineteenth century, New Orleans's benevolent women operated on a set of principles and precedents of female reform stretching back many decades.[54] They insisted that charity must be face-to-face, where the giver and the receiver meet and come to know one another—so many benevolent women continued to give cash handouts to the poor. Even the Ladies' Unsectarian Aid Society, directly affiliated with the COS, continued to operate and publicize a soup kitchen, where "anyone who chooses to apply is furnished with a large size slice of bread and bowl of soup free of cost," despite the COS's specific condemnation of soup kitchens.[55] One observer noted in 1895 that New Orleans still had a comparative lack of enthusiasm for charity organization, despite more than a decade of work by the COS.[56]

In fact many women's benevolent associations in the city were moving in the opposite direction during the 1890s, toward social reform rather than scientific charity. By 1890 the Ladies Unsectarian Aid Society had moved beyond sewing rooms and fund-raising, and had established a training school for nurses as one of their programs. Seven "progressive and prominent" physicians of the city conducted the classes, and the society gave students room and board, uniforms and textbooks.[57] The benevolent women who founded and operated this school envisioned it as a place where working-class women could learn skills that would gain them higher pay than the needlework of the Provident Sewing Society.

Other women's organizations in the city took a more aggressive approach than the COS in preventing poverty and hardship. Rather than waiting for destitute or abandoned women to arrive at the COS offices, one group of benevolent women tried to protect vulnerable young women from the dangers of the city. A committee of volunteers for the Home for Homeless Young Women would board arriving ships docking in the ports of New Orleans and offered to take young women to the home until they could find employment and safe housing. These volunteers found themselves in competition with "certain reprehensible characters . . . that would lead the young women to their ruin." Although they found it a "disagreeable duty," these women felt "called upon to perform it in the interests of humanity and of womankind."[58] These women volunteers clearly rejected the COS's presumption that poverty was caused by character flaws. Their actions suggest that they saw economic vulnerability as an important cause of destitution and demoralization of young women.

The Christian Woman's Exchange, which had earlier seemed disposed to support charity organization, had never fully committed itself to scientific almsgiving and turned now to social reform instead. It began by operating an employment bureau. "We have now on file applications for situations embracing almost every office possible for women to fill—housekeepers, governesses, teachers in art, music, languages, cooking, dressmaking, sick nurses, clerks, etc."[59] Their experiences with the needs of working women led them to a broader vision: by 1900, the CWE was experimenting (not too successfully) with operating a day nursery for working mothers.[60]

Operating along similar, but distinctly separate, lines, black clubwomen were building reform organizations of their own. The Phyllis Wheatley Club added a program of visiting nurses to its extensive program of community services. These clubwomen also established the first kindergarten for black children in the city.[61]

Other benevolent women in the city joined the settlement house movement and its ambitious agenda of social reform. Originally founded by women of the Episcopal Diocese as an urban mission, Kingsley House became a residential settlement in 1899.[62] With its philosophy of community solidarity as a means of empowerment of the working class, Kingsley House represented a clear alternative to the methods of the COS. The goals of the settlement houses were in many ways diametrically opposed to those of the charity organization movement. Settlements attempted to work with communities in order to produce fundamental reforms; charity organization societies intended to cut down on the alleged fraud in philanthropy. Settlements, Kingsley House included, emphasized the environment rather than individual moral weakness as the root of poverty. Their programs were intended to improve the environment in which children grew up in order to give more opportunities to create independent adults.[63]

Kingsley House also came to challenge the assumptions of gender in the city's benevolent activities. For professional social workers soon ran Kingsley House. And those professional workers, unlike those of the COS, were women.[64] From its founding until the 1950s, the Kingsley House staff was predominantly female, and all but one of its head residents were women.[65]

Despite the successes and popularity of Kingsley House and regardless of the growth of a progressive reform movement in the city, the charity organization movement gradually overpowered both the more traditional face-to-face charity of the past and the more reform-oriented organizations of the Progressive Era. First, new charity organizations emerged: New Orleans's Jewish community created its own version of the COS, called United

Hebrew Charities, in 1904. Like its Protestant counterpart, the UHC warned against assisting "professional beggars, tramps, and other men unwilling to work." The UHC soon claimed to have "effectively stopped fraud and checked the career of the imposter" through its scientific methods.[66]

Second, financial federations, such as the Community Chest, helped to push "scientific philanthropy" onto resisting evangelicals. Financial federations especially appealed to businessmen by promising the efficient coordination and organization of the community welfare machinery and by expanding the base of support that would relieve the pressure on the small circle of large givers. The financial federation principle succeeded because it united the financially powerful with the professional distributors of social welfare in a common cause.[67] New Orleans's first federation formed in 1914, although it was short lived.[68] But in 1921, a second effort, spearheaded by the professional social workers in the city, was more successful. The COS movement was well represented on the committee that drew up the federation plan: Charles Patterson of the COS and Julius Goldman of United Jewish Charities served on the committee, as did others who supported the principal of charity organization.[69]

Third, charity organization principles came to dominate professional social work and were then disseminated even further by a school of social work at Kingsley House. Eleanor McMain, head worker at Kingsley House, helped to organize a "school of applied sociology" in order to train social workers in the city. Classes began in November 1914 and were conducted at Kingsley House, making this the first program in the South for the professional training of social workers.[70] Although the school had originated in Kingsley House, financial difficulties dogged the directors; they eventually approached Tulane University with a plan to have the university take over the program. In 1917 Tulane officially acquired the school, reorganized it as the department of sociology, and ran it according to professional social work standards.[71]

Like schools of social work throughout the country, the Tulane University School of Social Work demonstrated a strong COS influence. Founders included COS leaders, and curricula included instruction on charity organization. Mirroring the national trend (the first training school of social workers in the country had been established by the New York COS), charity organizers strongly supported professional training for social workers and then helped to install "casework" as the centerpiece of that training.[72]

Like other such schools in the South, the Tulane University School of

Social Work was quite self-consciously "southern." The charitable and reform communities in the South had long realized that the "shortage of social workers in the South is so great at present that the growth of the profession and the extension of the lines of activity it represents have been distinctly handicapped," and they began efforts to establish centers for training social workers in the region.[73] The leaders of these efforts believed that southern social welfare agencies needed to employ native southerners, assuming that the South had its own special problems to solve and that only "real" southerners could understand them. As the promotional literature for one southern school put it, "[E]ven when trained workers have been brought to the South from the Eastern schools the problem had not always been solved. A graduate of a school in another section of the country, however capable or well trained he or she may be, is inevitably handicapped at the start by ignorance of local conditions and local ways of doing things."[74] The School of Social Work at Tulane hired southerners almost exclusively for the faculty and catered to students from southern states. As a result, southern schools of social work tended to produce graduates little inclined to tackle their native region's Jim Crow system or the industrialization that had so changed the nature of poverty in the region.

In conclusion, by the 1920s COS principles and personnel had thoroughly infiltrated the larger social welfare system of New Orleans. Charity organization became one of the fundamental principles of the School of Social Work at Tulane, of the several financial federations, and of numerous charitable institutions. Yet the triumph of the COS ideal also meant the reinforcement of the racial, religious, and ethnic configurations of charity in the Crescent City. Fund-raising might become more streamlined as a result of financial federation, but it would not challenge what Roy Lubove labeled the general fragmentation of communal life.[75]

Ostensibly gender neutral, in reality the triumph of the COS meant the rejection of both the nineteenth-century style of female benevolency and the Progressive Era's faith in change through social reform. Charity organizers and professional social workers alike adopted the rational, objective, scientific language of professionalism, or what Regina Kunzel has termed "the legitimizing rhetoric of science."[76] Even institutions founded by female reformers, like Kingsley House, came to be run by professionally trained social workers whose interests lay in casework and professionalization rather than reform.

Finally, the ascendancy of COS philosophies also meant that southern social welfare workers would be little inclined to challenge the southern post-Reconstruction racial settlement. Social workers found their collective attention diverted away from reform. Individuals could still pursue an interest in race relations or other reforms. Emeric Kurtagh, for example, the head resident at Kingsley House during the 1940s, pioneered a biracial recreational program for children, despite opposition from the settlement's board, from the city, and from white parents.[77]

Likewise, Elizabeth Wisner, on the faculty of the School of Social Work at Tulane, directed literally dozens of students toward research topics on blacks in the South, and she regularly placed students in social welfare agencies that served blacks.[78] But her School of Social Work remained white, as did the university upon which it was financially dependent, providing clear limits on her activities.

If New Orleans can serve as a reasonable predictor of trends in the rest of the urban South, then future studies should test for some of the possible trends identified here: the contest between benevolent women and scientific charity; the role of the charity organizing movement in reinforcing sectarianism, racial segregation, and the New South Creed; and the emphasis on southern "distinctiveness" in the formulation of schools of social work in the region. And if New Orleans can illuminate regional trends, then southern Progressive Era reformers would appear to have been bound not only by the region's racial views and social conservatism but also by the conservatism produced by charity organization and by the professionalization of social work. Regional mores and national trends combined to rein in southern social welfare policies that might have challenged racial policies or class relations. In a sense then, southern progressivism reconciled progress and tradition, but it also reconciled southern systems with national trends.

NOTES

This essay is based upon papers delivered at the Annual Meeting of the Social Science History Association ("Gender and Charity: New Orleans in the Progressive Era"), and the Annual Meeting of the Southern Historical Association ("Southern Settlement Houses and the Emergence of Professional Social Workers in the South"). Both conferences were held in 1994. I thank the participants in those sessions for constructive and encouraging comments.

1. John Fredrick Nau, *The German People of New Orleans, 1850–1900* (Leiden: E. J. Brill, 1958), 91.

2. I am purposefully broadening the time frame of this essay beyond the traditional periodization of the Progressive Era. It is my contention that "progressivism" was as much a response to the economic dislocations of the 1870s as it was a response to the economic troubles of the 1890s, and that the organizational activities of the 1870s were often identical to those of the 1890s, which are regularly considered "progressivism."

3. Louisiana, as a former Spanish and French colony, had not inherited the English poor law. Periodic efforts to pass statewide poor laws had failed. Not until 1880 did the state pass such a law, compelling the parishes to support their poor and infirm. Elisabeth Wisner, *Social Welfare in the South* (Baton Rouge: Louisiana State University Press, 1970), 26–27, 86–87.

4. Gilles Vandal, "The Nineteenth-Century Municipal Responses to the Problem of Poverty: New Orleans' Free Lodgers, 1850–1880, as Case Study," *Journal of Urban History* 19 (November 1992): 30–31.

5. Jo Ann Carrigan, "Impact of Epidemic Yellow Fever on Life in Louisiana," *Louisiana History* 4 (Winter 1963): 24. For example, German Catholics founded an orphanage in 1854. The Hebrew Benevolent Society opened a home for widows and orphans in 1856. Nau, *German People*, 91, 93.

6. Wisner, *Social Welfare in the South*, 92.

7. Robert H. Bremner, *The Public Good: Philanthropy and Welfare in the Civil War Era* (New York: Knopf, 1980), 91.

8. Vandal, "Nineteenth-Century Municipal Responses," 37.

9. Wisner, *Social Welfare in the South*, 98.

10. The state closed one public institution for delinquent girls in 1873, and the girls were transferred to a private institution. Evelyn Campbell Beven, *City Subsidies to Private Charitable Agencies in New Orleans: the History and Present Status 1824–1933* (New Orleans: Tulane University, 1934), 25.

11. Elizabeth Wisner, *Public Welfare Administration in Louisiana* (Chicago: University of Chicago Press, 1930), 188–89, 191–93.

12. Wisner, *Public Welfare*, 28–29.

13. Beven, *City Subsidies*, 21.

14. Beven, *City Subsidies*, 9, 28–29; Wisner, *Social Welfare in the South*, 93.

15. *Fifty-eighth Annual Report of St. Anna's Asylum* (1910), 4. Louisiana Collection (vertical file), Howard-Tilton Library, Tulane University, New Orleans.

16. *Second Annual Report of the Society of the Home for Homeless Men* (1897–98), 5. Louisiana Collection (vertical file), Howard-Tilton Library, Tulane University, New Orleans.

17. See Charter of the Home for Homeless Young Women. Louisiana Collection (vertical file), Howard-Tilton Library, Tulane University, New Orleans.

18. *Annual Report of the Christian Woman's Exchange* (1884–85), unpaginated. Louisiana Collection, Howard-Tilton Library, Tulane University, New Orleans.

19. Edison Allen, *A Little History of the Little Sisters of the Poor and Their Foundation in New Orleans* (New Orleans: n.p., 1972), 27.

20. John W. Blassingame, *Black New Orleans, 1860–1880* (Chicago: University of Chicago, 1973), 167–71. These benevolent societies were extremely popular and important through-

out the South. According to Claude Jacobs, four-fifths of New Orleans's population (black and white) belonged to some kind of benevolent society. "Benevolent Societies of New Orleans Blacks During the Late Nineteenth and Early Twentieth Centuries," *Louisiana History* 29 (Winter 1988): 22. A rare set of records for one of these benevolent associations—the Ladies' Friends of Faith Benevolent Association—is housed at the Amistad Research Center of Tulane University.

21. Dorothy Salem, *To Better Our World: Black Women in Organized Reform, 1890–1920* (Brooklyn: Carlson, 1990), 76.

22. Beven, *City Subsidies*, 27.

23. *Second Annual Report Conference of Charities* (1885), 5. Louisiana Collection, Howard-Tilton Library, Tulane University, New Orleans. James Leiby, "Charity Organization Reconsidered," *Social Service Review* 58 (December 1984): 523–38.

24. Roy Lubove, *The Professional Altruist: The Emergence of Social Work as a Career 1880–1930* (Cambridge: Harvard University Press, 1965), 8.

25. Frank Dekker Watson, *The Charity Organization Movement in the United States* (New York: MacMillan, 1922), 357–58.

26. As analyzed by Paul M. Gaston, *The New South Creed: A Study in Southern Mythmaking* (New York: Knopf, 1970).

27. Watson, *Charity Organization*, 159.

28. Philip W. Ayers, "Charity Organization in Southern Cities," *Charities Review* 4 (1895): 260. Ayers goes on to note that COSs formed in Louisville in 1884 and Memphis in 1893. (The New Orleans Conference of Charities was reorganized and renamed the COS in 1897. To prevent confusion, I will refer to the organization throughout as the COS, which is the "generic" name for these agencies.) Dewey Grantham reported that the New Orleans COS was organized in 1897 in response to the yellow fever epidemic in that year. The COS predated the epidemic, but it may be the case that the epidemic inspired the reorganization of the charity group. *Southern Progressivism: The Reconciliation of Progress and Tradition* (Knoxville: University of Tennessee Press, 1983), 224.

29. Gladys Geraldine Soule, "A History of the Family Service Society, vol. 1, The Charity Organization Society 1883–1925" (M.A. thesis, Tulane University, 1947), 18.

30. Lubove, *Professional Altruist*, 6.

31. Soule, "A History of the Family Service Society," 178.

32. Lubove, *Professional Altruist*, 16.

33. Robert Hunter, "The Relation between Social Settlements and Charity Organization," *Journal of Political Economy* 11 (1902): 75.

34. Soule, "A History of the Family Service Society," 20.

35. *Second Annual Report Conference of Charities* (1885), 4.

36. *Fourth Annual Report Conference of Charities* (1886–87), 24–25. Louisiana Collection, Howard-Tilton Library, Tulane University, New Orleans. Charity organizers argued that the work test "is a device sometimes used to determine in certain cases where other means are impossible, whether a given individual is 'work-shy' or not. In brief it is an aid in diagnosis." Watson, *Charity Organization*, 121.

37. *Fourth Annual Report of the Charity Organization Society of New Orleans* (1900), 2. Louisiana Collection, Howard-Tilton Library, Tulane University, New Orleans.

38. John Cumbler has noted that a local Associated Charities in Massachusetts developed a laundry, where women could be put to work in order to test their willingness to do so. Cumbler, "The Politics of Charity: Gender and Class in Late Nineteenth-Century Charity Policy," *Journal of Social History* 14 (January 1980): 104.

39. *Second Annual Report Conference of Charities* (1885), 19 (case number 2026).

40. *Second Annual Report Conference of Charities* (1885), 21, (case number 1929).

41. *Second Annual Report Conference of Charities* (1885), 18–19.

42. Regina Kunzel, *Fallen Women, Problem Girls, and the Professionalization of Social Work* (New Haven: Yale University, 1993), 33. In New Orleans, the Memorial Mercy Home established a children's annex in 1902 to care for the young children of the home's inmates who had found jobs outside the home. Ruby Brewster, "The Memorial Mercy Home-Hospital" (M.A. thesis, Tulane University, 1942), 19.

43. Here, COS workers foreshadowed policies of later professional social workers. See Kunzel, *Fallen Women,* 66.

44. The Mothers Pension Act of 1920, reenacted as the Children's Aid Law of 1930, should have made it possible for needy mothers to care for many children in their own homes. But neither the parish nor the state adequately funded this plan, and it did not serve the purpose of keeping children with their mothers. Beven, *City Subsidies,* 22. Although scholars have often noted that orphanages housed children who were not truly orphaned, little attention has been paid to the forcible removal of children from their parents as a condition of assistance.

45. Lubove, *Professional Altruist,* 13.

46. Irma M. Isaacson, "A History of Jewish Philanthropy in New Orleans," (M.A. thesis, Tulane University, 1937), 38.

47. Soule, "Charity Organization Society," 24. Elizabeth Wisner dryly observed that it was "no wonder that this voluntary charity could make no dent on the extensive poverty throughout many sections of the city, for its first report shows that only $298.65 was spent that year." Wisner, *Social Welfare in the South,* 99.

48. *Second Annual Report Conference of Charities* (1885), 9.

49. Florence Jennings, "A Study of the W. E. and Frances Roberson Memorial Home" (M.A. thesis, Tulane University, 1933), 9.

50. Grantham, *Southern Progressivism,* 226; Blassingame, *Black New Orleans,* 167.

51. *Annual Report of the Christian Woman's Exchange* (1885–86), unpaginated.

52. *Annual Report of the Christian Woman's Exchange* (1885–86), unpaginated.

53. *Fourth Annual Report Conference of Charities* (1886–87), 26–27.

54. Anne Firor Scott, *Natural Allies: Women's Associations in American History* (Urbana: University of Illinois, 1991), chaps. 1 and 2.

55. Soule, "Charity Organization Society," 48–49. Evidence from New Orleans certainly confirms the recent observation by Regina Kunzel that the professionalization of social welfare went slowly and was contested at every turn. Women's benevolent groups especially resisted this new view of professional relations between trained workers and their "clients." Kunzel, *Fallen Women,* 3.

56. See Ayers, "Charity Organization in Southern Cities," 260. Ayers asserted that the mild winters of New Orleans meant that the city had "less occasion for large gushes of benevo-

lence" and thus the "very poor have not had impressed upon them at intervals the assurance of public support."

57. Soule, "Charity Organization Society," 49.

58. New Orleans *Times-Democrat,* October 17, 1890, p. 3.

59. *Annual Report of the Christian Woman's Exchange* (1884–85), unpaginated.

60. *Annual Report of the Christian Woman's Exchange* (1900), 31. Louisiana Collection, Howard-Tilton Library, Tulane University. The annual report noted that the CWE was having trouble attracting mothers to the day nursery because they were suspicious it was really an asylum. Why the mothers felt this way remains undocumented.

61. Dorothy Salem, *To Better Our World: Black Women in Organized Reform* (Brooklyn: Carlson, 1990), 76, 81.

62. Isabelle Dubroca, *Good Neighbor: Eleanor McMain of Kingsley House* (New Orleans: Pelican Publishing, 1955), 40.

63. Elizabeth Lasch-Quinn, *Black Neighbors: Race and the Limits of Reform in the American Settlement House Movement, 1890–1945* (Chapel Hill: University of North Carolina Press, 1993), 50.

64. On Kingsley House, see Eleanor McMain, "Kingsley House, New Orleans," *Charities* 11 (December 5, 1903): 549.

65. Emeric Kurtagh, head resident from 1941 to 1949, was the only male to serve.

66. Isaacson, "Jewish Philanthropy in New Orleans," 38.

67. Lubove, *Professional Altruist,* 183.

68. Lubove, *Professional Altruist,* 186.

69. Dubroca, *Good Neighbor,* 111.

70. John P. Dyer, *Tulane, the Biography of a University, 1834–1965* (New York: Harper & Row, 1966), 195; Dubroca, *Good Neighbor,* 88–89; flyer announcing school opening, in Kingsley House Papers, Box 1, Board Correspondence.

71. Dyer, *Tulane,* 195.

72. Lubove, *Professional Altruist,* 139–42.

73. Southern Woman's Educational Alliance, *Social Work as a Profession in the South* (Richmond: n.p., 1921), 3.

74. Catalog of School of Social Work and Public Health, Richmond, Virginia, 1918–1919.

75. Lubove, *Professional Altruist,* vii.

76. Kunzel, *Fallen Women,* 37. Daniel Walkowitz has also made the point that objectivity and rationality were conventionally associated with male professional culture. "The Making of a Feminine Professional Identity: Social Workers in the 1920s," *American Historical Review* 95 (October 1990): 1051.

77. Paul H. Stuart, "The Kingsley House Extension Program: Racial Segregation in a 1940s Settlement Program," *Social Service Review* 66 (March 1992): 112–20.

78. Florence Jennings, "A Study of the W. E. and Frances Roberson Memorial Home (An Institution for Dependent Negro Children)" (M.A. thesis, Tulane University, 1933), is just one of the many theses on black institutions or race relations that Wisner directed.

Are You or Are You Not Your Sister's Keeper?

A Radical Response to the Treatment of Unwed Mothers in Tennessee

MAZIE HOUGH

In 1872 Lide Meriwether, a member of elite society in Memphis, Tennessee, confronted her southern sisters on their attitudes toward fallen women. Their husbands, she suggested, routinely stopped to assist a man who had fallen to drink or gambling, but they refused similar help to a woman fallen from virtue. Instead they condemned her to the life of an outcast for having succumbed once to the "master passion," shutting her out of society, work, and family on account of her reputation. Warning that "the voice of thy Sister's blood crieth unto me from the ground," Lide Meriwether urged them to take a more active role in helping fallen women and asserted that every woman could do something if she would. "Hold up the mirror of your husband's course," she urged them, "and then answer to your own soul the question, 'Guilty, or not guilty, concerning my sister?'"[1]

Meriwether's assertion that women were responsible for the fate of other women—that all women, rich as well as poor, faced the same temptations, and that exclusive attention to a woman's chastity caused more harm than good—directly challenged the traditional response to unwed mothers in Tennessee. Tennessee law and custom placed control of women's sexuality in male hands, emphasized the absolute importance of a woman's reputation for chastity, and it separated women by class as well as race.

Nevertheless, in 1875 and 1876, as if heeding Meriwether's call, evangelical women in Knoxville, Nashville, Chattanooga, and Memphis opened homes for unwed mothers. These homes were among the first in a series of homes that women organized throughout the country. Some began as refuges for prostitutes, others as temporary homes for homeless women and children; most turned quickly to serving young pregnant women. By 1946 the Children's Bureau would estimate that two-thirds of the two hundred operating maternity homes opened their doors between 1876 and 1900.[2]

Historians have found a uniformity in these homes. Volunteer Protestant women organized them to offer "sympathy, sisterhood, and piety" to their fallen sisters. They considered the pregnant women to be victims of male seduction. They encouraged the women to keep their babies and offered them salvation through Christianity and hard work. While the Tennessee homes had much in common with homes elsewhere in the country, to consider them as only part of a national movement obscures their historical significance.[3]

Mary Ritter Beard, a key figure in modern women's history, warned that "the political economy in which feminism has to function is the prime consideration." It is only by placing the Tennessee women's actions in context that we can see how radical was their challenge to the social order and at the same time how their inability to acknowledge the bonds of gender across race undermined this challenge. In Evelyn Nakano Glenn's terms, the failure of the early radical Protestant women reformers of the South revealed that "tackling gender hierarchy requires simultaneously addressing race hierarchy."[4]

Before the Civil War, Tennessee's bastardy and seduction laws had defined the options for unwed mothers and had made clear the social hierarchies of race, class, and gender. These laws differentiated between black and white, rich and poor, male and female and limited certain rights to only one side of the equation. They excluded black women from the courts, punished poor white women, reinforced male control of women's sexuality, and placed a high and absolute value on a woman's reputation for chastity.

Race was a primary dichotomy. Children born to slave mothers inherited their mothers' slave status and therefore had no legal standing in court. At the same time miscegenation laws prohibited interracial couples from marrying and thus ensured that all children born to such couples were "illegitimate."

The ability of white single mothers to sue men for support of their children depended upon the mother's class. Poor women could participate in a bastardy suit, but the suit offered them little. When a court found a man to be the father of a child born out of wedlock it could force him to pay no more than ninety dollars. After three years the laws determined that all "allowances shall cease . . . and the County Court shall dispose of the bastard child as most conduce to its interest, either by giving it to the reputed father, or binding it out to some suitable person." As the suit was brought by the state on behalf of the state and the father paid his money directly to the commissioners of the poor, the woman benefited but little.[5] A wealthy woman, on the other hand, could participate in a seduction suit and gain as much as ten to fifteen thousand dollars for the "dishonor and suffering visited upon the family."[6]

Rich or poor, however, women had little control over the suit designed to compensate them for seduction and betrayal. Only a justice of the peace could initiate a bastardy suit, and he could compel a woman to name the father of her child whether she wanted to or not. Only a man could bring a seduction suit unless the woman could prove that the man had offered her marriage first. And any white man could legitimate his child born out of wedlock at any time so long as he made the child his heir. He had only to petition the court and state his reasons for the request. Once legitimated the child was "as if . . . born to the former in lawful wedlock."[7]

And for all white women, their standing in court, their right to be believed, depended exclusively upon their reputation for chastity. In 1825 the court determined that a woman should not be compelled to testify in court in a bastardy suit: "It requires little knowledge of the female character to predict that such an open exposure of the frailty and vice of the woman would tend to tear away the film of modesty she had left and turn her loose upon society profligate and shameless . . . she would have almost irresistible temptations to commit perjury." Ten years later the court noted: "It would be monstrous to fix a stigma on a man's character and a burden on his estate, upon the unsupported affidavit of a woman whose character was so abandoned that no one would believe her."[8] If a man charged with seduction and breach of promise could prove that when he offered her marriage he had "supposed that the plaintiff was modest and chaste, and it turned out she was not," the woman could not win her suit. On the other hand men could, and did, testify to have slept with a woman in order to discredit her testimony and suffer no legal consequences.

Tennessee legal tradition relied upon white males to deal with birth outside of wedlock. When the social disruptions of the Civil War and the federal mandates of Reconstruction undermined that white male authority,

Protestant women stepped in to create their own solution to the problem of out-of-wedlock pregnancy. In less than two years they opened homes for "fallen" women in all four of Tennessee's largest cities and attempted in these homes to minimize the importance of a woman's reputation and to give women, in addition to men, some control of their fates. The homes accepted all women who applied and offered them redemption through religion as well as food and shelter. All four homes reported facing "much prejudice" and severe economic problems in their early years. One group closed its home; two groups survived only by aligning themselves with the National Florence Crittenton Association.[9] The third, the Woman's Christian Association Mission, working with and on the principles of Lide Meriwether, survived only by compromising its radical premises. For almost two decades, however, it successfully challenged the dominant construction of illegitimacy and offered women opportunities that their status, by virtue of class and reputation, did not generally allow.

Memphis reflected in microcosm the challenge to male authority and the social disruption in the postbellum South. The riverboat town established in 1840 exploded in terms of economic and population growth as it grew into a cotton-trading center, a distributor of goods for a one-hundred-mile radius, and a lumber town. It was the fastest-growing city in the nation in the 1850s and by 1860 had become the sixth largest city in the South. Between 1864 and 1866 alone its population doubled and by 1890 had more than doubled again.[10]

Numbers tell only part of the story. Union troops controlled the city from 1862 to the end of the Civil War. Recently freed men and women poured into the city, first seeking refuge in the Union Army, later seeking jobs and a new life. The tension over the arrival of a large free black population erupted in a riot in 1866 that killed forty-six African Americans. In 1867, 1873, and 1878, successive yellow fever epidemics decimated the city's population. In the last and worst epidemic more than half of the population left the city. The epidemics brought a major shift in demographics as many of the recent German and Irish immigrants left the city and never returned. By 1900 the city was 49 percent African American and virtually devoid of foreign-born inhabitants. The immigrants who continued to arrive came from the surrounding countryside.[11]

Simultaneously the men of Memphis lost control of the city twice in two decades. In 1862 the Union Army took control of Memphis and continued to rule under federal mandate. In 1870 locally elected officials regained control, but eight years later—their city devastated by the yellow fever epidemic—they surrendered the city's charter to the state yet again.[12]

As a result of the rapid growth, social fragmentation, and confusion over municipal authority, the city failed to provide even minimal services for the influx of immigrants from the countryside. Statistics from the end of the century suggest the social disorder that grew through previous decades. By 1903 Memphis had 504 saloons, more than four times the number in other comparably sized cities.[13] The murder rate in Memphis by the turn of the century was the highest in the country, and the suicide rate was far above the national average.[14]

White women of Memphis began to respond to the social chaos by creating a large number of organizations that sought to gain for women some control in a wide arena that included politics, commercial development, criminal justice, and education. The women who were organizing this movement were white, and their families had a stake in the city. They organized on the basis of gender and race and were not timid in their demands. Sometimes, but not always, they claimed the special prerogatives of women as they took advantage of the uncertain governance of the times to assert their right as women to participate in the reordering of the society.[15]

The Woman's Christian Association (WCA), founder of the city's home for fallen women, was one of the oldest and largest of these women's organizations. Organized "for the good of women carried on wholly by women" in 1875, it developed an array of programs, several of which lasted well into the twentieth century. (While it began with projects that directly benefited the urban middle- and upper-class of Memphis, it very quickly created a program that challenged one of the underpinnings of male dominance—male control of illegitimacy.) Its history suggests the ways that its founders—white women married to men who were making their fortunes in the city—negotiated the conflicting alliances of class, gender, and race. What began as an effort to promote class interests quickly developed into an assertion of rights for women.

The WCA started modestly with a small extension of women's traditional duties in an interdenominational sewing circle called the Memphis Bethel. These "prominent citizens" taught sewing to poor scholars and "by force of example," taught them "the way, the truth and the light."[16]

The president of the Memphis Bethel was Elizabeth Fisher Johnson, daughter of a state senator and prominent planter. Johnson had attended the Emma Willard School before her marriage to a plantation and cottonseed oil–mill owner. Although she moved to the outskirts of Memphis in 1872, she visited the churches in the city several years later to exhort women to join an interdenominational women's organization. In November 1875 the newspaper announced the creation of the Ladies Christian Association (hereafter WCA).[17]

The WCA's first concerns were directly related to their class.[18] Its mission, as its first report stated, was "to enlarge and systematize the missionary and benevolent work assigned to ladies as their legitimate field." The idea, the *Memphis Daily Appeal* explained, was to bring together "a body of Christian workers from all denominations" so they might "cordially unite in their labors" and "may impart and receive information as to the best methods of carrying on their work." The association planned to divide the city into seven districts and send a board of visitors to each district to determine which children failed to attend Sunday school and which families needed relief. The association also planned to open an employment agency "to procure good homes for worthy applicants without charge to them, and to furnish employers with reliable help at the moderate charge of one dollar."

The missionary effort, the *Appeal* reassured its readers, will be "mainly directed to the reading and distribution of the Bible and religious literature, and to persuade all to attend church and Sabbath school. The benevolent efforts will be mainly directed toward furnishing employment." These efforts directly benefited the WCA founders whose husbands were making money in the growing commerce of the city. Historian Marsha Wedell was able to identify the profession of the husbands of four of the ten founding members as a bank president, a plantation and cottonseed oil–mill owner, a lawyer and investor, and a clergyman of independent means who made his money largely through real estate. Soon the association also included women who were married to men prominent in the cotton business, judges, lawyers, railroad board members, physicians, and wholesalers of groceries and chemicals. Two husbands were officers in the Taxing District, two had been mayors, and one was a state legislator.[19] In a city that relied upon private donors to provide for the needs of an increasing and potentially disruptive poor population, the WCA's proposal to systematize private charity "so that unworthy parties may not be draining the treasury of each at the same time" was clearly in the best interest of those donors.

While the plan to systematize private charity supported the WCA founders' class, the plan for an employment agency promised specifically to benefit the women of the association's class. Historians have noted that finding a reliable supply of domestic servants had been an ongoing problem for wealthy American women and that this problem was intensified in the South after the Civil War.[20]

While the early WCA neatly fit the needs of women of their class, within a year the association began to branch out to encompass a number of more challenging reforms. Within the first decade the WCA would open a women's hospital, a women's cooperative, and a prison-visiting program. It began its most radical work, however, soon after it opened the employment agency in 1875. To support the working women who came to the agency, the WCA had opened a lunchroom with several rooms above for temporary lodgings. "Presently," a WCA historian noted in 1894, "it became evident that something must be done for a class of women who timidly sought those doors, one after another, but whose moral leprosy barred them from entrance."[21] In January 1876 the WCA opened up the Navy Yard Mission for these "moral lepers" in the Commandant's House on Promenade Street. In 1880 the group, unable to accommodate the large number of applicants, moved the mission to larger quarters on Alabama Street.[22]

For eight years the mission on Alabama Street operated as both a support of the social construction of gender, class, and race and as a contradiction to those things. It offered poor white women from the countryside an opportunity to improve their status by imbuing them with middle-class standards of industry, cleanliness, and order, and it excluded black women. At the same time it purposefully and indiscriminately mixed virtuous and nonvirtuous women by serving all white women who came to its doors and inviting middle-class women into the mission. And it insisted that women could protect and support other women.

The mission encouraged white women to apply on their own (rather than have others seek admission for them) and accepted all who did so. Meriwether reminded readers that "reformation of women thoroughly steeped in sin is only an occasional chapter in the great volume of reform recorded in houses like this." The WCA was particularly interested in helping young women from the countryside. "First, young girls often come in from the country or small towns in the vicinity seeking work and finding none. Meantime, money is gone and temptation meets them on every side," Meriwether noted in a report on the mission to the public. "But any kind man or woman finding her in such peril can direct her to the home." Meriwether also noted that the mission took in young girls whose parents or guardians found them hard to control or who "being wage earners, are compelled to spend most of their time away from them."[23] A report from the mission in 1884 noted, "We can only tell you of the homeless, friendless women, sometimes deserted wives, coming to us for protection and shelter until some way may be open by which they may honestly earn their daily bread." Included were those "without any means of support or friends to provide for daily wants, whose constitutional infirmities render them incapable of fighting life's battle." In its first twenty years the mission served from forty to sixty women a year.[24]

Evidence suggests that many of the women who came to the mission were poor rural women from Tennessee and surrounding southern states. In 1892 *The Gleaner* reported donations from a "grateful though heartbroken mother in Mississippi," who sent fifty dollars "wrung out, no doubt, in toil, self-sacrifice and tears," from a domestic who sent twenty dollars "to defray part of the expense of another girl, an old friend brought there in deepest trouble from Arkansas," and from a "humble, grateful woman" dismissed several years ago, "never forgetful of the hands that rescued her" who sent four dollars from her earnings in the kitchen."[25]

Every year from 7 to 20 percent left "without permission." No doubt some of these "pretended to reform, just for the use of the home until it suited them to take up again the dance of death," as the women's home in Chattanooga noted of its own departures. Others, however, clearly found more than food and shelter. As one former resident wrote, "I would like to be back in the Home, if only for one evening, and hear the same voices in the chapel, and go over the lessons once again. There I received so much help and so much strength." And another said, "[I was] bitter against the world when I came here, but I have learned in a measure to understand God's love and kindness. . . . I know he is my friend and has given me friends here."[26]

The mission offered "moral and religious instruction with training in every department of household labor." The women in the home did all the housework under the direction of a matron and her assistant while the WCA members visited regularly to provide instruction. By 1884 the home provided residents with regular Sunday church services performed by local ministers, Thursday services performed by the women of the WCA, and the word of God taught morning and evening. Each inmate was required to learn a portion of the scripture for daily recitation.[27] One visitor commented in 1881: "Each hour of the day is set apart for particular duties. There are so many hours set apart for devotional service, so many for labor and so many for recreation. No noise or confusion of any character ever mars the quietude of the establishment or its surroundings and morning, noon and night witnesses the observance of the most perfect discipline."[28]

The WCA reported that it considered industry as "one of the greatest helps in forming or remodeling character" and consequently kept the women in the mission working at various jobs. The industry was not only good for the women, it was necessary for the home, which was constantly struggling for funds. In 1881 the managers reported that they had been planning to open a laundry, but because of lack of water and conveniences, the severe winter, and want of means, they had not yet succeeded. The board, they told the press, had "found considerable difficulty in obtaining remunerative employment owing to the inexperience of their workers and the low prices paid." Three years later the mission opened a laundry, which brought in $242. That year the residents also sewed for local establishments, made a silk quilt that they sold for fifty dollars, and considered opening a rug industry.[29]

The income from all these efforts, however, was not enough to support the home. In 1880 the WCA began to board children who had at least one parent living. The board provided a welcome income while the children themselves provided good public relations.[30] The WCA members appealed to class biases when they pointed out that "many worthless parents will cling to their children and drag them down" but would bring them to the mission if they could see and talk with them. We make the best use of time, the WCA stated to the press, "hoping to plant seed that may bring forth fruit in eternal life." The WCA provided for the children physically as well as spiritually, and WCA reports at this time suggest that the WCA was fully aware of the good public relations that this service to young children provided.[31]

The WCA made every effort to bring together women of good reputation and women who had fallen. The WCA was open to "any woman of good moral character." Members of the mission committee met weekly and urged other members to volunteer their services in the home or to help run its weekly all-women prayer sessions. They invited the female public to visit during the weekly afternoon social hour, to attend the biweekly religious services, and to come to lectures.³²

The women who managed the mission clearly wanted to transform the residents by teaching them cleanliness, industry, order, and religion. They also, however, wanted to transform the larger society. They called on Christianity to minimize the distance between women who had fallen and women of good moral standing, and they asked women to take a direct role in determining the fate of fallen women. They did so at the very same time that their male counterparts—white southern men, who were on the rise—were jostling for power by emphasizing the crucial role white men played in protecting white women's chastity.

The 1870s and 1880s were a period of sharp racial conflict in the South as white men of means attempted to retain control of government by undermining poor black-white alliances, limiting black participation in government, and ensuring racial separation in the society at large. In 1875, the year the WCA was founded, Tennessee legislators passed a law that prohibited blacks from traveling in first-class accommodations and allowed innkeepers and recreational establishments to exclude blacks. African Americans contested this law in the assembly and the streets. In the conflict that followed, white women's purity—their innocence and chastity and need for protection—played a critical role as white men relied upon the threat of lynching to reassert white superiority and justified lynching by accusing black men of rape.³³

Ida B. Wells, who began her crusade against lynching in Memphis, claimed that lynching, along with the "midnight outrages of KKK, political massacres," and segregation legislation, was another means by which the white South rendered "our freedom a curse rather than a blessing." She described in detail how the threat of lynching successfully limited African Americans' actions and at the same time how claims of black attacks on white women's virtue justified the random white brutality. "Humanity abhors the assailant of womanhood, and this charge upon the Negro at once placed him beyond the pale of sympathy," she asserted.³⁴

The WCA spoke out against the first lynching in Memphis in its own newspaper, *The Gleaner,* but did not question its cause. Acknowledging that they did not "pretend to know the sentiments of white *voters,*" the paper's editors wrote in 1892, "we feel competent to speak for the women; the intelligent clear eyed wives, mothers, sisters, daughters of this community and we know they are horror stricken." They did not absolve the African Americans but noted that even where "ignorance, idleness and insolence of a large part of a large negro population has long been a menace and a danger, two wrongs do not make a right."[35]

In many ways the mission, which minimized the importance of a woman's reputation and which stressed women's responsibility to protect other women, contradicted the social construction that supported lynching. For lynching was a brutal show of force that could only gain support by asserting that black men needed to be violently curtailed in their attacks on innocent white women. The defense of lynching rested upon the assumption that white men had to protect white women because all white women were innocent and virtuous, all white men were the natural protectors of white womanhood, and all black men would stop at nothing to rape a white woman. In Memphis at the end of the century the white newspapers emphasized the "truth" of these constructs daily.

Women, the white newspapers insisted in a variety of ways, were innocent and naive. This innocence was innate and needed protection. As the *Appeal* commented on a nationally popular song about a woman who "had quaffed to the lips the unholy chalice of sin," it expressed a "tardy admission of the fact that virtue with women is innate, and that her degradation comes from contact with masculine turpitude."[36]

If women were by nature innocent, men were by nature sexually aggressive. In answer to a citizen petition to "abate nuisances of bawdy houses," the city's Legislative Council determined that to regulate these houses of prostitution would be unwise "because the question will never be satisfactorily solved until men have their passions under perfect control." They had not yet, the *Appeal* concluded, and to close the houses "would result in more evil than good."[37]

While white men were the seducers, they were also the protectors. For example, when Maud Stafford entered a house of prostitution in Memphis because her lover had ruined her reputation, the police encouraged her to come with them to the police station. When young men crowded to the station house and offered to post bail for her, it was the police again who kept them at bay. When her father came to get her he warned, "[Y]ou who are the heads of families . . . beware of the prowling wolves of society, who are all about you, seeking an opportunity to slake their thirst. . . . You cannot be too watchful." The *Appeal* concluded in 1904: "Today after centuries of progress we have reached a plane where there are other things dearer than life, and chief among these is female virtue. When this is slain . . . the avenger has the right to go forth in quest of blood-atonement. . . . There is a higher law . . . and that law readeth 'Thou shalt protect female virtue at all hazards.'"[38]

While society could appeal to white men's sense of chivalry as a way to curb their natural sexual aggression, there was nothing short of violence that would control the lust of black men. The *Appeal* suggested that in the decades following the war the ex-slaves had "lost in large measure the traditional and wholesome awe of the white race which kept the Negroes in subjection even when their masters were in the army." It warned that there were no longer any restraints upon the "brute passion of the Negro," and added: "The 'Southern barbarism' which deserves the serious attention of all people north and south . . . is the barbarism which preys upon weak and defenseless women. Nothing but the most prompt, speedy and extreme punishment can hold in check the horrible and bestial propensities of the Negro race." In proof, the papers printed almost daily stories of the rapes that led to lynching throughout the South. Black men, the stories repeatedly suggested, would stop at nothing.[39]

The radical implications of the writings of WCA founders Lide Meriwether and Elizabeth Fisher Johnson can only be understood in this context. Though Meriwether published her essays on the fallen woman in 1872, she and Johnson continued to speak on behalf of the fallen woman throughout the 1880s. They called on women to minimize the importance of a woman's reputation, to recognize that a fall from purity did not ruin a woman forever, and to rely on faith to equalize women before God.

Society women, Meriwether suggested, literally had the power of life and death over other women. They could offer them social acceptance and jobs, or they could ostracize them and deny them a means of earning a living. True Christian women, she asserted, would recognize their bond with other women and recognize that a fall from chastity did not have to ruin a woman forever. For more than forty years she herself had "taken young girls with their children" into her home, and they had "gone out and led good, pure, clean lives and died triumphant deaths."[40]

Perhaps even more radically, Meriwether suggested that all women shared an understanding of physical passion. They should not discriminate against a woman who was "overtaken by strong temptation." Their own children were of like passion and infirmities and might also fall. She consistently pointed out that she was happy not only as a mother but as a wife. She asked that others acknowledge the attraction of sex: "I ask, not of the 'lilies' and 'angels'; neither of the clods and icebergs that are formed and fashioned as women; but of every honest, candid, true woman, with a warm, impassioned heart beating in her bosom. Is the power of the master-passion of humanity a less temptation than the sparkle of the wine cup or the rattle of the dice?"[41]

What separated the women in the mission from the women who ran it was not moral superiority but education and opportunity, she stressed. The residents had been "sent out among the ravening wolves of starvation wages and strong temptations" and had not had access to "wholesome truths contained in great thoughts" and "the means of self control that only thought and study can impart."[42]

And finally, faith was more important than sexual purity. Meriwether suggested that to fail to help someone in need was more sinful than to fall, and Johnson reminded the public of Rahab, the prostitute, whom God saved because she alone had faith.[43]

In many ways the WCA Mission gave form to these ideas. It mixed in one shelter women "steeped in sin" and those seeking employment, those deserted by their husbands and those like Mary Love, member of Lauderdaid Presbyterian Church who, "being unable to support herself was placed here by friends. Humble, loving child of God, Bible her constant companion."[44]

When the women moved the mission from the navy yard to Alabama Street, they brought the home into the heart of the city where it was a visible reminder that not all white women were chaste. They also invited the public into the home to share the regular Thursday services and to attend talks. One by a female physician offered information on "anatomy and physiology of the human body illustrated with a life-size mannikin."[45] In addition, by keeping women and children together in the home, it offered single mothers an opportunity to keep their children and to support themselves without having to turn to male assistance.

Not only did the WCA women support women without the support of men, but they also actively interfered in class relations by supporting poor women in their negotiations with wealthier men. In 1882, for example, the

Appeal noted "about as dirty a piece of work as ever came to light in this city." According to the *Appeal*, "a young lady who had been ruined and cruelly deserted by a prominent citizen" had entered the mission. After making several unsuccessful attempts to contact the woman, the prominent citizen arranged for another young woman to apply to the home in the early hours of the morning. Suspecting something, the WCA board member refused to admit the young woman. The next day she discovered that the prominent citizen had sent the young woman to arrange a compromise or intimidate the pregnant woman into withdrawing her suit. Perhaps, the paper postulated, he was even arranging "to kidnap her and put her where she would cause no further annoyance to the gentleman of prominence who had wrought her ruin." The WCA Mission stood fast.[46]

The WCA women relied on religion to help them stand against society's norms and find a connection with fallen women. Acknowledging the "difficulties were great" the women reported, "For comfort and encouragement we have admonition. 'Let us not be weary in well doing for in due season we will reap if we faint not.'"[47]

Their faith also encouraged them to find connection with the women they served. In 1884 the Rev. N. M. Long called upon those who attended the annual service at the mission to "have faith in those for whom you work." Though one had fallen to the depths, still, he claimed, "there are principles in him on which God is building and on them we may build with confidence." Long suggested that all humanity held a sense of justice, a consciousness of right and wrong, and sympathy that "links us in fellowship with all our kind." "I say therefore," he urged, "judge them by yourself, not by the meanness simply but by the good." The WCA women in *The Gleaner* endorsed the idea of the equalizing role of sympathy. "Sympathy means like suffering," they claimed. "Therefore those who have had sorrows and suffering can come nearer to the heart of the creature in distress."[48]

The WCA also relied on religion to redeem what appeared to be an "irrevocably ruined life." A fallen woman once redeemed might be "made a source of power in the salvation of others." In fact, "thankful to be allowed to walk in the footsteps of their blessed Lord," she might be a more successful missionary than those who had never fallen.[49]

While the WCA challenged the class and gender hierarchies, it did not challenge the racial one. Unable or unwilling to challenge the racial constructions that underlay lynching, it was unable to sustain its challenge to the gender constructions. In 1892 the *Memphis Ledger* noted: "If Lillie Bailey, a rather pretty white girl, seventeen years of age now at the city hospital, would be somewhat less reserved about her disgrace there would be some very nauseating details in the story of her life. She is the mother of a little coon." According to the *Ledger,* Lillie was a "country girl" from Hernando, Mississippi, where her father had a farm. She came to Memphis to go to the mission where she remained almost three months before the child was born. At its birth, "the ladies in charge of the Refuge were horrified" and sent her immediately to the city hospital.[50]

The WCA's fate was inextricably tied to the racial constructs that it would not challenge. Unwilling to defy racial solidarity, it was unable to sustain its argument that a white woman's reputation was insignificant at the same time when the protection of white women's chastity was increasingly emphasized in white men's bid for power. The WCA always had trouble gaining support for the mission, but the inability to maintain its claim that all white women support one another regardless of their reputations ultimately led to the home's closing.

The mission was never a popular cause even among the WCA members. Although more than three hundred women volunteered their services and gave money to the WCA annually, most chose to donate to programs other than the mission. In 1881 WCA secretary Mrs. T. A. Fisher reported that while there were more than one hundred inmates in the mission, the entire expense was supported by one individual. Necessity, she stated, compelled this one-sided support. "Others would not, or did not give and what we feel to be an unjust proportion of the burden was cheerfully assumed by one."[51]

Lack of support for fallen women was apparently widespread throughout the South. Later that year Johnson gave a talk in St. Louis to the International Conference of Woman's Christian Associations in which she called for the WCA to support reformatory work. Pointing out how WCAs were establishing boarding homes, Bible classes, mothers' meetings, and the like, she noted "how few report any efforts made or work done in" the direction of the sinful and erring. She pointed out that only once did a WCA national meeting address the subject of reformatory work. "We acknowledge, dear friends, it is not pleasant work, but we think it necessary work and Christlike work." The refuge, the WCA leadership conceded in 1892, was "never very popular work."[52]

In addition, in spite of Meriwether's call to all Christian women to hire the fallen women, few women did. Although one of the first things the WCA developed was an employment agency specifically designed to find appropriate domestic help for families, and although domestic work was the ideal job for a woman with a child, there is little indication that the mission placed it inmates in domestic positions. Instead they trained them as seamstresses and laundry workers because this work taught the inmates the "independence of being self helpful and being *partly* self sustaining."[53]

While the mission suffered from lack of funds and lack of opportunities for its inmates, it suffered even more from overt community hostility. In 1881 neighbors complained to the Shelby County Grand Jury that the mission was a "nuisance to the neighborhood." The grand jury, after summoning witnesses pro and con, concluded that it was "fully impressed with the fact that institutions of this class are detrimental to any thickly settled neighborhood, by depreciating the value of property and detracting from its desirability as a place of family residence." The grand jury therefore recommended that the "lady managers" as "early as practicable" move the department devoted to fallen women to "a more suitable locality outside of the city limits."[54]

The WCA instead increased its campaign to present the mission as a worthy cause and forestalled the move for seven more years. Finally in 1888, suffering from lack of funds, community pressure, and a political conflict that emphasized white women's chastity, the WCA voted to "divide the dual work carried on by the Mission" and "establish a separate home for women in a retired place." It moved the "Magdalenes," as they were now referred to, out to "a most eligible place" near Fort Pickering but left the children in the Alabama Street home. A year later it opened a boarding home for women. Finally, with three separate boards for three separate missions—children, working women, and fallen women—the WCA abandoned its challenge to the state's construction of legitimacy.

The separation of "Magdalenes" from the children meant that the refuge women could no longer support themselves by taking care of others' and their own children. The creation of a separate boarding home for "pure" working women provided ample opportunity for the society to distinguish between those who had fallen and those who had not, and to provide ample support to those who had not.

The separation between the women of the boarding home and the women of the refuge was so complete that in 1895 even Lide Meriwether, who had written so forcefully on the harm created by reputation, was calling for a temporary home for working women who were waiting admittance to the boarding home. "They should not be sent to the Refuge," she insisted, "for a nameless cloud will rest upon them, however innocent they may be, if they are seen going and coming, even for a few days, in search of work."[55]

By the 1890s, then, the compromise of the radical experiment was complete. No longer did the WCA urge its members to use their sympathy to connect with the fallen women but suggested instead that they undertake the work as "a cross and self-denial." Where once they called on their members to recognize their common humanity, they now called on them for the godliness of self-sacrifice. No longer did the refuge challenge men's authority to protect women or question the importance of a reputation. Instead, it reflected the dominant social construction that relied on men to protect women's reputations and that emphasized the absolute importance of a woman's reputation.

Stories of the refuge after the turn of the century suggest that the institution became a place of punishment and a means to force young women to comply with the society norms. Fathers brought their daughters to the home; the staff pressured women to give up their children to save their reputations; and the matron called the police on women who ran in an effort to keep their children.[56]

In its early years, the demand for shelter at the mission outstripped what the mission, with its meager resources, was able to supply. As the WCA altered its practices and its theory, it lost its appeal to the women it planned to serve. Gradually the number of applicants declined until, even in the midst of the depression when it offered free care, many rooms remained empty. In 1937 the home closed. "The tiny bundle that was once YOU, no doubt filled your mother's heart with joy," the WCA announced in its last appeal for funds. But "that joy is not for every mother. Sometimes there is only shame." As the appeal made clear, the WCA had severed the connection between the fallen woman and all others and had accepted the importance of reputation. It had come a long way from Meriwether's charge that women find their common connection, "Guilty or not guilty, regarding your sister?"[57]

NOTES

1. Lide Meriwether, *Soundings* (Memphis: Boyle & Chapman, 1872), 152, 159.

2. Maud Morlock and Hilary Campbell, *Maternity Homes for Unmarried Mothers: A Community Service* (Washington, D.C.: U.S. Department of Labor, Children's Bureau Publication, 1946), 309, 4.

3. Regina G. Kunzel, *Fallen Women, Problem Girls: Unmarried Mothers and the Professionalization of Social Work, 1890–1945* (New Haven: Yale University Press, 1993), 2, 13.

4. Evelyn Nakano Glenn, "From Servitude to Service Work: Historical Continuities in the Racial Division of Paid Reproductive Labor," *Signs* 18 (Autumn 1992): 36.

5. *State v. Howard*, 1 Swan 134; *Kirkpatrick v. State*, Meigs 124.

6. *Thompson v. Clendenning*, 1 Head 288; *Love v. Masoner*, 6 Baxt. 25.

7. *McReynolds v. McCallie*, 69 Tenn 260; *McKamie v. Baskerville*, 86 Tenn 459; *Murphy v. Portrum*, 95 Tenn 695.

8. *Goddard v. State*, 10 Tenn 98; *State v. Coatney*, 16 Tenn 210; *Conn v. Wilson*, 2 Overton 234; *Goodall v. Thurman*, 1 Head 209.

9. The clippings files of the Nashville and Chattanooga Public Libraries hold various accounts of the Nashville and Chattanooga Florence Crittenton Homes. See also Otto Wilson, *Fifty Years' Work with Girls, 1883–1933* (Alexandria, Va.: National Florence Crittenton Mission, 1933).

10. Roger Biles, *Memphis in the Great Depression* (Knoxville: University of Tennessee Press, 1986), 10.

11. Herbert G. Gutman, *The Black Family in Slavery and Freedom, 1750–1925* (New York: Random House, 1976), 24; William J. Cooper Jr. and Thomas E. Terrill, *The American South* (New York: McGraw-Hill, 1991), 400; William D. Miller, *Memphis during the Progressive Era* (Memphis: Memphis State University Press, 1957), 3–7.

12. Thomas B. Alexander, *Political Reconstruction in Tennessee* (Nashville: Vanderbilt University, 1950; reprint, New York: Russell & Russell, 1968); Works Progress Administration, *Tennessee* (Viking Press, 1936), 207.

13. The cities were Fall River, Massachusetts, and Birmingham, Alabama. Miller, *Memphis during the Progressive Era*, 91.

14. Miller, *Memphis during the Progressive Era*, 91, 92, 26; Biles, *Memphis in the Great Depression*, 15.

15. By 1895 a network of women's organizations, the Woman's Council, boasted a membership of forty-eight organizations and more than three thousand women. "Woman's Edition," *Memphis Commercial Appeal*, February 14, 1895. Marsha Wedell, *Elite Women and the*

Reform Impulse in Memphis (Knoxville: University of Tennessee Press, 1991), thoroughly examines the women's reform movement in Memphis following the Civil War.

16. This and the following paragraphs on the origins of the WCA come from the *Memphis Daily Appeal*, February 23, 1875, p. 4.

17. Thereafter the newspapers referred to the organization as the Woman's Christian Association.

18. Glenda Gilmore suggests in her study of race and gender relations in North Carolina that the most important division between white politicians was between those who chose to live in the city and those who chose to live on the farm. The women of the WCA were women marked by their incomes, which enabled them not to work, and by their families' involvement in the expanding commerce of Memphis. See below and Glenda Elizabeth Gilmore, *Gender and Jim Crow: Women and the Politics of White Supremacy in North Carolina, 1896– 1920* (Chapel Hill: University of North Carolina Press, 1996), 256 fn15.

19. Wedell, *Elite Women and the Reform Impulse*, 149 fn22.

20. Jacquelyn Jones, *Labor of Love, Labor of Sorrow: Black Women, Work, and the Family from Slavery to Present* (New York: Basic Books, 1985), 112; David Katzman, *Seven Days a Week: Women and Domestic Service in Industrializing America* (Urbana: University of Illinois Press, 1981), 184–224. The "Woman's Edition" of the *Memphis Daily Appeal* confirms that this was true for Memphis women as well. *Commercial Appeal*, February 14, 1895.

21. *Memphis Commercial Appeal*, February 14, 1894.

22. *Memphis Women's Christian Association Yearbook, 1892–1893*, 7; *Memphis Daily Appeal*, March 6, 1881, p. 4.

23. *Memphis Daily Avalanche*, April 14, 1889, p. 10.

24. *Memphis Daily Appeal*, June 1, 1884.

25. *The Gleaner* 2, no. 5 (March 1892).

26. *Tennessean*, February 6, 1898; *Memphis Daily Avalanche*, June 3, 1883, p. 3, and June 17, 1884.

27. *Memphis Daily Appeal*, June 17, 1884; *Memphis Daily Avalanche*, March 6, 1881, p. 6.

28. *Memphis Daily Avalanche*, July 17, 1881.

29. *Memphis Daily Appeal*, June 17, 1884.

30. From 1881 to 1888 there were regularly twice as many children as adults in the Mission. In 1883 children's board brought in $500 and laundry and sewing combined, $317.35. *Memphis Daily Appeal*, March 26, 1881, p. 6; June 19, 1883, p. 3; and June 17, 1884.

31. This public relations approach was effective. In March the *Appeal* published a front-page editorial praising the mission's work. *Memphis Daily Appeal*, March 26, 1881, and June 15, 1881.

32. *WCA Annual Report*, 1893; *Memphis Daily Appeal*, July 19, 1881, and March 26, 1881, p. 2; *Memphis Daily Appeal*, January 26, 1878.

33. Robert E. Corlew, *Tennessee: A Short History*, 2d ed. (Knoxville: University of Tennessee Press, 1990), 361–64.

34. Ida Wells-Barnett, *Crusade for Justice* (Chicago: University of Chicago Press, 1976), 18, and *Selected Works* (New York: Oxford University Press, 1991), 61, 62, 201. Historian Jacquelyn Dowd Hall agreed with the Wells-Barnett analysis of the role of lynching in the South,

and Gilmore traces the white urban elite's increased reliance on racial antagonism to retain political power. See Hall, *Revolt against Chivalry: Jessie Daniel Ames and the Women's Campaign against Lynching* (New York: Columbia University Press, 1979), 129–57; and Gilmore, *Gender and Jim Crow*, 71–74.

35. *The Gleaner* 2, no. 5 (March 1892).

36. *Memphis Commercial Appeal*, October 2, 1898.

37. *Memphis Daily Appeal*, April 24, 1881.

38. *Memphis Daily Appeal*, April 19, 1881, p. 2; July 28, 1881; and June 7, 1904.

39. Wells-Barnett, *Selected Works*, 32–33; *Memphis Daily Avalanche*, June 27, 1878; *Memphis Daily Appeal*, January 15, 1881, January 19, 1881, and June 6, 1882, 2.

40. Meriwether, *Soundings*, 103; *Memphis Daily Appeal*, April 14, 1889, p. 10.

41. Meriwether, *Soundings*, 13, 14, 27.

42. *Memphis Daily Avalanche*, April 14, 1889, p. 10.

43. Meriwether, *Soundings*, frontispiece; *Memphis Daily Appeal*, January 22, 1882.

44. *Memphis Daily Appeal*, June 19, 1883, p. 3.

45. *Memphis Daily Appeal*, January 26, 1878. When the home moved locations, it also changed names. Thus in the subsequent text, the home is referred to as both "the mission" and "the refuge."

46. *Memphis Daily Appeal*, June 15, 1882.

47. *Memphis Daily Appeal*, June 15, 1882.

48. *Memphis Daily Appeal*, June 17, 1884; *The Gleaner* 2, no. 8 (June 1892):123.

49. *Memphis Women's Christian Association Yearbook, 1892–1893*, 31.

50. That Lillie put herself beyond the bounds of white society is made clear by the fact that she was named. No other residents ever were. Wells-Barnett, *Selected Works*, 203–5.

51. *Memphis Daily Appeal*, June 15, 1881.

52. As reported in *Memphis Daily Appeal*, January 22, 1882; *The Gleaner* 2, no. 8 (June 1892).

53. *Memphis Daily Appeal*, March 17, 1880, June 19, 1883, and June 15, 1881. (The emphasis is mine.) The refuge claimed only once to have placed women in domestic positions.

54. *Memphis Daily Appeal*, June 29, 1881.

55. *Woman's Edition, Memphis Daily Appeal*, February 14, 1895.

56. *Memphis Women's Christian Association Yearbook, 1892–1893*, 11; *Annual Report*, 1902–3, 14; interview with Denny Glad of Tennessee's Right to Know, June 3, 1994.

57. "Mother's Day" flyer from the Ella Oliver Home clippings file in the Memphis Public Library; *Memphis Press Scimitar*, December 24, 1936, and June 17, 1937.

Anxious Care and Constant Struggle

The Female Humane Association and Richmond's White Civil War Orphans

E. SUSAN BARBER

Theda Skocpol, Megan McClintock, Amy Holmes, and, in this volume, Susan Hamburger have each contributed to our understanding of the postwar experiences of northern and southern widows and other adult female dependents of Union and Confederate soldiers. Relatively little scholarship has emerged, however, that documents the experiences of dependent children orphaned by the war. This essay examines the effects of the American Civil War on the care of orphans in Richmond, Virginia—in particular, white female orphans under the protection of the Female Humane Association of the City of Richmond. The Civil War generated an acute but short-lived crisis for Richmond institutions involved in the care of destitute children by rendering earlier fundraising strategies ineffective at the same time that wartime casualties greatly increased the number of orphans in need of assistance.

Richmond women's benevolence did not begin in 1861. From the beginning of the nineteenth century, white women in the Virginia capital created a variety of reform-minded associations whose agendas mirrored those of organizations established by northern women during the same period of time. During the 1810s and 1820s, Richmond women were active in female chapters of the American Anti-Slavery Society and, between 1820 and 1850, they organized women's auxiliaries to several temperance associations, including the Martha Washingtonians and the Sisters of Temperance.[1] In 1836 they founded the Union Benevolent Association, a group aimed at assisting impoverished white women by selling the women's handiwork.[2] During the Civil War, the Union Benevolent Association expanded its role by serving as home visitors for the Richmond Soup Association, a quasi-municipal agency that provided soup for a nominal fee to thousands of indigent white and black Richmonders.[3]

Formed in 1805, the Female Humane Association of the City of Richmond was one of the city's oldest charitable groups. An ecumenical organization composed of women from the city's Episcopal, Methodist, Baptist, and Presbyterian congregations, the association operated a nonsectarian Christian asylum for "the relief and comfort of distressed females," as well as a day school for poor white girls, on the corner of Charity and St. John Streets near the northwest city boundary.[4] The association's founding occurred within the context of the creation of numerous orphanages by women's benevolent groups throughout the United States during the early decades of the nineteenth century, a trend initiated, in part, by a desire to remove poor children—especially girls—from the harmful effects of the almshouse.[5] Four years before the Richmond asylum came into existence, female reformers in Boston, Massachusetts, and Savannah, Georgia, had organized two similar groups, and, by 1815, the Richmond, Boston, and Savannah orphanages were joined by comparable institutions in New York City, Cincinnati, Ohio, Washington, D.C., and Petersburg, Virginia.[6] Although most of these organizations focused primarily on relieving the suffering of destitute white children, in 1836, two Quaker women—Mary Murray and Anna Shotwell—formed the New York Colored Orphan Asylum for boys and girls in New York City.[7]

During much of the nineteenth century, the asylum operated by the Female Humane Association of Richmond took in full- and half-orphans; provided them with a rudimentary education in "reading, arithmetic, needle work, knitting, spinning, and every kind of domestic business," and then bound a number of them out for domestic service in the homes of affluent white families in Richmond and the surrounding counties.[8] Throughout much of the nineteenth century, "placing out," as it was called, increasingly became the preferred strategy for dealing with demands of caring for homeless children.[9] Although the asylum staff and the number of residents it served was originally quite small, during the antebellum period it grew to include a matron, one or more assistant matrons, several teachers, a visiting doctor, and a variety of domestic workers who cooked and cleaned for the asylum's residents, usually fifteen to twenty girls between the ages of two and seventeen.[10]

The benevolent association that operated the asylum was composed of white women from the more affluent sections of Richmond. Among the association's founders were Jean Moncure Daniel, a sister-in-law of Supreme Court Chief Justice John Marshall, and Eliza J. Carrington, the wife of a Revolutionary War hero.[11] Other organizers were Mary Nicholas, the wife of a Virginia attorney general, and Elizabeth Wirt, the wife of a prominent Virginia attorney. A list of members for 1860 included the names of women who were wives and daughters of a number of prominent Richmonders—clergymen, lawyers, politicians, and business owners.[12] Mrs. Joseph R. Anderson, the wife of the Tredegar chief; Mrs. Bolling Haxall, the wife of a Haxall Flour Mill scion, and Nancy Bierne Macfarland, whose husband later served as president of the Richmond Common Council, were all association members. Women of good standing in the community were nominated to join the association, pending approval by the majority. On the eve of the Civil War, the association's membership totaled fifty-four.[13]

With the exception of the three male trustees who executed adoptions and apprenticeship indentures and annually reviewed the association's finances, the day-to-day operation of the asylum was supervised by the female members and officers, which included a president, a secretary, two stewards whose duty was to pay out the association's funds, six solicitors to engage in the door-to-door fund-raising, and six visitors. In 1811 the asylum was incorporated by an act of the Virginia legislature, a move that permitted the mostly married female members to operate the asylum independent of the laws of coverture that restricted married women's roles throughout much of the nineteenth century. Incorporation enabled the women, without male support, to buy and sell property, receive and administer bequests, and serve as the girls' legal guardians.[14] In 1829, when the association replaced door-to-door solicitation with benefit fairs, the solicitors were eliminated and a seven-member board of directors assumed the task of seeing that the property was properly maintained and of making periodic visits to the asylum to monitor the girls' treatment.[15]

During the antebellum period, the work of the association was financed largely through the collection of membership dues of four dollars per year, an annual fair or door-to-door fund-raising campaign, and a few modest bequests, which the women occasionally invested in bank stocks and other securities. In 1843 an endowment from the estate of Edmund Walls—a flour inspector for the port—enabled the association to erect a larger facility near the city's northern perimeter.[16] From time to time, older girls contributed to their room and board by sewing aprons, drawers, chemises, petticoats, dresses, flannel shirts, and cloaks worn by themselves and the younger inmates.[17]

As its symbol the association chose a standing female figure surrounded by children. The figure held a naked infant in her left arm, while her right hand clutched the hand of a little girl; another child to the left clung to her skirt.[18] This image underscored the ties between women's personal and social mothering and emphasized the maternal role the association expected to play to the young girls who became their wards. It also demonstrates that southern women utilized the concept of women's moral and social maternalism, which served to defend northern women's antebellum benevolence.[19] An 1827 history of the association reflected this apotheosis of the "[a]ssociation as mother" in its account of an early resident of the asylum who eventually became its matron, a position she held until her death at the age of seventy-three.[20] No male figure is present in the image, suggesting not only the dependent and orphaned or semiorphaned status of the children clinging to the female form but also suggesting the association's intention to assume the primary role in decisions concerning the children's welfare. In accepting children into the asylum, the association preferred full orphans, including female children who had been abandoned at birth and living in the almshouse, to children with a surviving parent who sought temporary placement because of illness or desertion but who might interfere with the association's plans by reclaiming the child at some future date.

The women of the association were no doubt motivated by a genuine altruistic concern for relieving the misery they saw reflected in the lives of their female wards. But their actions were also informed by contemporary middle-class attitudes about the working poor, as well as white southerners' attitudes regarding race. The constitution and bylaws of the association and the annual reports were replete with statements about the women's determination to rescue these girls from "the haunts of vice and . . . viciousness," where they would become "a tax upon the citizens," and to send them forth into the world, "strong in virtuous principles, and rich in useful knowledge."[21] This "useful knowledge" consisted primarily of the skills necessary to render them efficient seamstresses or domestic servants in the homes of upper- and middle-class women like those of the association members.

By establishing an orphanage for female orphans that was administered by a board of female "directresses," the members of the association were also staking their own claim to a portion of the public sphere and a voice in Richmond society that was often denied to elite and middle-class women by the gender prescriptions of the nineteenth century.[22] Mothering the city's motherless children provided Richmond women with a rationale to justify leaving their homes to enter the public arena in order to engage in social reform politics.

By the mid-1840s, the Female Humane Association had been joined in its mission to minister to the city's impoverished children by two additional groups. In 1834 the Sisters of Charity of St. Vincent de Paul founded the St. Joseph's Female Academy and Orphan Asylum on the corner of Fourth Street and Marshall for white German and Irish Catholic girls whose parents either had died or were too impoverished to care for them.[23] The Richmond Male Orphan Society was opened in 1846 "to provide a home for [white] orphan boys, and boys with . . . parents who are morally or physically unable to provide for their children." According to popular legend, this latter organization came to life at the insistence of a Female Humane Asylum "directress" who urged her husband and other male philanthropists to establish a home for orphaned boys shortly after encountering a homeless male urchin at the asylum's door, begging for food on the day after Thanksgiving.[24] Like orphans at the female asylum, boys at the Male Orphan Asylum were also trained to become productive, albeit menial, laborers in the Richmond economy. In the decades before the war, this training consisted of placing teenaged boys in the surrounding countryside as farmhands or manual laborers.[25]

None of these groups accepted orphans of color. Despite the fact that southern white women's benevolence was frequently made possible by a bevy of African American domestic workers and household slaves, no female orphans of color were ever admitted to the Richmond Female Asylum or the St. Joseph's Female Academy.[26] (As late as 1960, the Richmond Male Orphan Society still adhered to a policy of accepting only white boys between the ages of six and sixteen as residents.)[27] In 1867 the Richmond Society of Friends, in cooperation with black Richmond church leaders, succeeded in petitioning the Richmond Common Council for permission to build a black orphanage. Until its opening in 1869, however, black Richmond orphans either remained in the city almshouse, were cared for by a network of real or surrogate kin, or came under the protection of one of the hundreds of secret black philanthropic groups that blossomed in the postwar capital.[28]

The Female Humane Association experienced temporary financial reverses in the depression following the War of 1812 and had once considered closing the asylum in the late 1820s; but nothing in its history prepared it for the challenge to its resources posed by the American Civil War.[29] The death of more than six hundred thousand soldiers left thousands of children without fatherly support. No reliable figure for the number of Civil War orphans exists, but given the fact that at least 30 percent of the men who lost their lives in the Civil War were married, and that approximately one-third to one-half of these men were fathers to two or three dependent children, a conservative estimate would place the number of northern and southern children who emerged from the Civil War as either full or half-orphans between 123,000 and 275,000.[30] In the postwar South, this figure translated to between 51,000 and 116,000 children between infancy and eighteen years of age. By the end of the war, officials in Boston, Massachusetts, placed the number of homeless children at approximately six thousand. In New York City, the estimate rose to more than thirty thousand.[31] By 1866 Governor Patton of Alabama estimated the number of Civil War orphans in that state, alone, at sixty thousand.[32] A sizable number of these children no doubt remained in the care of their mothers or else were absorbed into a broader network of family relations that included grandparents, aunts and uncles, cousins, or adult siblings. Others, however, swelled the poorhouses, or the rolls of existing orphanages where their presence placed an increased demand on the institutions' limited postwar funds.

In Richmond the situation was complicated by the fact that the city's population grew from approximately 39,000 in 1860 to more than 120,000 in 1863, as thousands of refugees swarmed into the city to avoid Union invaders or to seek work. Midway through the war, the Richmond papers were filled with accounts of half-starved children clustered outside the walls of Libby Prison, vying for scraps thrown through the barred windows by Union prisoners.[33] Letters to the editor of the *Richmond Examiner* related tales of homeless women and children sleeping on city streets or feeding themselves from the offal of Chimborazo Hospital, a medical facility for sick and wounded Confederate soldiers located on the eastern edge of the city.[34] Others complained about gangs of unruly boys who engaged in rock-throwing battles that occasionally injured innocent passersby.³⁵ In April 1862 fourteen-year-old orphan Eliza Dickinson was brought before the city court on the charge of engaging in prostitution to provide food and shelter for herself and her two younger brothers. Dickinson's widowed mother had died shortly after the family arrived in the city.³⁶

Unfortunately no wartime minutes for the Female Humane Association or the Richmond Male Orphan Association have survived, and records for the St. Joseph's Female Academy and Orphan Asylum are virtually nonexistent, so it is impossible to know precisely how many children were cared for by these institutions during the war and the immediate postwar period. But scattered evidence from annual reports presented to the Richmond Common Council, which were sometimes published in the Richmond papers, indicates that the number of inmates at both of the female orphanages increased dramatically. In 1863 and 1864, for example, the Female Humane Association reported a population of more than sixty girls, a number triple the fifteen or twenty residents it averaged in the 1820s or 1830s.³⁷ Many of these new girls were the daughters of Confederate soldiers killed in battle, or girls whose mothers, according to the association, had died after being "worn out by the care and toil of providing for the wants of a family left upon her hands by this relentless war."³⁸ In October 1867 Sister Mary Rose reported a parallel population increase at St. Joseph's Female Asylum in an appeal for funds to the Richmond Common Council. "We have at present in the Asylum sixty-three orphans," she wrote, "totally dependent [and] without any income . . . which we count upon your charity to furnish."³⁹ Four years later the orphans at the St. Joseph's asylum numbered sixty-five.⁴⁰

The number of inmates in the Richmond Male Orphan Asylum increased as well, from thirty boys in 1857 to fifty in 1861. All boys of military age eventually enlisted in the Confederate Army or Navy. Several served together aboard the Confederate steamer *Patrick Henry*, and at least three may have fallen in battle: one at Manassas, another at Charlottesville, and a third during the Petersburg siege.⁴¹

A five-thousand-dollar legacy the Female Humane Association received in 1861 from the estate of a wealthy benefactor no doubt eased its financial burdens for a time; but during the war other sources of income evaporated, while the number of orphans in the asylum grew. The Richmond school fund was forced to withdraw its annual stipend in 1862, and contributions from such other organizations as the Richmond Literary Fund and the Richmond Musical and Dramatic Association simply disappeared from the association's financial records. By the spring of 1862, the matrons were instructed to restrict the girls' food to "the plain necessaries of life," which required the exclusion of tea, coffee, and molasses.[42] In January 1863 the asylum sold some of the older girls' needlework for $190.[43] And although the Richmond Common Council had routinely allocated one thousand dollars per year to each of these institutions during much of the antebellum period, by the end of 1864, the city's precarious financial situation made further donations impossible.

The Female Humane Association attempted to recoup its financial losses and meet the needs of its expanding population through appeals to the local churches and by reinvigorating its door-to-door campaigning. This fund-raising strategy may have been necessitated in part by a shortage of available spaces for holding benefit fairs because many municipal buildings had been requisitioned by the Confederate government for use as office buildings or military hospitals. In 1863 six of the local churches contributed more than forty-five hundred dollars to the asylum's operating budget, and door-to-door campaigns in the city's three wards in 1864 and 1865 netted $7,308, an astounding figure given the straitened economy of the Confederate capital in the closing years of the war.[44] As impressive as these amounts may seem, they did little to offset the rising inflation rates for market commodities, which, by mid-1863, had soared to 900 percent.[45] For a short time in 1865, a year the association's secretary later characterized as one of "anxious care and constant struggle," the girls were forced to subsist on a diet of bread and water, until a Confederate battalion stationed in the city sent a day's rations of bacon, flour, rice, and meal.[46] When Richmond fell on April 3, 1865, even this source of aid vanished.

Richmond's surrender virtually bankrupted the Female Humane Association, while the resulting fire that leveled the city's financial district reduced its securities to piles of ash. Confederate defeat also rendered worthless thirty-nine hundred dollars in Confederate bonds and the remainder of the forty-two hundred dollars in Confederate currency collected during the association's March 1865 door-to-door campaign.[47] With no place else to go for help, the asylum registered with the federal authorities occupying the city, which permitted the girls to draw rations of meat and meal on a regular basis. At the same time, the association reduced the number of residents from sixty to thirty-one, in part by returning some girls to their relatives but more often by binding out more girls into domestic service, usually to fill vacancies created in white households by the departure of former slaves.[48]

Not all these binding-out arrangements were mutually satisfactory, in part because the girls sent out were often younger and were either poorly trained or homesick or both. "A white girl from the Orphan Asylum has come out on trial," Emma Mordecai wrote of the young girl named Annie who arrived on the morning of May 7, 1865, shortly after the Mordecais' servants announced their intention to leave. "[She] is unhappy & lonesome, and doesn't intend to stay. She does not seem to be very competent." Within a week, Annie was back at the asylum while the Mordecais were left to rely on the labor of an untrained former field hand and her two young sons.[49]

In its effort to preserve the girls' privacy, the minutes of the Female Humane Association's meetings are frustratingly circumspect about specific problems concerning outplacement, but other such arrangements must have proved more mutually beneficial. Throughout the late 1860s and the 1870s, the association continued to cope with the added drain on its resources by placing ever-younger girls in Virginia households. Although most girls in the antebellum period had remained at the asylum until they were fourteen or fifteen years of age, by the mid-1880s, girls of nine and ten were routinely sent out to work.[50]

The decision to put younger girls into domestic service met with disapproval, not only from some association members who, in 1877, attempted unsuccessfully to fix the minimum age for placement at fifteen, but also from surviving relatives who complained that the girls were being released "before their moral and mental training is completed." In 1874 the association moved to curtail family interference by adopting a resolution requiring absolute *in loco parentis* control over any child it accepted.[51] Despite this new policy regarding placement, the association still attempted to exercise a measure of compassion and good judgment by reclaiming girls from homes where abuse was suspected and by denying adoptions of girls in ill health or by relatives the association deemed "unsuitable."[52]

Rather than placing out younger boys, the Richmond Male Orphan Asylum coped with its dwindling postwar reserves by putting the boys to work manufacturing tobacco products. In 1870 the association purchased Camp

Grant, a former Confederate hospital on Richmond's southwest side that had more recently served as a barracks for Union troops during federal occupation. Two of the four buildings were made into dormitories while the remainder were converted to sheds for stemming and processing tobacco. In 1875 other boys were sent to work at a matchbox factory in nearby Rocketts, folding and gluing boxes for fifteen cents an hour. When that factory closed in 1877, boys of fourteen years of age or older were employed in rolling cheroots. During the first year, they manufactured more than 360,000 cigars for a profit of $600.[53] This option was not available to the Richmond Female Association, however, since white women and girls were not involved in the large-scale manufacture of tobacco products until the early to mid-1880s.

A second way in which the Female Humane Association coped with its wartime reverses was by altering its financial strategy. Financial evidence for the period from 1866 to 1871 is extremely sketchy, but it suggests that the asylum led a rather hand-to-mouth existence, depending to a large extent on door-to-door contributions and handouts from several charitable groups and private donors to piece out its daily needs. Some of these donations came from sympathetic northerners, such as the women of the New York Ladies' Southern Relief Association, a short-lived organization of New York women with roots to the former Confederacy that supported Confederate orphanages throughout the South.[54] During this period, between 83 and 93 percent of the Female Humane Association's yearly budget was derived from such sources as these, while interest and dividends on stocks and bonds supplied less than a tenth of that budget.

Between 1872 and 1880, the association shifted its fund-raising strategies once more. During this time, the women conducted only one door-to-door campaign and began systematically to invest in the major railroad lines serving the metropolis, a move made possible by a generous bequest from the estate of William A. Barrett, a wealthy Richmonder who burned to death in a fire in his Cary Street home.[55] In 1872 the women purchased stock in the Richmond & Petersburg line, and in 1874 they acquired shares in both the Orange & Alexandria and the Danville. By 1876 they also owned stock in the Clover Hill and the Virginia & Tennessee lines. Money for these purchases came from bequests by two Female Humane Association members. The association also leased property on Pearl Street to several Richmond merchants.[56]

The association had maintained a small portfolio of state and municipal bonds from the early 1810s, but, for much of the antebellum period, it had relied on membership dues and community largesse to fund most of its yearly expenditures and had usually incorporated any interest it realized from these investments into the asylum's operating budget.[57] The investment decisions of the 1870s, however, indicate a shift away from door-to-door solicitations and a more concerted effort to rely on financial investments in stocks and bonds as a more dependable source of income, a strategy the association had only flirted with briefly during its antebellum years. Between 1872 and 1880, the amount of yearly income from dividends on stocks and bonds rose from 21.4 to 82.7 percent while income from charitable contributions fell from 76.1 percent to as low as 8 percent (Table 1).

This shift from charitable contributions to investments as the primary source of revenue reflects a newer and more sophisticated financial strategy that was forged by the "anxious care and constant struggle" of the women's wartime experience. No longer content to beg door-to-door for whatever the hand of charity would provide, throughout the 1880s and early 1890s the association continued to reinvest its dividends and expand its investments through the purchase of municipal bonds and stocks.[58] By 1895 it possessed an investment portfolio valued at more than $150,000. The Female Humane Association's new investment strategy parallels that of the male philanthropists at the head of the Male Orphan Asylum who, for decades before the war began, had systematically speculated in Richmond real estate, a practice they resumed in the postwar decades.[59]

Anne Firor Scott has observed that, for some groups formed in the antebellum period, the war's special demands diverted the women's attention away from their work for the poor. For instance, leaders of the Boston Fragment Society, which had been formed in 1812 to minister to needs of widows and orphans, worried that the war's overwhelming carnage would harden both members and supporters to the daily destitution of women in their community and would also drain the group's energies and resources. And for a time it did, causing the Boston Fragment Society to examine its custom of holding an annual social event for its subscribers, on the basis that the funds could be more suitably spent on the poor.[60] But although the Female Humane Association was initially devastated by wartime changes, the Civil War ultimately served to focus and concentrate its energies, in part

Table 1. Female Humane Association Yearly Income, 1860–1880, by Percent

Year	Dues	Donations	Stocks & Bonds	Bequests
1860	4.8	45.7	49.5	—
1861	2.3	78.2	19.5	—
1862	1.7	63.6	34.2	—
1863	1.7	64.6	12.0	21.6
1864	1.2	83.0	15.3	0.4
1865	2.4	72.3	25.2	—
1866	1.6	88.6	3.5	0.5
1867	3.5	86.6	3.5	0.5
1868	6.0	83.0	10.4	0.6
1869	3.0	86.5	10.4	—
1870	2.6	93.4	4.0	—
1871	3.6	85.4	10.9	—
1872	2.6	76.1	21.4	—
1873	1.4	32.3	25.7	40.6
1874	1.8	17.9	80.3	—
1875	1.5	23.2	75.2	—
1876	0.6	1.1	58.2	40.0
1877	3.7	19.0	73.9	3.4
1878	1.3	8.0	73.9	16.7
1879	1.7	9.0	74.8	14.5
1880	1.1	15.6	82.7	0.7

Source: Account Books, December 1858–December 1867, December 1866–December 1899; Minute Book, December 1875–October 1894, Memorial Foundation for Children Records, 1827–1935, Library of Virginia.

because its work was now infused with a patriotism born of caring for the orphans of Confederate soldiers. It also forced the Female Humane Association to take a hard look at its fund-raising strategies. It emerged from Reconstruction not only on sounder financial footing but also with a more sophisticated understanding of fund-raising strategy forged by the exigencies of civil war.

Although the Civil War posed an acute crisis for the city's white orphanages, its effects were essentially short-lived. By the late 1880s, all the children orphaned by the Civil War had either reached the age of majority or had died, so their drain on the institutions' resources had passed. The Female Humane Asylum, the Richmond Male Orphan Society, and the St. Joseph's Female Academy all continued their mission to indigent white orphans well into the twentieth century. In 1931 the St. Joseph's Orphan Asylum celebrated the dedication of a new Catholic orphanage—St. Joseph's Villa—comprised of fourteen buildings and a church.[61] And in the mid-1960s, the Richmond Home for Boys and the Memorial Foundation for Children—as the Richmond Male Orphan Society and the Female Humane Asylum were later called—continued to care for white boys and girls from the Richmond community.

Over the course of decades, however, declining enrollments and changing attitudes toward the treatment of indigent children led to shifts in both the mission and the strategies of the Female Humane Association. The nationwide movement away from institutionalizing indigent children in orphanages and toward placing them in foster homes in the late nineteenth century ushered in a more relaxed approach to the girls' treatment.[62] Rather than keeping them cloistered within the asylum's walls, the girls were now permitted to go on picnics, to take walks outside the asylum, or to participate in other forms of recreation. When the asylum moved to the country in 1916, the gingham dresses and somber capes that had long been the girls' identifiable uniform were replaced with pleated skirts, middy blouses, and brightly colored ties of the girls' own choosing. The resident teacher was dismissed, and the girls began to attend the public schools. In the 1930s declining enrollments forced a second shift as the institution—now called the Memorial Home for Girls—moved away from caring for the impoverished female orphans who had been the focus of its benevolence for more than 130 years, and concentrated its energies, instead, on emotionally disturbed girls who were accepted into the institution based on referrals from the Children's Memorial Clinic, a municipal agency associated with the Medical College of Virginia.[63]

Orphaned children were the Civil War's youngest casualties. As their fathers fell in battle at Cold Harbor, Gettysburg, and the Wilderness, Confederate orphans in Richmond, Virginia, strained the capacity of the city's existing institutions. Caring for Confederate orphans was not just an economic necessity. It was also a patriotic duty owed to those who had given their lives in the struggle for southern independence. The women of the city's Female

Humane Association responded to the challenge of caring for the war's most innocent victims with a mixture of foresight and practicality. Placing younger girls into domestic service was a practical decision that helped to relieve the immediate burdens caused by overcrowding. The decision to alter completely its fund-raising techniques positioned the association not only to meet the immediate postwar challenges but also enabled it to enter the twentieth century with a secure financial base, thus ensuring its mission to the city's motherless and fatherless children until the Civil War had all but faded into distant memory.

NOTES

1. Marie Tyler-McGraw, *At the Falls: Richmond, Virginia, and Its People* (Chapel Hill: University of North Carolina Press, 1994), 116–18; Elizabeth Regine Varon, "'We Mean to Be Counted': White Women and Politics in Antebellum Virginia" (Ph.D. diss., Yale University, 1993), especially part 1; and Patricia C. Click, *The Spirit of the Times: Amusements in Nineteenth-Century Baltimore, Norfolk, and Richmond* (Charlottesville: University Press of Virginia, 1989), 78–81. Some historians have suggested that southern women's organizational politics lagged behind that of northern women and that their reform activism was frequently limited both by religious and communal expectations, as well as an overwhelming desire to avoid involvement with any cause related to abolitionism. (Elizabeth Fox-Genovese, *Within the Plantation Household: Black and White Women of the Old South* [Chapel Hill: University of North Carolina Press, 1988], and Jean E. Friedman, *The Enclosed Garden: Women and Community in the Evangelical South, 1830–1900* [Chapel Hill: University of North Carolina Press, 1985]). The evidence for Richmond supports neither conclusion, however. Instead, Richmond women's organizational activity was a vibrant part of the antebellum community.

2. Varon, "'We Mean to Be Counted,'" 31–33.

3. *Richmond Dispatch*, November 26, 1864; Soup House Association Papers, Eleanor S. Brockenbrough Library, Museum of the Confederacy, Richmond, Virginia; Richmond City Papers, Minutes of the Common Council, various bundle dates, Library of Virginia, Richmond, Virginia (cited hereafter as MCC).

4. *Female Humane Association* ([Richmond]: John Warrock, 1827), 6, Memorial Foundation for Children Records, 1827–1935, Library of Virginia, Richmond, Virginia (cited hereafter as MFC Records). Throughout this article, I am using "association" to refer to the benevolent organization known as the Female Humane Asylum of the City of Richmond. I use "asylum" to refer to the orphanage this group established.

5. Henry W. Thurston, *The Dependent Child: A Story of Changing Aims and Methods in the Care of Dependent Children* (New York: Columbia University Press for the New York School of Social Work, 1930), 15–59; Marilyn Irvin Holt, *The Orphan Trains: Placing Out in America* (Lincoln: University of Nebraska Press, 1992), 41–79.

6. Thurston, *Dependent Child*, 40–59; Suzanne Lebsock, *The Free Women of Petersburg: Status and Culture in a Southern Town, 1784–1860* (New York: Norton, 1984), 202–12; Clark, *Institutional Homes for Children*, 57.

7. Thurston, *Dependent Child*, 60.

8. *Constitution and By-Laws of the Female Humane Association of the City of Richmond, Adopted April 1, 1833* (Richmond: John Warrock, 1833), 14. Throughout much of this period, however, African American women made up 90 percent of Richmond's domestic labor force. White female orphans provided a portion of the remaining 10 percent. Angela Catherine Bongiorno, "White Women and Work in Richmond, Virginia, 1870–1884" (M.A. thesis, University of Virginia, 1978), 19–21; and Tracey M. Weis, "Negotiating Freedom: Domestic Service and Household Relations in Richmond, Virginia, 1850–1880" (Ph.D. diss., Rutgers University, 1994), 26–29.

9. Holt, *Orphan Trains*, 42–77.

10. MFC Records, various dates.

11. Varon, "'We Mean to Be Counted,'" 12.

12. Virginia [Mrs. Edwin] Cox, "The Memorial Foundation for Children," 1–2; *Constitution and By-Laws* (1833); Account Book, December 1858–December 1867, all in MFC Records.

13. List of Subscribers for 1860, MFC Records.

14. Lori D. Ginzberg, *Women and the Work of Benevolence: Morality, Politics, and Class in the Nineteenth-Century United States* (New Haven: Yale University Press, 1990), 48–53; Anne Firor Scott, *Natural Allies: Women's Associations in American History* (Urbana: University of Chicago Press, 1991), 26; and Lebsock, *Free Women of Petersburg*, 199–201.

15. *Female Humane Association* (1827), 2; *Constitution and By-Laws* (1833), 8.

16. Cox, "Memorial Foundation for Children," 6–7; W. Asbury Christian, *Richmond: Her Past and Present* (Richmond: L. H. Jenkins, 1912), 146–47; Virginius H. Dabney, *Richmond: The Story of a City* (rev. ed., Charlottesville: University Press of Virginia, 1990), 137.

17. Annual Reports, December 1, 1877; December 6, 1880, MFC Records.

18. *Constitution and By-Laws* (1833), 11.

19. Ginzberg, *Women and the Work of Benevolence*, 1–35. The importance of the mother-child bond in nineteenth-century families is discussed in Barbara Welter, "The Cult of True Womanhood, 1820–1860," *American Quarterly* 18 (Summer 1966): 151–74. Discussions of motherhood in the South can be found in Julia Cherry Spruill, *Women's Life and Work in the Southern Colonies* (1938; reprint, New York: Norton, 1972), 43–63; Sally G. McMillen, *Motherhood in the Old South: Pregnancy, Childbirth, and Infant Rearing* (Baton Rouge: Louisiana State University Press, 1990), 180–85; and Suzanne Lebsock, *Virginia Women, 1600–1945: "A Share of Honour"* (rev. ed., Richmond: Virginia State Library, 1987), 65–68.

20. *Female Humane Association* (1827), 8; Cox, "Memorial Foundation for Children," 8. Although neither of these accounts names this particular matron, she may have been Mary A. Lipscomb, who died on February 26, 1882, and was eulogized in the association minutes. Minutes, March 6, 1882, Minute Book, December 1875–October 1894, MFC Records.

21. Annual Report, Female Humane Association, Year Ending December 1, 1865, bundle dated January 29, 1866, MCC; *Constitution and By-Laws* (1833).

22. Welter, "Cult of True Womanhood," and Barbara J. Berg, *The Remembered Gate: Origins of American Feminism: The Woman and the City, 1800–1860* (New York: Oxford University Press, 1978).

23. Polly Daffron, "Beautiful St. Joseph's Villa, Elaborate and Modern Catholic Orphanage, to Be Formally Dedicated Here Next Sunday with Brilliant Ceremonies," *Richmond Times-Dispatch*, November 1, 1931, section 3, p. 1; James Bailey II, *History of St. Peter's Church, Richmond, Virginia: 123 Years, 1834–1959* (Richmond: Lewis Printing Co., 1959), 20–30.

24. Constitution and By-Laws of the Richmond Male Orphan Society, Virginia Historical Society, Richmond, Virginia. This account of the home's founding is found in George W. Rogers, "Richmond Home for Boys—110 Years of Service to the Community," *Richmond News-Leader*, July 17, 1956. Another apocryphal account claims the boy was begging for pennies. "Boys Repay 119-Year-Old Debt," unidentified newspaper clipping in Richmond Home for Boys File, Valentine Museum, Richmond, Virginia. Similar stories about children begging for food or money surround the founding of the Richmond Female Asylum.

25. W. Leigh Carneal, "Home Where Homeless Boys Are Happy," unidentified newspaper clipping in the Richmond Home for Boys File, Valentine Museum, Richmond, Virginia.

26. Varon, "'We Mean to Be Counted,'" 27–29.

27. "Yesterday, a Boy Was Homeless," pamphlet, [1960–61], Richmond Home for Boys File, Valentine Museum, Richmond, Virginia.

28. Howard N. Rabinowitz, *Race Relations in the Urban South, 1865–1890* (Urbana: University of Illinois Press, 1980), 135, 143–45; Peter Rachleff, *Black Labor in Richmond, 1865–1890* (Urbana: University of Illinois Press, 1989), 13–33.

29. *Female Humane Association* (1827), 8; *Constitution and By-Laws* (1833), 4.

30. I am basing this on a casualty rate of 618,222 men. Maris A. Vinovskis, "Have Social Historians Lost the Civil War? Some Preliminary Demographic Speculation," and Amy E. Holmes, "'Such Is the Price We Pay': American Widows and the Civil War Pension System," both in *Toward a Social History of the American Civil War: Exploratory Essays*, Maris A. Vinovskis, ed., 1–30 and 171–96. (New York: Cambridge University Press, 1990).

31. Holt, *Orphan Trains*, 74.

32. *Report of the Ladies' Southern Relief Association of Maryland, September 1st, 1866* (Baltimore: Kelly & Pet, 1866), 12, in Records of the New York Ladies' Southern Relief Association, 1866–67, Eleanor S. Brockenbrough Library, Museum of the Confederacy, Richmond, Virginia (cited hereafter as NYLSRA Records). Since Patton's figures appeared in the context of an appeal for funds for Confederate widows and orphans they may have been inflated.

33. F. F. Cavada, *Libby Life: Experiences of a Prisoner of War in Richmond, Va., 1863–65* (Lanham, Md.: University Press of America, 1985), 132.

34. Judith Brockenbrough McGuire, *Diary of a Southern Refugee during the War* (New York: E. J. Hale & Son, 1867; reprint, New York: Arno Press, 1972), 252–53.

35. *Richmond Whig*, May 14, 1863.

36. Dickinson's father had died some time earlier. *Richmond Enquirer*, April 29, 1862. Similar descriptions can be found for homeless children in the North. Holt, *Orphan Trains*, 74–77.

37. *Southern Churchman*, January 4, December 14, 1865.

38. Entry dated April 4, 1861, Account Book, December 1858–December 1867, MFC Records; Annual Report, Female Humane Association, in *Southern Churchman*, January 4, 1865.

39. Letter to the Richmond Common Council from Sister Mary Rose, Sister of Charity, October 5, 1867, MCC, bundle dated October 14, 1867.

40. Letter to the Richmond Common Council from Sister Mariana of St. Joseph's Female Orphan Asylum, February 6, 1871, MCC, bundle dated February 20, 1871.

41. "Boys Repay 119-Year-Old Debt."

42. Annual Report, Female Humane Association, Year Ending December 1, 1862, in *Southern Churchman*, May 22, 1863.

43. Entry dated January 27, 1863, Account Book, December 1858–December 1867, MFC Records.

44. Entries dated June 1 through December 11, 1863; January 1 through June 18, 1864; and March 20–29, 1865, all in Account Book, December 1858–December 1867, MFC Records.

45. Thomas Senior Berry, *Richmond Commodity Prices* (Richmond: Bostwick Press of the University of Richmond, 1985), 1.

46. *Southern Churchman*, January 4, 1865; Annual Report, Female Humane Association, Year Ending December 1, 1865, bundle dated January 29, 1866, MCC.

47. Entries for March 20–29, 1865, Account Book, December 1858–December 1867, MFC Records.

48. Annual Report, Female Humane Association, Year Ending December 1, 1865, bundle dated January 29, 1866, MCC. As the recession of 1873 deepened, these numbers rose. By 1872 the number of female orphans stood at forty-nine, and by 1873 it was fifty-five. *Richmond Dispatch*, December 5, 1872; Annual Report, Female Humane Association, Year Ending December 1, 1877, MFC Records.

49. Entries dated May 6, 7, 11, 13, and 16, 1865, Emma Mordecai Diary, Virginia Historical Society. Fifty-two-year-old Emma Mordecai was living with her widowed sister-in-law, Rosina Young Mordecai, on a farm on Brook Road in the city's north end.

50. *Constitution and By-Laws* (1833), 10; Minutes December 4, 1876 and June 4, 1877; Annual Report, Female Humane Association, Year Ending December 1, 1877; Annual Report, Female Humane Association, Year Ending November 20, 1886. Minutes, June 5, 1876; October 1, 1877; March 4, 1878; March 3, 1879; October 2, 1880; November 20, 1886. All these sources are in the MFC Records.

51. Amendments of the Constitution of the Female Humane Association, March 11, 1874, loose paper inside Minute Book, December 1876–October 1894, MFC Records.

52. *Southern Opinion*, December 14, 1867; Minutes, December 3, 1877; March 4, [1878]; December 12, 1878; March 3, [1879]; June 7, 1880; and October 21, 1895, MFC Records.

53. "Once a Barracks, Now a Real Home," *Richmond Times-Dispatch*, September 5, 1965, Richmond Home for Boys File, Valentine Museum, Richmond, Virginia.

54. NYLSRA Records.

55. Account Books for December 1859–December 1867 and December 1866–December 1899, MFC Records.

56. Account Book, December 1866–December 1899, MFC Records.

57. *Constitution and By-Laws* (1833), 3.

58. Minutes, March 5, 1883, December 5, 1887, and October 29, 1888; Cox, "Memorial Foundation for Children," 12–16, all in MFC Records.

59. Virginia Home for Boys in Richmond, Inc., miscellaneous microfilm reel #1340, Library of Virginia, Richmond, Virginia.

60. Scott, *Natural Allies,* 26–36.

61. Daffron, "Beautiful St. Joseph's Villa."

62. Eve P. Smith, "Bring Back the Orphanages? What Policymakers of Today Can Learn from the Past," in Eve P. Smith and Lisa A. Merkel-Holguin, eds. *A History of Child Welfare* (New Brunswick, N.J.: Transaction Publishers, 1996), 107–33.

63. Cox, "Memorial Foundation for Children," 10–15.

I Certainly Hope That You Will Be Able to Train Her

Reformers and the Georgia Training School for Girls

LEE S. POLANSKY

By the time Betty Foster turned seventeen in 1914, she was well known to authorities in Atlanta, Georgia.[1] Arrested numerous times for prostitution, Betty had been incarcerated in—and abruptly thrown out of—both the town jail and a missionary-run home for prostitutes. Betty's first failed escape was from the Atlanta Juvenile Hall. Her second escape entailed convincing Jack, a young orphan boy being held at the hall, to steal some boys' clothing for her.

Donning long pants, a plaid shirt, and a newsboy cap, Betty persuaded Jack, who had been left in charge while the hall officers went to lunch, to unlock the door for her. Betty and her friend Helen Taylor, another young prostitute, ran into the nearby woods, where they wandered, lost, for the next two days. Conceding defeat, they called the juvenile officer and begged him to rescue them. The girls' escapades, complete with Betty's picture, received prominent notice in the newspapers.[2]

For several years before Betty's adventure, Atlanta's papers had been reporting frequent stories about young girls behaving in rebellious ways. Sudden elopements were frequent front-page items, as when the papers reported how "Inez," aged fifteen, sneaked out to the "moving picture show" and returned—newly married to T. R., aged twenty-three. Her parents were stunned.[3] Atlanta reacted quickly to what seemed to be falling moral standards and a lack of control over teenagers of all classes. Movies would be censored for scandalous treatments. The chief of police banned "spooning" in the park; young couples seen kissing in public would be arrested. A Grand Jury convened to investigate "the girl problem," but could offer no solution.[4] Like other southern cities at the time, Georgia's cities were finding that they had no place for girls who broke the social and moral codes of behavior appropriate to the white southern "lady."

While Rhoda Kaufman was not much older than Betty and Helen, she had a very different adolescence. Her father, a German-Jewish immigrant, had owned a prosperous business in Columbus, Georgia, and Rhoda graduated from Vanderbilt University in 1909.[5] Kaufman planned a career in social work, which was fast becoming an acceptable and popular field for educated women. Realizing that the citizens of Columbus, with its small-town atmosphere, would view her ambitions with suspicion, Kaufman moved to Atlanta. She quickly joined the Southern Association of College Women (SACW), a "women's club" of like-minded, college-educated women interested in pursuing literary and philanthropic interests.

Kaufman found that her degree in biology hardly prepared her for what she would see while volunteering as a "friendly visitor" for the SACW and the Atlanta Associated Charities. As a visitor, Kaufman called on poor and working-class families throughout the city and in the surrounding mill villages, instructing them in proper nutrition, good health, and keeping a budget. On one routine visit, Kaufman was shocked to come upon a "notably fast and forward girl," who, at the young age of fourteen, already worked as an "incorrigible" prostitute. Kaufman spotted another girl, who, at thirteen years of age, seemed destined to follow in her mother's footsteps into a life of crime.[6] As Kaufman strolled through downtown Atlanta, window-shopping in all the fine stores, she no doubt saw the many young girls "hanging around" the streets, dressing in "short dresses" and flirting with men.[7]

Kaufman and other observers of Georgia's urban landscapes wondered what would happen to girls like Betty and Helen. While cities as diverse as Boston and Chicago had been experiencing this problem for years, Atlanta's newspapers had started warning a decade previously that the problem of prostituting and wayward girls might become as "serious and pitiable" as it had become in the North.[8] Nationally the "girl problem" conflated anxiety about changing gender roles and the role of working- and middle-class girls. In Georgia the so-called "girl problem" posed a serious threat to a New South vision of harmony and social order. Most important it threatened continued white supremacy. Within the context of the South's strictly defined racial and social hierarchy, wayward girls seemed to present an even more pressing problem than in the North. As future mothers of white children, and thus of a large portion of the white race, these girls might produce a degenerate, irresponsible, and possibly rebellious generation. Wayward girls, thought reformers, must be saved from lives of crime, immorality, and dissolution.

Worries about "race suicide" had become a national obsession. But they had particular resonance in a southern city with a black population that had rapidly risen to 40 percent and showed no signs of slowing.[9] The 1906 race riot and the 1913 lynching of Jewish factory manager Leo Frank still resonated in the memories of many Georgians. A state that claimed to be "progressive" and aspired to attract business and commerce could not ignore the racial and class divisions those traumatic events signified. In a city obsessed with its image, the prediction that blacks might soon outnumber whites, and that wayward and prostituting white girls might give birth to a race of inferiors caused panic.

Rhoda Kaufman, familiar with contemporary social welfare developments, knew that girls' reform schools had been touted by juvenile delinquency experts since the first one opened in 1856 in Lancaster, Massachusetts. Purporting to reform girls arrested for acts of "moral turpitude," the school had provided a home to girls not unlike Betty and Helen.[10] Proposing that Georgia open a training school to "adjust" white girls to their rightful place in the community as mothers, Kaufman rallied a network of reformers together consisting of clubwomen, businessmen, social workers, and church groups. By exploiting fears of race suicide and by playing on Georgia's pretensions to progressivism, these groups would establish one of the most respected southern girls' reformatories.

Historians have pointed out that Progressive-Era women reformers, especially middle- and upper-class women working from women's clubs, used their traditional roles as wives and mothers to argue that public involvement in child welfare was a natural and laudable extension of traditional gender roles. While southern women reformers also used this argument to rationalize participating in the public sphere, they did not intend to use progressive practices to apply northern interpretations of "social change" to southern society. Rather, southern progressives, including those who inaugurated the girls' training school, used reform to preserve the status quo of a New South social order founded on white supremacy and a strictly defined class hierarchy. Like the middle- and upper-middle-class reformers analyzed by James Leloudis and David Carlton, Georgia's women used reform for their own means: to widen the strictures of being a "southern Lady" and to construct a stable social environment ordered by race, class, and gender.[11]

By training girls to be proper mothers, a training school would ultimately serve a middle and upper class that needed an abundant white labor pool and social quiet in order to attract business. Reformers were also motivated by altruism and found the sight of young white prostitutes troubling. They were drawn to the tragic lives of these girls and sought to give them a better life. Yet they refused to address the structural reasons that caused girls like Helen and Betty to prostitute. Reformers preferred to blame not poverty and industrialization for Betty and Helen's behavior. Rather, they blamed the parents of the wayward girl herself. Furthermore, they refused to see the need for education and child-saving in Georgia's black community, which also had a "girl problem." Examining reformers' motivations behind their call for a training school, as well as their relationships with the girls they termed "wayward," illuminates elite and middle-class attitudes toward poor and working-class whites. And by revealing the lives of girls like Helen and Betty, we can see how they were affected by lives of poverty, as well as how the reform school was an attempt to redefine them as "ladies."

By 1914 Atlanta had made a miraculous recovery from its inauspicious beginnings and was considered the premier southern city by many. Possessing the advantages of a large northern city, including a symphony and a museum, Atlanta's downtown bustled with fine shops. There was a thriving upper and middle class of businessmen, lawyers, and entrepreneurs. Atlanta had earned its appellation as "Gateway to the South," seeing spectacular growth in an extraordinarily short time. From 1880 until 1920, the city's manufacturing capacity increased ninefold, establishing Atlanta as a leader in national and regional "trade, distribution, insurance, and banking."[12]

But not all was perfect. Within walking distance of the tony shops and cozy teahouses of downtown were mill villages where dirty children ran down rutted and filthy streets. Young girls haphazardly dressed in frayed petticoats took care of baby brothers and sisters as their mothers worked in the mills. Rhoda Kaufman realized that these girls belonged to Atlanta's new white working class. Fleeing the depressed rural South and Appalachia, large numbers of rural migrants, both black and white, flocked to Georgia's cities throughout this time. Out-of-luck tenant farmers and sharecroppers and their families clamored outside factory doors, eager to work for the meager wages paid. Confectionery makers, overall factories, cotton mills, and other industries, attracted by a probusiness atmosphere and a thus-far docile and poorly paid white work force, provided a seemingly limitless source of low-skill jobs. Unfortunately life in Atlanta and in Georgia's other industrializing cities was not as prosperous as workers had hoped. Long working hours, crowded housing, low pay, and the disintegration of family ties challenged traditional family bonds. Parents would find the isolation, stresses, and strains of urban life difficult and sometimes overwhelming. Helen and Betty would be tempted by the newly discovered urban pleasures Atlanta offered: boys, car rides, friends, clothes, freedom. Families fell apart under the pressures of modernization, and girls like Helen and Betty lived the consequences.

After her father died, Helen, aged fourteen, followed her mother to work at the local broom factory to help support the family. Growing tired of the monotony of factory life, she soon met up with Betty Foster, and the two began staying out all night. During the day, they would "entertain" men at Helen's house while her mother worked. Helen found that this was a profitable venture and after Betty's arrest, she moved on to a house of prostitution. Ever resourceful in the pursuit of money and excitement, Helen also fenced stolen goods for a gang of boy burglars.

Helen soon met a boy, and like many other girls, counted herself lucky when they married. Unfortunately, any hopes Helen had of living a "respectable" life were shattered when her husband forced her back into prostitution and onto the streets. Helen was soon arrested again and sent to the city's juvenile detention hall. Rhoda Kaufman thought it was scandalous that a state as modern as Georgia had only a detention hall (which, after all, was meant for boys) to send a girl like Helen, who had possibilities of reformation and training for motherhood. As newly elected president of the Southern Association of College Women, Kaufman decided she would use the energy and enthusiasm of the state's women's clubs to establish a reformatory.[13]

Northern women's clubs have been traced to antebellum times, but Georgia's women had their first sight of club work only at the 1895 Atlanta

Cotton Exposition. The Atlanta Women's Club was established shortly thereafter and would become Atlanta's most exclusive club. Much like its northern sisters, the AWC had a membership consisting of the city's elite and middle class. Club leaders and members were mostly southern-born and -educated, and were usually the wives of prominent businessmen and entrepreneurs. More than half the AWC members were listed in the 1907 *Blue Book*, Atlanta's social register. They lived in the most affluent sections of the city, organizing "teas" and debutante balls, garden parties and charitable events.[14]

Clubwomen also engaged in an extraordinary range of public-minded and educational endeavors, from the literary to the charitable.[15] Inspired by charitable work undertaken by northern women's clubs and the progressive emphasis on civic work as a means to improve the lives of urban dwellers of all classes, Georgia's women's groups initiated "healthy baby" campaigns and successfully petitioned the city council to ban spitting on sidewalks. The women also lobbied the state legislature for such causes as the abolition of convict labor. Clubwomen felt it was right that they engaged in these public activities—activities that had previously been considered "unladylike" for southern women. These causes served the public good and the good of the state.

Children's causes were an important issue with women's clubs all over the country. Georgia's clubwomen also "adopted" working-class and poor children, together with their adolescent siblings, as a central focus for their charitable and fund-raising enterprises. Who better to take up the gauntlet for children than clubwomen—mothers themselves? Georgia's clubwomen professed a "surplus of mother love"; they were maternal soldiers and "peace armies" fighting to improve children's lot.[16]

Like their sister clubs in other parts of the country, southern women's clubs took varied approaches to child-saving and the wayward child. They ran study groups and read specialized books and attended lectures on subjects from the general to the mundane, from child psychology to proper diet. Others engaged in charitable activity, fund-raising, and administering child-care institutions. With the help of church volunteers and business organizations, clubs started orphanages and the like.[17] By the end of the 1920s, largely thanks to women's clubs, Atlanta and Georgia boasted a number of orphanages, day-care centers, nurseries, after-school centers, and a juvenile court system.[18] Clubs had proven the worth of women's activism in a region previously resistant to all but the most "ladylike" behavior. Even their failed attempts at instituting child-labor laws, compulsory education, and free statewide kindergartens showed the clubs' dedication and tenacity in fighting for children.[19]

The decade-long legislative battle for free statewide kindergartens symbolized the importance of education to child-saving. Education would provide the means to prepare white children to take their rightful place in the New South social order. While day-care centers, after-school programs, and kindergartens taught working-class white children middle-class behaviors and values, black children were explicitly excluded from educational pursuits. White children were trainable; black children were not. Clubwomen pointed out that education could convince the unruliest white child to "WANT to be neat and clean, to be courteous and kind and helpful."[20] Educational means would inspire "habits of accurate observation, attention, patience, perseverance, self-control, and self-denial for the good of others," the perfect characteristics for a new industrially based order.[21] While this view of children's training undeniably resembled northern progressive views of education, southern reformers never intended that white working-class children would actually aspire to—or move up to—middle-class status. Rather, education would cement the childrens' place within the social structure.

Despite the best intentions of clubwomen, however, some children inevitably fell into the delinquent life. The "wayward" child had been a national preoccupation for some time.[22] Several assumptions undergirded the most popular ideas about delinquency's origins, including a bad environment, peer and parental influence, and heredity.[23] With women's clubs again helping to lead the way, progressive reformers across the country addressed delinquency by opening juvenile courts and reformatories to "adjust" the delinquent to his or her environment.

The North had confronted juvenile delinquency when it became aware of "street Arabs" and "wayward children" during early industrialization. The problem came to the South only with the urbanization of the late nineteenth century, when Atlanta's industrialization brought not only fame and fortune but a juvenile crime wave that city authorities were unprepared to address. In 1903, while visiting the city stockade, National Convention of Charities and Corrections delegates revealed that "criminals of both sexes and all ages . . . both white and colored" were housed together in the same room, a practice other regions had disposed of long ago. Rather than waiting until they "returned to their northern homes," the delegates decided to call attention to this "shame and disgrace to Christian civilization." Arguing that mixing ages and races together led to the "learning of meanness and devilishness to children," they urged Georgians to emulate northern ways and place the "little children" in a "department to themselves."[24]

Georgia's reformers, including women's clubs, missionaries, progressive businessmen, and social workers, consciously trod a path laid by northern reformers. But southerners held a different ideology that led them to battle a legislature reluctant to fund or intercede in "private" and "family" matters. But with the city stockade debacle fresh in their minds, by 1905 the state's women's clubs had successfully lobbied for a juvenile court, a detention center, and a boys' reform school.[25] Now, the wayward girl problem beckoned. Georgia's reformers had attempted to address the economic and social needs of the many young women who had been attracted to the city with the burgeoning employment opportunities of the early 1900s. Missionary workers opened night schools and ran settlement programs; they started inexpensive residences for the women. But the needs of the younger girl (who often also worked) were ignored, and, in an effort to remove their presence from the streets, the emphasis gradually shifted to arresting girls who displayed wayward behavior.

The juvenile court, detention center, and reformatory ostensibly addressed the problem of the delinquent boy. But to the reformers, girls—as future mothers—were even more important. As the newspaper urged funding for a wayward girls' "home," it reminded readers that "the influence of an evil woman is worse than the influence of an unreformed man." Training wayward girls for "moral self-support and useful citizenship" was necessary for the future of the state.[26] Southern reformers rationalized the need to separate girls from their families for training by arguing that the parents of such girls were themselves responsible for their plight in life and their poverty. Unlike northern social reformers who often addressed and sometimes attempted to ameliorate the social and economic inequalities causing poverty, southern reformers blatantly ignored the reality of workers' lives. Northern social workers pointed out that young girls prostituted because of "various causes, social, economic and individual," and were "ignorant" and "untrained and unskilled workers."[27] Georgia's workers blamed girl prostitution on parents too ignorant to know better. While the foremost contemporary social-work theorist noted that "social reform and social case work of necessity progress . . . together," in Georgia and the South the two were mutually exclusive.[28]

Southern workers and reformers held steadfastly to the idea that "Georgia Crackers," as native whites, were genetically superior. At the same time, they believed that working-class southern whites were intrinsically an "unpromising element" and "an impressive example of race degeneracy."[29] Reformers described the southern migrant as "in many cases unmoral, reverential and sincere, but sensitive . . . and suspicious." These qualities clearly required the "sympathetic and friendly guidance" of the charity worker and friendly visitor. "Nothing will suffice," said one expert, "short of personal service . . . born of friendship and sympathy."[30] Southern social welfare experts agreed that one should "segregate the mentally unfit and educate the rest," and this prescription fit perfectly with the ideals of a training school.[31]

Mill families were especially denigrated. One worker described a wayward girl's relatives as "mill people but they are far above the average."[32] Parental ignorance and "feeblemindedness" was routinely blamed for the children's delinquency, and the only solution was family separation. One clubwoman who volunteered in the mountains claimed that the "moral conditions" of one "mountain district" were so lax as to be "almost unbelievable." She said one family's children could be "helped," but only if separated from their parents. She begged welfare authorities to assist her in taking the children "legally," explaining that "the mother will not give them up willingly."[33] That a mother might not so easily relinquish her children was seen as an unnatural act. Northern workers had believed in separation of such families as these—in the nineteenth century. They had since shifted to the idea that parents could be trained to raise their own children properly. Southern reformers, however, persisted in believing that dividing a family was the best way to save the children, testimony to their often callous disregard for the poor.

Georgia's clubwomen and welfare workers held indistinguishable views of the wayward child and the role for which he or she should be "trained." Both groups, whether originally southern or northern, expressed the same assumptions about the racial and class underpinnings of a southern society. The divisions between the two groups often blurred as clubwomen performed welfare work, albeit usually as volunteers. City and county administrators generally refused to fund welfare work; agencies were happy to supplement their tiny (usually one person) staffs with untrained, but sympathetic, volunteers. Many workers (such as Rhoda Kaufman) gained entrée into the professional world of social services through volunteer charity work. Disabled and never married, Kaufman was not the "typical" clubwoman, who was usually married and did not work. Kaufman did, however, use her club connections and volunteer work to fulfill her ambitions. Other social workers entered the field as unpaid missionary workers or church workers. The state's only "training school" for white settlement workers was a church mission; entrance required merely a desire to help "the people." Other individuals, especially those who worked in the juvenile courts, were political appointees. As social work outside the South moved toward "professionalization" and away from the volunteer "friendly visitor" approach, Georgia's social welfare programs remained resolutely nonprofessional and personally based. Workers attempted to change the individual and not the structure.[34]

While Georgia's clubwomen were usually married to prominent or affluent men, little is known about the social workers who would become directly involved with the girls' reformatory. At a time when social work outside the South self-consciously sought to define an image and identity around professionalism and specialization, few of Georgia's female social workers possessed more than a normal school degree. Some, including the future superintendent of the girls' reformatory, lacked even that. Social workers comprised a small and tightly knit group with a strong sense of mission and purpose. They had no qualms about sharing information about their "cases" and about the various wayward girls they brought to juvenile court. "Case work" was highly personal and paternalistic, and social workers gained their sense of entitlement and power through community and professional ties. They derived their power from their assumed profession and were respected by townspeople and authorities, such as court officers and police. They were both feared and deferred to by their clients. Social workers at orphanages, county juvenile courts, missions, or mills had personal knowledge of many of the girls who would be sent to the school and thus had a powerful influence on their lives.

Social workers found girls like Betty Foster, a runaway, a challenge. The state urgently needed to find a place to train her for proper motherhood. Her family, poor and chaotic, would prove typical of the families of those committed to the Georgia Training School for Girls. Betty's parents had separated when she was nine, and she went to live with her mother. Her mother realized she could not care for her children; she awarded custody of them to the juvenile court, an unusual step at a time when most troubled families "gave" their children to relatives. Eventually Betty went to live with her aunt.

Unable to afford further schooling, Betty left school at eleven and went to work. Atlanta's businesses had an insatiable demand for unskilled labor, and Betty had no problems finding a succession of menial jobs. But at fourteen, bored by the monotony and regimentation of factory life, Betty married. While she admitted her husband "made a good living for her," allowing her to stay at home, Betty preferred the excitement of the streets. Eager to make some easy money, she started prostituting. Betty was soon arrested and sent to the detention hall. She too would end up at the training school.[35]

The lobbying effort inspired by girls like Betty and Helen enlisted many of Georgia's most influential citizens, who felt that wayward girls should be removed from parents too lax and too stupid to discipline them. They also believed that some girls were naturally criminally inclined and should be kept from the community. One social worker noted about one of her charges: "The only thing to do with the girl is to place her in some industrial institution where she will be taught how to live and also kept from mischief.... She steals anything she can get hold of."[36] A training school, supporters asserted, would protect girls from amoral families, while protecting the community from the girls. And, most important, by training girls to be proper wives and mothers, the school would guard the supremacy of the white race. While the school itself was modeled on progressive notions, its underlying arguments were inherently conservative and based on the ideals of shoring up the New South order.

In her campaign to open a reformatory, Rhoda Kaufman knew she would need the help of the community's most prominent citizens. She enlisted the help of E. H. Peacock, a well-respected missionary-turned-philanthropist. A. K. Hawkes, a wealthy businessman, donated land for the school, proposing that the school be privately funded like Georgia's other child welfare institutions. Supporters called for an "industrial home for the sake of wayward girls, who are not blessed... with a proper protector, and necessary influence to guide them." The "great cry" for funds attracted pledges of two thousand dollars, mostly from businessmen and church groups.[37] E. A. Peacock toured different girls' reformatories, soliciting advice on starting a modern reformatory.[38]

By 1913, however, proponents of the Home for Wayward Girls realized that they would not be able to raise enough money to open the home. They convinced a state representative to file a bill requesting a seventy-five thousand-dollar appropriation, a large amount for a welfare institution. The group, which encompassed women's clubs, social welfare activists, businessmen, and evangelical groups, argued that the state's reputation demanded this school. It was humiliating that a city as admired by other cities as Atlanta should be forced to ship wayward girls to out-of-state institutions. That delinquent girls were often housed in adult facilities was a disgrace.[39] While several southern states had already opened training schools, proponents claimed that Atlanta would be the first southern city to have a girls' school, proving the city's progressive mettle yet again.[40]

The central role of the school would be to preserve "the race," and the issue was "not one of sentimentality and philanthropy, but of *simple racial preservation and justice*." Emphasizing the sacredness and necessity of training young white girls in continuing the southern way of life, they pointed out that the school would "make" girls into "available mothers and industrial workers."[41] Pleas were made to save the "white girls gone wrong, and going wrong," who would ultimately "go to [their] doom" without the protection of the Home for Wayward Girls.[42]

The legislative campaign was multifaceted, requiring skillful organization by the women's groups, social reformers, and evangelicals. Using personal contacts, Rhoda Kaufman collected support from the state's most influential businessmen.[43] The newspaper of the Georgia Federation of Women's Clubs urged clubwomen to contact their representatives, reminding their members to "[t]ell them you want this bill to pass and why you want it."[44] Clubwomen appeared daily in the state house gallery to monitor the legislative debates about the school.[45]

Not all legislators approved of the women's participation in political matters. Nor did they approve of the school, thinking it a waste of state money. At least one senator took umbrage at the sight of women flurrying around the chamber lobby. He snorted at the cause and disparagingly scoffed, "The time will come . . . when we legislators will have to divorce ourselves from these good women who congregate around here and lobby for bills. These women will come up here next and lobby for hospitals for dogs and cats." This legislator apparently disagreed with contemporary thinking that wayward children could be saved, stating, "I don't know of any satisfactory disposal we can make of young boys and girls. In my own county is a school for wayward boys and it doesn't do any good.... I say, don't let's give 'em anything."[46]

The gentleman was promptly rebuked by both the clubwomen and his fellow senators, with one clubwoman commenting on the "flippant manner in which members of the Georgia legislature have sought to dispose" of the school. A religious group published advertisements in the newspapers publicly censuring legislators holding the bill back, imputing the worse motives to the men. While we cannot know whether the advertisements had any effect, they were so large that they were impossible to ignore. At least one senator resented the ads: "I favor this bill in spite of its advocates, rather than because of them."[47]

Most of the state's legislators took the matter quite seriously, appealing to both human and racial superiority. One rebuked his recalcitrant colleagues, saying, "It is indeed startling ... to hear on the floor of this chamber a senator treating this subject with levity, comparing girls with dogs and cats." He noted that the state already had "an institution which cares for sixty-nine white boys, and it is a wonderful institution. We should be proud of it." He exclaimed that even African Americans had criminal institutions: "We have a Negro reformatory. And no senators get up here [to] object to paying its annual appropriation. You care for Negroes, for young boys, and yet this senator gets up here and says you might as well provide for dogs and cats as girls. This senator says, 'don't appropriate a few thousands, let these girls go, and care for the boys and the Negroes, let them go on in the way of crime, and not do a thing about it.'" The assumption that it was shameful to rehabilitate "Negroes" while sacrificing white girls to the streets remained unchallenged. Often accused of pandering to African Americans by providing them with the most basic of services (such as education), legislators were highly vulnerable to racially based attacks. Reformers regularly attacked southern legislators for providing educational facilities to black children at the expense of white children.[48]

One debater invoked the visceral fear of the young innocent white girl cruelly exploited, perhaps by a "foreigner" or "Negro": "When the vice crusade went over Atlanta," he claimed, "one girl was found playing dolls—

she was young." He called to his fellow white men to protect the girl: "Be men, senators, and vote for this bill."[49]

The girls' training school finally won legislative approval on August 15, 1913. Its appropriation had shrunk to twenty thousand dollars from the original seventy-five thousand, but the bill passed overwhelmingly in the Senate, thirty-two to zero.[50] Faced with severe budgetary constraints, the governor had vowed to veto the bill. After he found his office flooded with telegrams from school supporters who stressed the responsibility of the state to "save" these girls, he signed the bill on August 19, 1913.[51]

June 20, 1914, saw the triumphant opening of a new "model" training school that would provide "shelter for unfortunate girls from ruin and guide them upward to useful and happy lives."[52] Set "in a grove on a knoll," the building had "two long wings . . . flooded with light and air" flowing "through windows on every side." The stone facade was stern and forbidding as a haunted house. We can only imagine how frightened Betty and Helen must have been as they walked reluctantly up the long winding drive to the front entrance. Supporters felt sure that these girls who wore the "pallor and splotched complexions" of the city would soon "take on the clear pink flush of young health, after some days in their home on the high hills in the woods, among their gardens and chickens."[53] The site of the Georgia Training School (GTS) carefully followed progressive ideas, which held that the city was a negative environment. Situating the school ten miles outside Atlanta would expose the new residents to healthy rural living and allow them to avoid the temptations of urban life.[54]

The GTS was similar in its location to the location of northern reformatories. Unlike some northern reformatories, however, the GTS lacked the funding to educate girls beyond the eighth grade. Nor did it offer factory training or courses in business. The GTS conformed strictly to traditional gender divisions: its girls would be wives and mothers. Girls would thus learn to farm, garden, milk cows, and feed chickens. Jewell Hill would proudly write her mother, "We have a garden apiece and they sure are cute. I am going to raise beans and lettuce in my garden."[55] Delinquency theory held that "for a large majority of girls . . . farm work is therapeutic." But in the South, it was merely practical to train girls in domestic skills when their return home would require them to garden, babysit younger siblings, cook, and clean.[56]

The GTS quickly filled up with girls from all over Georgia. Committed from its streets, detention halls, prisons, and orphanages, they came from the growing urban areas of Valdosta, Rome, Savannah, Columbus, and Atlanta. About one-third of the GTS girls were committed for prostitution. Most, however, were committed for "wayward" behavior, ranging from having sex with a boyfriend to disobeying a parent.[57] There was no shortage of concerned parties eager to bring girls to the juvenile court and from there to the school.[58] County probation officers, court workers, police, and mill-village social workers (and parents) all recommended girls to the school.

A concerned social worker brought the Lock children to juvenile court, complaining that Mrs. Lock was "unable . . . to control" the children. Mrs. Lock worked in a cotton mill all day, and Mr. Lock was dead. Sally Lock was only ten years old but already associated "with vicious and immoral people and . . . is incorrigible." Her sister Annie, who was thirteen, had worked steadily in the mills since she was ten. Both girls had been seen with "bad company" and dated "mill boys." Since "mill people" had come to symbolize the social disorder attendant to industrialization, a girl who "went around with" the sons of mill workers was assumed to be wayward. After stealing a coat and hat from another girl while in the detention center, Sally was described as "without a doubt one of the worst little creatures I ever came in contact with." But the worker nonetheless had faith in the power of the school to change Sally's future, writing, "I certainly hope that you will be able to train her."[59]

Cynthia Embree was hired as superintendent shortly after the school opened and would have a powerful and lasting impact on the GTS and its girls. While Embree was not from Georgia and lacked a college education, she had a background in social welfare. Most important, the GTS Board of Managers and the social welfare community were well acquainted with her through her work as an Atlanta court probation officer. Yet despite her social service background, Embree carried a deep distrust of social "case work," which was the social worker's claim to efficiency and professionalism. Commonplace in other training schools by now, no social workers would be employed at the school during Embree's tenure or for years afterward. Embree's only concession to case work was to institute two administrative forms including an "intake form," which recorded the girl's demographic information, and a "record," which recorded the girl's behavior during her stay at the school and after.[60]

While Embree disliked case work, she enjoyed the collegiality from her contacts with her "professional" associates, such as court workers, social workers, and probation officers. She forged a strong relationship with social workers all over Georgia, and she relied upon them to "report" on girls who had left the school. And the social workers relied on Embree to give their cause credibility. One probation officer, who committed at least six girls to the training school, wrote, "I find girls for you where ever I go.... None of these girls had ever known what a chance was." Clearly concurring that most of the girls direly required the intervention of the court, she wrote, "If we can ever get juvenile courts ... and ... welfare work organized in each county it will mean much to your work as well as humanity in general. I know your heart is with us in this work we are trying to organize over South Georgia."[61]

Clubwomen became less involved in the school after its opening, and Embree had little contact with them. She and board members occasionally gave talks about the school at club meetings. She also paroled girls to work as housemaids in clubwomen's homes, where the girl could live in a "family environment." Embree once asked one clubwoman (who was very active in social welfare) for the "name of some good woman to whom I could parole Lillian M. and who would look after her."[62] But clubwomen continued to take it upon themselves to "rescue" poor children, who were sometimes sent to the school. The Hill family had two daughters who would end up at the GTS. Mr. Hill was dead, and Mrs. Hill, a laundress, lived with her six children "in a home of squalor" in Columbus's "Negro quarters."[63] The Hills' direct challenge of racial convention disturbed townspeople. By living in a black neighborhood and by engaging in a line of work usually reserved for black women, Mrs. Hill and her family were sure to come to the attention of city authorities. In a social milieu where racial boundaries were sacrosanct, a group of clubwomen felt vindicated in "rescuing" the six children from their mother.

Edna Hill quit school after the first grade and went to work in a cotton mill when she was ten; Jewel Hill went to work at fourteen after having completed only the first grade. Left alone to care for their younger siblings in their few free hours, the girls found themselves drawn by the lure of pretty things their mother could not possibly afford. Like many other GTS girls, the Hill sisters took up prostituting. After their "rescue" by clubwomen, four of the siblings were adopted by "respectable" families. Edna and Jewel, too old to adopt out, were sent to an orphanage, but the girls were used to their freedom and refused to adapt to a rigid institution. They were eventually sent to the GTS.[64] In this case, then, the desired rehabilitation of the Hill sisters was entirely due to the intervention of a nonprofessional group of clubwomen.

To reformers, women like Mrs. Hill were eminently unsuited to raise girls who had the region's future in their very hands. Social workers believed that these girls' families were "dirty and disorderly" and lacked "moral distinctions."[65] Many of the families of wayward girls, such as the Hills, had long relationships with law enforcement and social welfare agencies, and commitment to the training school was often the culmination of a family's involvement with authorities. Welfare workers held a particular authority in communities that clubwomen may not have had. While southern life continued to be strongly oriented to the individual family, many parents felt they had no choice but to acquiesce to a social worker's demand for custodianship of their daughter. And, in fact, the GTS had legal guardianship over a committed girl until she was twenty-one.

Social workers unhesitatingly invoked their presumed authority over the families of wayward girls. Ethel Young had been married at fourteen and left her husband after two weeks because he drank and "wouldn't provide for her." She had been arrested for prostituting with soldiers and ended up at the GTS. Ethel Young's mother complained to Superintendent Embree that a social worker had come and "taken" Ethel away and "have done something with her I don't know what nor where." Mrs. Young tragically added that the social worker had forbidden Ethel to "tell me goodby and it is nearly bout to kill me."[66]

By 1915 the school was "home" to forty-one residents and had an impeccable reputation throughout the South for its training of girls. Superintendent Embree was known for adapting "methods," such as an "honor court," which were used by progressive training schools outside of the South. In general, however, her own methods were based on a close personal relationship with each girl and conformed to the paternalistic and familistic ways of the South. Social workers and others who sent girls to the school had little influence over the school's administration. Embree was a formidable woman who did things her own way without consultation with other professionals.[67]

Although we know little about daily life in girls' reformatories during this time, the GTS was probably similar to other schools—but for the central role played by religious training. The "rising bell" sounded at 6 A.M. Chapel was held twice a day and several more times on Sundays; evangelical and church groups often came to the school to hold special services. Celebrating a service for girls graduating from eighth grade, the "ladies" of one evangelical group "gave each girl a silver pencil." Girls studied and worked for half of the day and gardened or worked in the kitchen for the rest of the day. "Recreation" took up less than two hours a day; Superintendent Embree agreed with Martha Falconer, one of the foremost authorities on wayward girls, who counseled, "The great object . . . is to keep the girls so busy and happy at work and play that they have little time for idle gossiping and quarreling."[68]

Despite Embree's attempts to keep her "girls" active, most of them rebelled during their early days at the GTS. Betty Foster was, not surprisingly, wild and recalcitrant during her first few days. She tired of the routine by her second day and ran away for an hour. Two days later she set fire to a mattress, and she ran away two more times within two months. Helen Taylor also had a difficult time "adjusting" to the GTS. She joined Betty in setting fire to their mattresses, and she conspired with her mother and her own husband to run away from the school. Helen did more than her share of plotting, gagging a matron one time and helping several other girls to run away. After those adventures, however, both girls calmed down and were promoted to the senior cottage where they had more freedom and could wear their own clothes.[69]

Both Helen and Betty ended up happily married. Helen had an especially strong attachment to the GTS and to Superintendent Embree, and she corresponded with Embree for several years. "Miss Embree please come down . . . I know you need a rest. . . . I really want to see you and be with you all to my self."[70] Helen believed that the school had given her an advantage she had lacked before her stay, allowing her to attain a respectability she had been denied as a wayward girl. Moreover Helen seemed happy with her choices and even asked Embree if a young relative who "went wild" could be sent to the school. Appropriating the middle-class description of "waywardness," she perceived her relative's activities as shameful. "She has went to pictures and read novels until she's love mad. . . . She had boys to come in." Helen's "training" had served its purpose: it had socialized her to follow a traditional role within the southern hierarchy of race, class, and gender. Helen became a wife and mother, and her perception of the school reaffirmed her choices. "I don't mind the School. I just mind what I did before I got to the School. . . . I can truthfully say I am pure now. And always will be."[71]

NOTES

This quote in this title is taken from Sally Lock's file, letter to Superintendent Cynthia Embree from social worker, no date, Georgia Training School for Girls, Georgia Department of Children and Youth Services (DCYS). For their support and help, I would like to thank Elizabeth Fox-Genovese, Dan Carter, Mary Odem, Ann Chirhart, Elna C. Green, Joy Fishel, and the two reviewers. This project would not have been possible without the extensive cooperation of Sandra Stone and the DCYS.

1. The names of all girls sent to the Georgia Training School for Girls have been changed in accordance with confidentiality requirements set forth by the Georgia Department of Children and Youth Services.

2. *Atlanta Journal*, June 22, 1914. Betty and Helen were committed to the Georgia Training School for Girls (GTS).

3. Atlanta *Georgian and News*, January 20, 1914, 4.

4. *Atlanta Journal*, May 6, 1913, 9, and November 4, 1913, 6. *Atlanta Constitution*, November 2, 1911, 1.

5. Rhoda Kaufman Manuscript Collection, Box 1, Folder 3, biographical material, Georgia Department of Archives and History.

6. Speech, no date, Kaufman Collection, Box 1, Folder 3.

7. *Atlanta Constitution*, November 2, 1909, 1.

8. Historians who have examined the "girl problem" from a nonsouthern perspective include Ruth M. Alexander, *The "Girl Problem": Female Sexual Delinquency in New York, 1900–1930* (Ithaca: Cornell University Press, 1995); and Mary Odem, *Delinquent Daughters: Protecting and Policing Adolescent Female Sexuality in the United States, 1885–1920* (Chapel Hill: University of North Carolina Press, 1995). *Atlanta Constitution*, June 14, 1905, 7, and June 15, 1905, 6.

9. James Russell, *Atlanta: 1847–1890, City Building in the Old South and the New* (Baton Rouge: Louisiana State University Press, 1988), 242–43.

10. Barbara M. Brenzel, *Daughters of the State: A Social Portrait of the First Reform School for Girls in North America, 1856–1905* (Cambridge, Mass.: The MIT Press, 1983), 45.

11. James L. Leloudis, "School Reform in the New South: The Woman's Association for the Betterment of Public School Houses in North Carolina, 1902–1919," *Journal of American History* 69 (March 1989): 886; David Carlton, *Mill and Town in South Carolina, 1880–1920* (Baton Rouge: Louisiana State University Press, 1982), 180–88.

12. Nancy MacLean, "The Leo Frank Case Reconsidered: Gender and Sexual Politics in the Making of Reactionary Populism," *Journal of American History* 78 (December 1991): 921; Gretchen Maclachlan, "Women's Work, Atlanta's Industrialization and Urbanization, 1879–1929" (Ph.D. diss., Emory University, 1992), chap. 1.

13. Helen Taylor, intake file dated May 5, 1915. Girls committed to the GTS had "intake" statements recording demographic and personal information, which was subsequently entered into their "files."

14. Atlanta's Women's Club listing, *The Blue Book* (New York: Dua Publishing Company, 1907), 62–63, and Darlene Roth, "Matronage: Patterns in Women's Organizations, Atlanta, Georgia, 1890–1940" (Ph.D. diss., George Washington University, 1978), 107–9.

15. Mrs. John K. Ottley, "Georgia Federation Convention," General Federation of Women's Clubs, *Bulletin* 8, no. 3, December 1910, General Federation of Women's Clubs Manuscript Collection, Women's History and Resource Center, Washington, D.C.

16. Atlanta Federation of Women's Clubs, AFWC *Yearbook*, May 1912–13, 3, AFWC Papers, Box 1, Atlanta History Center (hereafter AHC). Mrs. A. O. Granger, "The Effect of Club Work in the South," *Annals of the American Academy of Political Science* 28 (July–December 1906): 248–56; *Atlanta Journal*, July 6, 1913, 6.

17. "Lion's Club to Lead Drive for Georgia Home Society," *Atlanta Constitution*, February 16, 1921, 3; "Atlanta Foundation," *Atlanta Constitution*, February 3, 1921, 1.

18. "Sheltering Arms Association Makes Fine Report for 1920," *Atlanta Constitution*, February 15, 1921, 7. "Mrs. Bethune Patterson—90 Years Old, Recalls Atlanta's First Club," *Atlanta Journal*, February 25, 1953, clipping in Sheltering Arms Day Nursery Association Collection, Box 1, Folder 1, AHC. Atlanta Kindergarten Alumnae Papers, Box 1, Folder 6, AHC.

19. Nancy Hewitt discussed northern women's activism in *Women's Activism and Social Change, Rochester, New York, 1822–1872* (Ithaca, N.Y.: Cornell University Press, 1984). The development of myths around southern "ladyhood" can be found in Anne Firor Scott, *The Southern Lady: From Pedestal to Politics, 1830–1930* (Chicago: The University of Chicago Press, 1970).

20. Madge A. Bigham, "Kindergarten Memories," 1937, Atlanta Kindergarten Alumnae, Box 1, Folder 8, AHC.

21. Pamphlet, "Kindergarten," no date, no publisher, Kindergarten Alumnae, Box 1, Folder 3, AHC.

22. See Steven Schlossman's historical examination of juvenile delinquency in *Love and the American Delinquent: The Theory and Practice of Progressive Juvenile Justice, 1825–1920* (Chicago: University of Chicago Press, 1977). There has been little historical work on southern juvenile delinquency.

23. For contemporary delinquency theory, see William Healy, M.D., and Augusta F. Bronner, *Delinquents and Criminals, Their Making and Unmaking: Studies in Two American Cities*, Judge Baker Foundation Publication No. 3 (New York: The MacMillan Company, 1928).

24. *Atlanta Constitution*, May 11, 1903, 1. By the 1920s most southern states held regular social welfare conventions modeled on that of the NCCC. Georgia was one of the last states to do so, however, according to Virginia Wooten Gulledge's study, "The North Carolina Conference for Social Service: A Study of its Development and Methods" (n.p.: The North Carolina Conference for Social Service, 1942), chap. 2.

25. The boys' reformatory was racially and occupationally segregated: white boys learned trades and black boys picked cotton. *Atlanta Journal*, "The Fulton Industrial Farm for White Boys," June 15, 1913. Granger, "The Effect of Club Work in the South"; and K. Cassatt, "Communications," *Annals of the American Association of Political Science* 28 (July–

December 1901): 293–96. By 1928 Georgia's forty-eight counties each had a juvenile court. "Jottings," *The Survey* (January 22, 1921): 613; and *Atlanta Journal*, February 2, 1921, 12.

26. *Atlanta Constitution*, August 20, 1914, 4.

27. Maude E. Miner, New York Probation and Protective Association, "Social Hygiene," National Conference of Charities and Correction, Forty-first Conference, *Proceedings* (1914): 197.

28. Mary E. Richmond, *Social Diagnosis* (New York: Sage Foundation, 1917), 25.

29. Clare de Graffenried, "The Georgia Cracker in the Cotton Mills," *Century Magazine* (February 1891): 483; James P. Kranz, Associated Charities, Memphis, "Scope and Limitations of Family Rehabilitation with Reference to Southern Conditions," National Conference of Charities and Corrections, *Proceedings*, Forty-First Conference (1914), 131–34.

30. "A Training School for Settlement Workers," *Churchman* 106 (August 3, 1912): 155.

31. Kranz, "Scope and Limitations," 131–34.

32. Sally Lock, file. Undated note concerns another girl.

33. Correspondence, Children's Bureau Collection, Record Group 102, Box 67, File 7340, National Archives.

34. Daniel J. Walkowitz, "The Making of a Feminine Professional Identity: Social Workers in the 1920s," *American Historical Review* 95 (October 1990): 1051, and "A Training School for Settlement Workers," *The Survey* 52 (September 15, 1924): 631, which also emphasized Georgia's lack of trained social workers.

35. Betty Foster, intake file, July 5, 1914.

36. Thelma R., file, court record, no date.

37. *Atlanta Journal*, July 14, 1912, 11.

38. *Atlanta Journal*, July 28, 1912, 6.

39. *Atlanta Journal*, editorial, July 1, 1912.

40. Virginia opened a girls' school in 1906, Alabama in 1908, and Texas in 1913. Margaret Reeves, *Training Schools for Delinquent Girls* (New York: Russell Sage Foundation, 1929), 411.

41. *Atlanta Constitution*, clipping, n.d.; clipping, March 21, 1913, Kaufman Collection, Box 1, Envelope 3.

42. Kaufman Collection, Box 1, Folder 3, typed text. Advocates for the Home for Wayward Girls neglected the black community's "girl problems." While several southern states had homes for wayward black girls by this time, Georgia had only a private home for "homeless" black girls. The GTS remained segregated until the 1970s. Reeves, *Training Schools*, 405–7; *Atlanta Constitution*, February 26, 1921.

43. Kaufman Collection, Box 5, Folder 1. Box 1, Folder 3, correspondence: Garland M. Jones, Esq., to Kaufman, June 16, 1913; telegraph from O. H. Elkins to Governor Slaton, August 19, 1913.

44. *Atlanta Constitution*, August 3, 1913, n.p.

45. *Atlanta Journal*, August 11, 1913, 7. *Atlanta Constitution*, August 2, 1913, editorial page, and August 20, 1913, 4. Jean M. Gordon, "Why the Children are in the Factory," The National Conference of Charities and Correction, *Proceedings* (1908): 346.

46. *Atlanta Constitution*, August 6, 1913, and August 17, 1913, n.p.

47. *Atlanta Constitution*, August 17, 1913. Atlanta *Constitution*, August 6, 1913.

48. Ibid.
49. Ibid.
50. *Atlanta Journal*, August 15, 1913, 9.
51. *Atlanta Journal*, August 19, 1913, 6.
52. *Atlanta Journal*, August 19, 1913, 6.
53. Board of Managers, "First Annual Report of the Georgia Training School for Girls," June 1, 1915, 12.
54. Reeves, *Training Schools*, 116. The original GTS buildings were demolished in the 1970s; the property is currently the site of a DCYS boys' facility.
55. Jewel Hill, letter from Jewel to her mother, dated June 1, 1917.
56. Reeves, *Training Schools*, 122.
57. GTS records were inconsistently maintained. They remain unprocessed and uncataloged, making it difficult to quantify them.
58. For legislation establishing Boys' Training School, see *Georgia Laws: Acts and Resolutions of the General Assembly of the State of Georgia, 1905*, Article I, Sec. 1237–1259. *Georgia Laws 1913: Acts and Resolutions of the General Assembly of the State of Georgia* (Atlanta: Charles P. Byrd, State Printer, 1913): Part I, Public Laws, Title 5, Miscellaneous, No. 257: 87–91, established the GTS. For juvenile court background, see State of Georgia Department of Public Welfare, *In Loco Parentis (In Place of the Parent): The Work of the Juvenile Court in Saving Georgia's Wards from Lives of Poverty and Crimes. A Handbook for Juvenile Court Judges, Advisory Boards, Probation Officers and Civic Organizations* (1922); and Jesse Carrell Larmore, "The Juvenile Court Movement in Georgia" (M.A. thesis, Emory University, 1942), 14–15.
59. Sally Lock, intake file; letter to Superintendent Embree from Evelyn Williams, State Department of Health, no date.
60. Embree was GTS superintendent from 1915 until 1921. Jonathan Magidoff of the Chicago Historical Society kindly provided me with information about Cynthia Embree and her work at the Chicago Home for Girls, where Embree worked from 1922 until 1936.
61. Bertha B. file, Agnes McKenna to Cynthia Embree, August 20, 1917.
62. Bertha B. file, Embree to Mary Raoul, November 13, 1916.
63. Jewel and Edna Hill, file intake reports from the *Atlanta Constitution*, no date.
64. Jewel Hill, file, letter from mother to Embree, n.d.
65. De Graffenried, "The Georgia Cracker in the Cotton Mills," 483–98.
66. Ethel Young, intake file, and letter from mother to Embree, May 30, 1920.
67. Reeves, *Training Schools*, 345; Board of Managers, "Annual Report," 1915: 12.
68. Martha Falconer, "Work of the Girls' Department, House of Refuge, Philadelphia, PA," The National Conference of Charities and Correction, *Proceedings* (1908): 391; and GTS "Annual Report," 1921.
69. Betty Foster, record; Helen Taylor, record.
70. Helen Taylor, letter to Embree, August 16, 1920.
71. Helen Taylor, letter to Embree, November 24, 1919.

The Colors of Social Welfare in the New South

Black and White Clubwomen in South Carolina, 1900–1930

JOAN MARIE JOHNSON

At the turn of the century, as the South continued to struggle with economic and social changes brought about by the Civil War, black and white clubwomen from South Carolina sought to define the New South through social welfare work. This essay argues that each group of women, although performing similar community services, drew motivation from different sources and worked toward different goals. Although historians have recently recognized women's significant role in Progressive-Era social welfare reform in the South, as well as in the nation, thus far they have not focused on how such women affected race relations in the New South.[1] A comparative approach reveals how clubwomen in South Carolina shaped the Jim Crow South: white women legitimized and strengthened segregation through their emphasis on southern identity and their outreach programs for whites only, while black women challenged Jim Crow through their own social welfare agenda.[2]

South Carolina white and black clubwomen infused social welfare work with meaning peculiar to their understanding of southern history and race constructions and social and economic visions of a New South.[3] However such meaning was radically different for black and white clubwomen. Many white southern clubwomen, drawn to social reform in part by a desire to honor the past, worked exclusively for whites. Women of the South Carolina Federation of Women's Clubs (SCFWC), led principally by Louisa Poppenheim, believed that their Confederate heritage foretold future glory for the South. They worked to build pride in the South by promoting southern literature and history and by supporting the Lost Cause, the movement to honor the Confederacy. At the same time, however, they recognized the economic needs of the postwar South, and they developed a social welfare agenda. This essay explores how, through educational improvement, establishing reformatories, and child-labor reform, these women aided poor whites, trying to make the South a prosperous region worthy of its honorable past. They supported economic change in order to bring about a New South, while hoping to ameliorate industrialization's negative effects. For white clubwomen in South Carolina, pride in the southern past was inextricably linked to social welfare as they advanced their own New South creed of industrialization and prosperity.

Black women, excluded from white women's programs, negotiated their own agenda for social welfare. By identifying and meeting the needs in their community, notably in education and reform for girls, African American clubwomen in South Carolina attempted to claim a place for themselves in the New South as legitimate members of southern society. Excluded from most new industrial jobs, although not neglecting liberal arts, black women advocated manual training in order to improve their economic status. Led by Mrs. Marion Wilkinson, the South Carolina Federation of Colored Women's Clubs (SCFCWC) fought to make the South Carolina legislature acknowledge the needs of young black girls with state appropriations to the Fairwold Home for Colored Girls. In this and many other ways, black clubwomen sought to partake in the prosperity promised in the New South and thus to uplift the race.

As the first state to secede from the union, South Carolina stood at the vanguard of southern nationalism and of pride in the past. At the same time, however, the state also led the movement for New South industrialization, as it was the third-leading producer of cotton textiles in the nation, with more than 140 mills and tens of thousands of mill operatives by the early twentieth century.[4] Thus white clubwomen from across the state, including the mill towns in the Piedmont region and the tradition-bound city of Charleston, all focused on southern identity, and citizens had to balance tradition and progress carefully. Blacks overwhelmingly remained mired in agricultural labor or domestic service, excluded from New South prosperity. Therefore, although the region remained predominately agricultural, especially for African Americans, the exploding presence of mills nurtured a predominate atmosphere of change in the state, which a concurrent emphasis on tradition could counter.

White clubwomen in the SCFWC, an umbrella organization for local women's clubs, created southern identity through the promotion of southern literature and history, the use of rhetoric designed to inspire and appeal to southern women, and cooperation with the United Daughters of the Confederacy (UDC), an association dedicated to the Lost Cause. Honoring the past was necessary, they believed, because only a proud past could inspire hope for the future. Unlike the UDC, however, which limited itself to memorializing the past, clubwomen were driven by the honor of the past to take up social welfare. Significantly, southern women, like northern women, justified their work in the public sphere by emphasizing their maternal duty to better the health and safety of children, but they also argued that as daughters of the Confederacy it was their duty to better the New South. The *Keystone*, a journal written and edited by Mary and Louisa Poppenheim, was the official organ of the SCFWC and the UDC, and it provides a compelling record of federation leaders' speeches. Through the speeches, clubwomen attempted to rouse the SCFWC members to embrace social reform by invoking a strong sense of place.

Louisa Poppenheim, SCFWC president from 1900 to 1902, argued that the past history of plantation life instilled in southern women the motivation for community service. She contended that "the plantation system in the South necessitating large tracts of land developed a permanency of residence which created an intense local pride and feeling of responsibility." These characteristics had not disappeared, according to Poppenheim, and uniquely qualified southern women for club work.[5] She called for women to look to the glory of the past and the strength of their foremothers for inspiration. "As [southern women] look out into the misty morning of the future," she wrote, "they receive fresh courage from the prestige of the past, for they believe that inspiration for the future can be secured through the contemplation of that past."[6]

Similarly one of Poppenheim's successors, Sarah Visanska, president from 1910 to 1912, argued that the New South should be built upon the progress and perseverance of the Old South. She reminded clubwomen, for example, that as one of the original thirteen colonies, South Carolina sounded "the bugle call of progress and reform," and that despite the Civil War, "those clarion notes have been stilled but never quite forgotten." Visanska envisioned a role for women in the return to that progress and reform in the New South. After using the past to motivate clubwomen to embrace reform, she issued an impassioned plea for attention to the plight of working women, for whom she demanded "equal pay, and equal respect, for equal work."[7] Visanska also called southern women to respond according to the example set for them by their ancestors. She told clubwomen, "In the past, untrained and unprepared, our women rose magnificently to the duties imposed by calamitous war and untold privations. To-day we must answer the call of new conditions!" Visanska enumerated the problems that southern women faced: the care of mill children, growing cities that needed parks, playgrounds, free libraries, and better sanitation, and the guarantee of safety for young working girls.[8]

Ida Lining, an SCFWC and UDC officer, was even more explicit in her appeal to the past to inspire social welfare work. She named George Washington, John C. Calhoun, Robert E. Lee, and others as worthy leaders who should erase any shame that the South might feel after the Civil War. "Is our pride humbled?" she asked, "Perish the thought, Southerners! We have nothing to be ashamed of. When 'our storm-cradled nation fell' and we furled our banner forever, it was with the applause of the whole world. Its tattered folds do not conceal honor." Southerners had risen above the hardships encountered and survived them. This legacy of perseverance meant that "[w]hen we take our education affairs in hand, we will overcome illiteracy. If we are 'let alone' we will settle the color question." Lining continued, "This is not a 'new South.' It is the same old South under changed conditions. . . . The re-incarnated spirits of our heroes, both men and women . . . should stimulate us to prove in the eyes of the world a 'just cause' and we are doing it." She concluded that in order to be "self-respecting Southerners," clubwomen needed to establish schools and libraries, aid the poor, and end illiteracy.[9] References to the Lost Cause were common to the UDC, but in this article, Lining addressed clubwomen, for they were the women who were building libraries, improving schools, fighting illiteracy, and aiding the poor.

Clubwomen and their work were crucial to the success of the New South. Although they honored the Old South, their desire for prosperity allowed them to embrace industrialization. Yet, because of their duty to children, to women, and to civic improvement, they also worked to ameliorate the negative consequences change brought. Women thus simultaneously embraced and critiqued the New South. Several historians have shown that women's clubs forced the state and local governments in the South (and the nation) to institute social welfare programs.[10] Because of their strong links to the Lost Cause, when women advocated change they were perceived as less threatening to the southern way of life. Therefore they were perhaps most successful at reconciling tradition and progress in the New South. Moreover, because women ensured that the South did not lose its cultural traditions, men were free to invest in cotton mills and to dedicate themselves to economic change. When the inevitable problems associated with industrialization arose, women took care of those problems without blaming the men or the mills.[11] South Carolina clubwomen eased the transition from farm to factory for many through education reforms that helped train the workforce needed in the New South. White clubwomen did not, however, criticize the economic system, in which segregation sustained depressed wages.[12]

Thus, despite their attention to the past, the SCFWC also hoped to shape the New South through social welfare work. Founded in 1898, charter clubs in the federation were purely literary, although most slowly expanded their purpose to include community welfare.[13] The federation promoted education, the establishment of libraries and kindergartens, and child-labor and juvenile delinquent reforms. By the 1920s the public welfare department, which contained the social and industrial conditions and the health committees, fought for labor legislation, such as minimum wages and maximum hours, and institutional aid not only for delinquent children but also for the feeble-minded, and for improved conditions in the penal system.[14]

As women and mothers, clubwomen throughout the nation naturally were concerned with children's education. The SCFWC focused on higher education for women, manual and domestic training, and kindergartens and libraries. Education was one of the most crucial needs in the postbellum South because there had been no free public school system before Reconstruction—due to the plantation system, rural isolation, and lack of support for such a tax-supported system. Therefore, after the war, states had to raise taxes, build schools, and train teachers. Despite northern philanthropic aid, southern clubwomen preferred to retain control, especially over southern literature and history in the curriculum, the shape of industrial training, and the regulation of spending on black schools.

The desire to control their own reforms, evident in Lining's article, was clearly linked to the "negro problem." For example, the editors of the *Keystone* reprinted an article from the *New York Tribune* that recognized education as the central problem in the New South, praised the South for meeting that problem head on, and finally advocated that the North stay out and let the South handle its own affairs without fear because the "South means to do its education duty by the negro."[15] As numerous historians have shown, southerners did not "do their duty" for black schoolchildren, and in fact spending on black schools only decreased in comparison to white schools. Under the influence of such state politicians as Ben Tillman, governor and senator and a virulent racist who did not want to spend the state's money on the education of black youth, South Carolina's record was among the worst in the country, with spending on white children more than six times the amount that spent on black children.[16] White clubwomen in South Carolina supported the state's inequitable policies by extending their aid to white children only.

Louisa Poppenheim and other chairs of the education committee focused primarily on two facets of reform: providing scholarships for higher education to females and improving local elementary schools.[17] The process of examining applicants for scholarships made clubwomen realize that a preponderance of unqualified girls indicated a lack of adequate elementary school training, and they quickly began to divide their attention between scholarships and local schools. For example, Poppenheim recommended that clubwomen make personal visits to their community schools, in addition to discussing education topics at a club meeting set aside as "Education Day." She recommended that clubwomen investigate school conditions, such as the number of pupils attending, as women's clubs throughout the nation were doing. However, as a southern woman and a member of the UDC, she also advocated asking what histories were being taught in order to ensure that they taught the "true" history of the Civil War.[18]

Clubwomen also debated the need for manual or industrial training in the South. Many white reformers saw industrial education as a necessity for white children to become skilled laborers in the newly industrial South, and in combination with liberal arts as training for all children in neatness, character, and other worthy traits. This was especially true for women, who could learn to be better homemakers.[19] Despite the federation's initial focus on higher education for girls, as education committee chair, Louisa Poppenheim advocated promoting industrial education. She argued that one problem of the New South was the overabundance of professionals and the lack of well-trained laborers.[20]

The debate over industrial education forced middle- and upper-class clubwomen to consider just whom they wanted to aid—their own children or the children of the poor, especially cotton-mill families. Most white clubwomen were married to successful businessmen, planters, lawyers, educators, and other professionals, and came from socially and politically prominent families in the state, yet they aimed reforms at poor white children.[21] For example, the *Keystone* printed the comments of a reader who signed him/herself only as "Angus" of Newberry following the federation's annual convention in 1904. In this letter, the writer praised clubwomen for the work being done with scholarships but questioned their focus on higher education. "Would it not be better," Angus asked, "to begin at the bottom and build up to a higher plane the poor white children of our state. An industrial department should be a feature of all public schools, especially in mill districts, where girls should be taught the useful handiwork of sewing, proper preparation of food and hygiene of their homes."[22] The SCFWC hoped to do both. Ultimately clubwomen aided their own children through scholarships and "needy" white citizens through industrial education in public schools and mill districts. They did not, however, include black children in their agenda.

Industrial education for white children prepared them as adults to have clean and well-kept homes, and such education provided basic skills needed for factory labor but did not train these children for opportunities beyond the mills. Ironically clubwomen translated Booker T. Washington's program of industrial education for black children into a similar program for white children—who, because they were white, could not be ignored but were not expected to transcend class distinctions. Rather they were "saved" by the opportunity to leave the farm and improve their lives and education by living in mill villages, while they provided the labor necessary for an industrial New South. Generally white southern reformers did not refer to Washington's influence, although at times, direct comparison could also be effective by hinting that as blacks learned skills, whites would have to work for them.[23] Martha Berry, who established a school for poor children in Georgia, declared, "A great deal has been spent upon the Indians and Negroes and they have institutions all over the Southland where they can receive practical industrial training." In comparison, however, white children had little of the same opportunity, and because cotton mills hired whites, not blacks, the progress of whites determined the progress of the New South.[24] In South Carolina white reformers' racial affinity with poor white children had its limits, however. Ironically such reformers as Louisa Poppenheim could at once perceive industrial education as a positive good and therefore something that should be taught to whites, while at the same time praise Booker T. Washington for asserting that blacks needed industrial, rather than liberal arts, education in order to keep blacks "in their place."[25]

Clubwomen's emphasis on education was evident also in their interest in kindergartens. The SCFWC kindergarten department worked to establish local kindergartens through the volunteer efforts of local clubs, to train kindergarten teachers through scholarships, and finally, to ask the state to mandate free public kindergartens as an essential part of the public school system.

South Carolina clubwomen explicitly linked the need for kindergartens to urbanization, industrialization, and the New South. Sarah Visanska detailed the trend toward urbanization during the nineteenth century, along with which, she contended, "has arisen another need—the feeble cry of the children of the poor has been heard in the land, and, fortunately, with the want has also come its relief—the free kindergarten." Rather than striving to alleviate the family's poverty, Visanska directed clubwomen's attention to the children. Clubwomen could readily extend aid by establishing kindergartens for children, she argued, whose working mothers could do little more than feed them, "while the poor little hearts and minds are starved or become hardened by neglect, and of ill-treatment." At the turn of the century in South Carolina, poor children, although predominately rural, increasingly lived in mill towns. Visanska exhorted clubs to open free kindergartens, which were "an absolute necessity for the children of the poor in factory towns and crowded city streets."[26]

In addition to their focus on education, South Carolina clubwomen also worked to establish a reformatory for delinquent white boys (and later girls). There, although black clubwomen stressed morality and protection in the need to care for delinquent black girls, white clubwomen were less concerned with morality than with progress. They worked diligently to aid white boys, whom they assumed to be morally fit but simply in need of another chance in life.[27] The reformatory fit into their program of industrial education and improved opportunities for poor white children in the state. The clubwomen hoped to build southern prosperity through "increas[ing] the number of efficient men and women citizens of their state."[28] Repeated attempts to gain funding were finally successful when in 1908 the legislature granted ten thousand dollars to the school, enough to build and staff it.[29] Once the school was established, clubwomen hounded county legislative delegations to maintain the full appropriation.[30] As work on the reformatory progressed, it underwent a series of name changes. Margaret McKissick, SCFWC president from 1906 to 1908, advocated the term "industrial school," reducing the stigma attached to the word "reformatory." Rather than viewing the boys as delinquents, McKissick saw them as wayward boys, who, in her words, needed "formation" rather than "reformation."[31]

Clubwomen also worked to ameliorate child labor in South Carolina, one of the leading cotton-mill states. Sarah Visanska was one of the first leaders to encourage southern clubwomen to address this problem, particularly pernicious in the New South. Visanska refrained from blaming mill owners or New South proponents, but rather she appealed to women, who formerly gave alms to the poor, to train them through better education, kindergartens, and industrial education in order to make "useful, happy citizens of tomorrow." In other words, the New South creed advocated by Henry Grady and others could not create a prosperous South for all whites without women to aid those adversely affected by industrialization.[32] Yet, because clubwomen were often married or otherwise related to mill owners, because they were reluctant to criticize the New South or to support federal legislation, and because mill owners, workers, politicians, and editors in South Carolina all protested legislative regulation of child labor in favor of welfare programs for mill children, clubwomen in South Carolina did the same. The legislative committee did not promote child-labor legislation with any of the same fervor applied to kindergartens or the reformatory. Instead, they worked to establish schools in cooperation with owners in mill districts. At the same time, most clubwomen and the Poppenheims promoted a positive view of mill conditions, rather than the common critical portraits of pale children laboring at the spindles. Clearly clubwomen's belief in the New South shaped their social welfare agenda.

Each of the reforms discussed above, inspired by a desire to build a prosperous New South upon the glories of the Old South, was provided by South Carolina clubwomen for whites only. Clubwomen were similar to their fellow southern progressive reformers in restricting welfare programs.[33] Yet, in combination with their espousal of the Lost Cause and because their efforts often were centered on children and education, women made certain that the segregation statutes enacted by southern white men would stand through time by transmitting their understanding of race to the next generation. Few southern white clubwomen gave aid to blacks at this time. Moreover South Carolina clubwomen may have been more reluctant than clubwomen in the Upper South to engage in interracial work because of the state's majority black population and history of race relations.[34]

References throughout the *Keystone*, federation yearbooks, correspondence, and reports indicate that the SCFWC consciously chose to exclude blacks from social welfare benefits. For example, in 1918, Louisa Poppenheim, as chair of the Committee on Matrons in the Police Station and County Jail, enlisted the aid of state senator Niels Christensen, who reported to Poppenheim that there had been approximately fifteen hundred female prisoners in the past year, one third of whom were white. Armed with this information, Poppenheim requested the cooperation of the federation in securing matrons "for these 500 white women prisoners."[35] Although aware of the plight of twice as many black female prisoners, she chose to extend aid to whites only.[36]

Moreover at other times, some white women were willing to sacrifice improvements for whites if blacks would share in them. One of the primary interests of the Castalian Club of Rock Hill, for example, was forming a public library. However these clubwomen refused to attempt to bring a Carnegie Library to Rock Hill "when it was brought out that by a ruling of the Carnegie Foundation, Negroes as well as whites would have access to it."[37] In thinking about race, then, it is important to consider that members of the SCFWC refused to aid blacks at considerable risk to the improvement of social and economic conditions of the state as a whole. Despite their desire to ignore African Americans in their community, on occasion the clubwomen felt obligated to extend services to blacks. The few times that white South Carolina clubwomen chose to assist blacks, however, were in cases where it appeared that such assistance was necessary in order to save whites. For example, when clubwomen nationally promoted aid for tuberculosis victims, the Poppenheims advocated such work in the South because "TB germs are easily transmitted from gentle black mammies to white babies, and so the protection of the black nurse may save its white charge."[38]

Their reluctance to aid blacks was perhaps based on their fear that black access to education and opportunity following emancipation would enable blacks to eclipse poor whites in economic prosperity and political power. For example, some women feared that black children would attend school while poor white children had to work in the mills.[39] Sarah Visanska reminded the federation of these concerns, claiming, "On the site of the old plantation, with its swarm of happy, child-like, improvident negro slaves, rises the modern factory with its village of pale, oft-neglected [white] children."[40] Visanska's rhetoric indicates that although fear of black progress at the expense of whites at times handicapped reformers, as with the Castalian Club's library work, it could also motivate clubwomen to work for child-labor laws and education reform for white children.

Although southern white clubwomen most often attempted to ignore the needs of African Americans in their community, when they did acknowledge the presence of blacks, they commonly referred to images of happy and loyal slaves. This reinforced the justness of the Confederate cause, which fought to retain slavery, emphasized black dependence on whites, and united white southerners in a common past, promoting a white southern identity. Clubwomen published book reviews and short stories in the *Keystone*, and they regulated history and literature in the schools and in libraries in order to disseminate their version of the history of slavery. In only one of many examples, in her review of *A Carolina Cavalier* by George Eggelston, Louisa Poppenheim praised his representation of African Americans, claiming that the character "Marlborough is the real Southern Negro, who knows of no greater distinction than to be the servant of his master."[41] Through the *Keystone,* the Poppenheims promoted a conscious bond among white southern women, trying, for example, to stimulate an interest in southern culture by printing such articles as "The Story of the Confederate Flag."[42]

Locally clubs read the *Clansman* and the *Leopard's Spots* and studied the life of author Thomas Dixon. Their minutes reveal support of the Klan in many forms, such as, when in 1914, the Amelia Pride Club was pleased to have Mrs. Hutchison, a charter member, display items worn by her father-in-law while he was a member of the Ku Klux Klan.[43] Similarly, although the promotion of libraries was one of the major social welfare efforts undertaken by clubwomen throughout the nation, southern clubwomen used libraries to promote southern identity. The Poppenheims printed a list, approved by the UDC, in the *Keystone,* advising southern clubwomen about appropriate books for donation. The SCFWC also called for a special topical traveling library on southern history and literature.[44] This focus on southern history, literature, and culture, although seemingly peripheral to clubwomen's social welfare agenda, was critical to fostering their notion of white southern identity. By promoting a positive image of slavery and the Klan, and by excluding blacks from social welfare and economic prosperity in the New South, members of the SCFWC undergirded segregation. Significantly South Carolina voted in its new constitution, which was intended to disfranchise African Americans, only three years before the SCFWC was founded, and the state, along with cities including Charleston and Columbia, continuously passed segregation statutes, regulating everything from street cars to mill entrances and exits, during the first twenty years of the federation's existence.[45]

African American clubwomen in South Carolina, however, fought both the Lost Cause version of history and the New South creed promoted by white clubwomen. Not only did they emphasize black history and literature, they also sought to share in the prosperity of the New South by instituting their own program of social welfare and attempting to extract from the state some of the same benefits extended to white citizens. For these black women, however, motivation for reform came not from a pride in the past but rather from strategies for race uplift, which included promoting manners, morals, and "respectability." Led by Marion Wilkinson, black clubwomen unsuccessfully asked the state to take over the girls' home started by members of the South Carolina Federation of Colored Women's Clubs (SCFCWC). However the home survived because clubwomen believed passionately in the need for an "enlightening influence" for the individual girls concerned, as well as for the benefit of race progress in general. That is, as part of their strategy of emphasizing the home and virtue in order to uplift the race, they sought to protect the most vulnerable class in South Carolina: young, homeless, indigent black girls.

In 1909 Wilkinson, Sara B. Henderson, and L. A. J. Moorer, all of Orangeburg, Celia Dial Saxon of Columbia, Susie Butler of Charleston, and others founded the SCFCWC at Sidney Park Church in Columbia. In a speech given to the National Association of Colored Women (NACW) in 1962, Mrs. Emily Albertha Johnston Murray recalled the founding of the SCFCWC, which she attributed to the need for organized racial uplift work.

"We felt the need of united and systematic effort and hop[ed] to furnish evidence of moral, mental, and material progress made by our people," said Murray. She then delineated the purposes of the federation, which primarily concerned women, children, and the home. The first purpose concentrated on black women's own self-improvement: "to promote education of colored women and to hold our education convention annually." The next three goals encompassed children and the home: "to raise the standards of the home; to work for social, moral, economic and religious welfare of mother and children; and to protect the rights of women and children who work." Finally the federation worked also for the race as a whole, hoping both "to secure and enforce civic and political rights for our group" and "to promote interracial understanding so that justice and good may prevail among all people."[46]

In the early years of the federation, clubwomen concentrated in part on improving rural schools in nearby communities. Like white clubwomen, black women in the state emphasized industrial training. For example, they advocated teaching cooking, sewing, personal cleanliness, and hygienic conditions in the home. Unlike white women, however, they hoped that these skills, taught alongside general education, would erase negative stereotypes of blacks and allow them to partake in New South prosperity.[47]

In South Carolina the emphasis on industrial training was due, in part, to Marion Wilkinson, whose husband, Robert, was president of South Carolina State College, a school that serviced black agricultural workers and teachers predominately. Robert Wilkinson worked to establish a vigorous agricultural extension program at the college, which reached farmers throughout the state. As president of the college and an influential leader of African Americans in the state, he tried to balance academic and industrial training. Wilkinson praised the increase in interest in "scientific training in agriculture, mechanics, and home economics," while at the same time noting that "the Negro Land Grant Colleges are being rapidly equipped and operated so as to give as much 'Liberal Education' as possible along with vocational training and specialized teaching. Culture and refinement are not being overlooked."[48] Like her husband, Marion Wilkinson also stressed teaching practical skills along with exposing children to culture and the arts. For example, she headed the Domestic Science Department of the NACW, but she also promoted a federation scholarship fund that would send a girl to Atlanta University, one of the few black southern schools that offered a liberal arts education.⁴⁹ The Wilkinsons' approach to education reveals a practical, if limited agenda: African Americans in South Carolina were largely excluded from mill jobs or skilled labor positions; therefore the Wilkinsons stressed those subjects that would give practical training in the most likely areas of employment, agriculture, and domestic service. At the same time, through art, literature, and other cultural events, the couple hoped to expose blacks to "the finer things" in life and encourage achievement. Moreover they believed that such training would uplift the race through eliminating accusations of inferiority.

In addition to education, the Fairwold Home for Delinquent Girls was the most significant reform project tackled by the SCFCWC. From 1917 to 1989, the SCFCWC spent significant amounts of time and money on this home for delinquent, later underprivileged, and eventually abused African American girls. Fairwold was such an important project for the federation, in fact, that many clubs were founded for the explicit purpose of aiding Fairwold. Some clubwomen even attributed the origins of the state federation itself to Fairwold, although it was founded several years before World War I, which is generally recognized as the impetus for the home.⁵⁰

During World War I, the government stationed military troops in Columbia. The presence of soldiers resulted in an increased number of arrests of young, and especially homeless, black girls for prostitution and other crimes. In order to aid those girls who, according to black clubwomen, had fallen victim to the dangers posed by the military presence, the federation decided to open a home for delinquent girls. They raised thirty thousand dollars to purchase an old farmhouse located near the railroad station in Fairwold (outside of Columbia). Originally named the Fairwold Home for Delinquent Girls, young black homeless girls found guilty of misdemeanor crimes were sent to the home instead of to jail. Despite the preponderance of judges who regularly sent girls to the home, in one incident, two girls sentenced to the reformatory were resentenced to the penitentiary because the home was not officially a "state reformatory."⁵¹

Decrying the fact that the state supported homes for black boys and white boys and girls—but not black girls—clubwomen, the sole financial supporters of Fairwold, appealed to the state for funding. In order to approach the legislature with more power, clubwomen realized that they needed to gain the support of prominent whites. In one of the only instances of cooperation in the first decades of their coexistence, black clubwomen turned to white clubwomen for aid, but they received only nominal support.[52] Instead, a committee of prominent whites and blacks, led by white Episcopal bishop Kirkland G. Finlay, approached the legislature and secured a two-thousand-dollar appropriation for Fairwold. In 1925 the committee asked the state to continue the appropriation and unsuccessfully lobbied for an official reformatory to be created by the state.[53]

Later that year, a fire destroyed the home, forcing the federation to return to the legislature for additional funding.[54] James C. Dozier, executive secretary of the state board of public welfare, supported the request, although he reasoned that a reformatory was necessary because "this class of Negro girls is a menace to her community and to the state at large."[55] African Americans hoped to appeal to the state for funding by arguing that white girls, as well as black and white boys had state-supported reformatories, and black girls deserved no less. A stirring editorial was published in the *Palmetto Leader,* a black newspaper in Columbia, demanding of state legislators, "Why have you neglected [colored girls]? Do you not think it more important to care for such girls [as opposed to boys]? Can not your Christian duty point the way? Are you contented to put the dollar against humanity? Do you take the position that colored girls of that kind are not worth caring for?"[56] Despite their reluctance to fund the home, the assembly finally approved an appropriation, which Governor Richards then vetoed, because, he argued, it was illegal to make a donation to a private institution, while neglecting to note the fact that there was no public institution of its kind.[57] The state legislature, therefore, refused to build a state-supported reformatory for black girls and only funded Fairwold for two years. Clubwomen persevered, however, and raised more than twelve thousand dollars to build a new home on land donated by the white Episcopal church.[58]

Once built, the operation of the home required constant fund-raising. Despite the generosity and inventiveness of club fund-raising, the lack of funding was such a problem for the SCFCWC that they actually changed the mission of the home in order to obtain funding from the Duke Foundation. In 1932 they decided that the program should be centered around orphaned and economically underprivileged girls rather than wayward girls or the "morally delinquent." Clubwomen did not give up their concern for delinquents but succumbed to practical constraints. According to the *National Negro Digest,* when the federation originally appealed to the Duke Foundation for funds, they were rejected because the foundation did not give to delinquent homes, although it did give to orphanages. Clubwomen changed the focus, and the Duke Foundation began granting the home an annual stipend. This adaptation indicates the extreme measures that black clubwomen had to take in order to keep the home running because, despite repeated appeals to the legislature, the state provided little support. African American clubwomen took matters into their own hands to provide social welfare services when the state refused.

Clubwomen did not stop at shouldering much of the financial burden of Fairwold. Led by Marion Wilkinson, they were also integrally involved in the programming of the home, and they tried to ensure that the girls received good training, care, and affection. Girls were taught sewing, handicrafts, cooking, housecleaning, laundering, poultry-raising, gardening, and dairying at the home. They were also exposed to "culture" through poetry or music programs during the evenings or talks on various subjects from the housemother. They attended church and Sunday school, and despite their own status, the girls brought "some form of cheer to the sick or the aged of the community."[59]

The SCFCWC's intense dedication to the reformatory went far beyond rescuing the twenty or thirty girls who lived at Fairwold in any given year. Rather, Fairwold embodied the strategy of racial uplift espoused by clubwomen in South Carolina and the nation. Most black clubwomen emphasized morality, manners, and "respectability" because they hoped these would decrease the oppression of a race thought to be undeserving of respect. Rescuing delinquent girls and guiding them to an upright home life could lessen the stigma of immorality attached to black women. Mary McLeod Bethune, NACW president who was originally from South Carolina, espoused a philosophy of education for black girls that perhaps best expresses how the protection and education of girls were inextricably linked to the progress of the race. She stressed the need for girls to learn "good citizenship in the home." Bethune believed that by teaching a young black girl morals, cleanliness, and how to make a good home, she learned how to raise her family; in a home presided over by a good mother, family members could become better citizens.[60] Thus the home made the citizen, which in turn dictated the experience of the race. The SCFCWC stressed these ideals, when, at its 1911 convention, for example, topics included, "Child Study as a Preparation for Moral Uplift," "How to Safeguard Our Girls," and "The Mother, Daughter, and Social Purity."[61]

In their emphasis on respectability, southern black clubwomen differed slightly in degree from northern clubwomen. Clubwomen across the nation believed that African Americans needed to adopt certain values that would make them appear "respectable" to whites. Historian Evelyn Higginbotham contends that black churchwomen worked to achieve "middle-class" manners: sexual purity, hard work, frugality, temperance, punctuality, neatness, and piety.[62] Such a strategy inevitably led to conflicts between middle- and upper-class clubwomen and the poor blacks whom they intended to aid.[63] Higginbotham argues that this practice was at once conservative and radical, as African Americans, although they worked to adopt the norms of the dominant society, were at the same time able to "transcend oppression" by demanding group respect.[64] In other words, by claiming these values and the respect that they commanded, African Americans wrestled them from the monopolistic grip of the white middle class. At the same time, white reformers were able to define themselves as "white" in relation to the cultural values that they attempted to impose upon poor whites, but not on blacks. The very meaning of whiteness would be threatened if blacks were able to realize the same middle-class cultural norms that whites had appropriated, for their race only, regardless of class.

Black women who embraced this strategy of uplift sought to protect young girls in particular. The sexual morality of the race was in the hands of its women, and therefore clubwomen desired to teach girls morality and to protect those who might have been easy prey for men, both black and white, or crime.[65] While a problem throughout the nation, the vulnerability of black girls and women was intensified in the South, where white men continued to commit sexual assaults on black women long after slavery ended—a factor that, according to Darlene Clark Hine, contributed to the migration of black women out of the South.[66] Because of the lack of respect for black girls particularly evident there, this strategy of race uplift had a more profound meaning in the South. "Chivalry," both before and after the Civil War, ensured that elite white southern women would be recognized for their purity, beauty, and morality; at the same time they were assumed to need the protection of white men. This justified the separation of the races, and in extreme form, resulted in white men lynching black men under the guise of protecting the sexual purity of white womanhood from the mythical "black beast rapist." In other words, chivalry "masked" racism as the source of such violence. Black southern women who promoted respectability undermined white justification for oppression. Furthermore, respectable middle-class black clubwomen confounded white supremacists by their own manners, and their elite economic status belied the rationale for segregation based in the presumed degraded status of blacks.

South Carolina black women were perhaps exceptionally concerned with morality and young girls because of the state's white political leaders. For example, Ben Tillman asserted that most black women were without virtue, and argued against raising the age of consent from fourteen to sixteen because, he reasoned, black girls would seduce white boys and then white boys would be punished.[67] Tillman was later succeeded by Gov. Coleman Blease, who expressed similar sentiments, contending that "[t]he negro race has absolutely no standard of morality. . . . They are, in that separate class by themselves as marital infidelity seems to be their favorite pastime."[68] Their actions encouraged an attitude in South Carolina that left black girls unprotected and allowed the legislature to get away with establishing industrial schools for all children, except black girls.[69]

Black women in South Carolina took on many of the same social welfare projects as white women, such as education and establishing a reformatory. However, as is evident in the case of Fairwold, many of these projects had special meaning for black women because there was precious little other aid available to the community, and because clubwomen hoped to prove their respectability through improving the morality and behavior of the black community. In South Carolina, even as white clubwomen fostered segregation through their support for a New South economy and social welfare programs that benefited whites only, through their promotion of the Lost Cause and a white southern identity, black clubwomen challenged those assumptions that buttressed Jim Crow by attempting to claim state support for black girls—and respectability for the race.

NOTES

1. Anne Firor Scott, *The Southern Lady: From Pedestal to Politics, 1830–1930* (Chicago: University of Chicago Press, 1970), and *Natural Allies: Women's Associations in American History* (Urbana: University of Illinois Press, 1991).

2. This case study of South Carolina suggests further research on clubwomen and regional influence is necessary. I seek to add to Linda Gordon's work, which, by examining leaders primarily from the North, found significant differences in black and white visions of social welfare, such as universal versus means-tested programs. "Black and White Visions of Welfare: Women's Welfare Activism, 1890–1945," *Journal of American History* 78 (September 1991): 559–90.

3. New South advocates promoted industrialization. See Paul Gaston, *The New South Creed: A Study in Southern Mythmaking* (New York: Knopf, 1970).

4. David L. Carlton, *Mill and Town in South Carolina, 1880–1920* (Baton Rouge: Louisiana State University Press, 1982), 7, 133–34.

5. Louisa Poppenheim, "The Southern Woman in Club Life," March 1909, South Carolina Federation of Women's Clubs Collection (hereafter SCFWC), Dacus Library, Winthrop University, Rock Hill, South Carolina (Winthrop), Box 19, Folder 65.

6. Louisa Poppenheim, "Woman's Work in the South," in *The South in the Building of the Nation*, vol. 10 (Richmond: 1909), 637.

7. *Keystone*, March 1900, 9–10.

8. *Keystone*, June 1903, 4.

9. *Keystone*, February 1904, 9.

10. See Scott, *Natural Allies*, and Marsha Wedell, *Elite Women and the Reform Impulse in Memphis, 1875–1915* (Knoxville: University of Tennessee Press, 1991).

11. Although Wedell found that women did criticize New South spokesmen for their commercialism (*Elite Women*, 87), I did not find similar criticisms by South Carolina clubwomen, perhaps because of the role of the mills there.

12. James L. Leloudis, "School Reform in the New South: The Woman's Association for the Betterment of Public School Houses in North Carolina, 1902–1919," *Journal of American History* 69 (March 1983): 906–9.

13. Yearbook, 1921–22, 21, SCFWC, Winthrop.

14. See yearbooks of the SCFWC, Winthrop, throughout the 1920s.

15. *Keystone*, December 1902, 6.

16. In South Carolina, for example, per capital spending in 1894 for whites was $3.82, for blacks, $1.58; by 1921 white schools received $11.97 and black schools $1.23 per student. Francis B. Simkins, "Race Legislation in South Carolina Since 1865," *South Atlantic Quarterly* 20 (April 1921): 170–71.

17. *Keystone*, June 1903, 5.

18. *Keystone*, August 1904, 5.

19. See, for example, Mary Frances Wickcliffe, "Some Results from Manual and Industrial Training," Southern Educational Association, 1906, Asheville, North Carolina, 188–97.

20. *Keystone*, August 1904, 5.

21. Louisa Poppenheim, for example, came from a long line of planters, and her father was a successful merchant in Charleston.

22. *Keystone*, July 1904, 10.

23. See, for example, Leonora Beck Ellis, "Educating Southern Factory Children," *Gunton's* 24 (May 1903): 459–70.

24. *Charities* 17 (November 3, 1906): 195.

25. Book review of Booker T. Washington's *Future of the American Negro*, in *Keystone*, March 1900, 13.

26. *Keystone*, June 1899, 8.

27. Clubwomen also may have focused less on morality because they worked for a boys' reformatory first and more intensively. For girls, they focused on scholarships, again emphasizing education, not morality.

28. *Keystone*, October 1911, 3.

29. *Keystone*, April 1907, 3; December 1907, 3; and March 1908, 3.

30. Yearbook, 1924–25, SCFWC, Winthrop.

31. *Keystone,* January 1906, 3.

32. *Keystone,* March 1905, 12–13.

33. On southern Progressivism and segregation, see C. Vann Woodward, *Origins of the New South, 1877–1913* (Baton Rouge: Louisiana State University Press, 1951).

34. Most interracial cooperation came from the temperance movement, the YWCA, and the Methodist church, not women's clubs. Furthermore timing seems to have been crucial, as efforts in the temperance movement in North Carolina in the 1880s and 1890s ended when the new segregationist state constitution was passed, and did not resume until World War I and the passage of suffrage brought about women's involvement in the Commission on Interracial Cooperation in the 1920s. Even then, in South Carolina, clubwomen gave little support to the state CIC. Jacquelyn Hall shows just how difficult it was for white women to cross racial lines in *Revolt against Chivalry: Jesse Daniel Ames and the Women's Campaign against Lynching* (New York: Columbia University Press, 1979).

35. Charleston *News and Courier,* May 16, 1918.

36. Officials probably would have been less receptive to funding both white and black matrons.

37. Lillie Neely, "The History of the Castalian Club," n.d., (c. 1939), Castalian Club Papers, Winthrop (hereafter CCP, Winthrop), Box 1, Folder 1.

38. *Keystone,* March 1909, 3.

39. Irene Ashby, "Child-Labor in Southern Cotton Mills," *World's Work* 2 (October 1901): 1290–95; Elizabeth Davidson, *Child Labor Legislation in the Southern Textile States* (Chapel Hill: University of North Carolina Press, 1939), 23–25.

40. *Keystone,* June 1903, 4.

41. *Keystone,* May 1901, 12.

42. *Keystone,* March 1911, 14–15.

43. Minutes, June 9, June 23, and July 21, 1902, CCP, Winthrop, Box 1, Folder 2. Minutes, February 3, 1914, Amelia Pride Club Papers, Winthrop, Box 1, Folder 3.

44. *Keystone,* May 1903, 4.

45. Simkins, "Race Legislation," 170–77, and Theodore Hemmingway, "Beneath the Yoke of Bondage: A History of Black Folk in South Carolina, 1900–1940" (Ph.D. diss., University of South Carolina, 1976), 53–60.

46. Speech to the National Association of Colored Women (hereafter NACW) 1962, and Constitution, Albertha Murray Papers, Folder 6, Avery Institute for African American History and Culture, Charleston, South Carolina.

47. *National Notes,* April/May 1917.

48. Columbia, South Carolina, *Palmetto Leader,* 1.

49. Minutes, NACW, 1912, *Records of the National Association of Colored Women.*

50. Interview with Mrs. Casselberry, Orangeburg, South Carolina, March 1, 1996; Asa Gordon, *Sketches of Negro Life and History in South Carolina* (Columbia: University of South Carolina Press, 1929; 2d ed., 1971), 182.

51. *Palmetto Leader,* September 25, 1926.

52. The State Commission on Interracial Cooperation, in which South Carolina Episcopalians were prominent, while clubwomen were not, led the effort.

53. *Palmetto Leader*, February 7, 1925. While the committee included Mrs. L. H. Jennings, president of the SCFWC, the federation did little else to support the home.

54. See *Palmetto Leader*, 1924–30, passim; interview with Mrs. Geraldine Zimmerman, Orangeburg, South Carolina, October 9, 1995; and Etta B. Rowe, "The Fairwold Industrial School for Colored Girls," *National Notes*, March 1926, 11–12.

55. *Palmetto Leader*, December 19, 1925.

56. *Palmetto Leader*, January 15, 1927.

57. *Palmetto Leader*, April 30, 1927.

58. *National Negro Digest* 4 (1940): 28–29.

59. *National Negro Digest* 4 (1940): 28–29.

60. Mary McLeod Bethune, "A Philosophy of Education for Negro Girls," n.d. typescript, Mary McLeod Bethune Papers, Amistad Research Center, Tulane University, Folder 13.

61. *The Crisis* 2 (1911): 211.

62. Evelyn Brooks Higginbotham, *Righteous Discontent: The Women's Movement in the Black Baptist Church, 1880–1920* (Cambridge: Harvard University Press, 1993), 95–96.

63. Black clubwomen were "elite" and were defined in the black community by their education and by their marriage to professionals, educators, ministers, and businessmen, as well as by relative wealth. For a critique of race uplift based on class and gender limitations, see Kevin Gaines, *Uplifting the Race: Black Leadership, Politics, and Culture in the Twentieth Century* (Chapel Hill: University of North Carolina Press, 1996).

64. Higginbotham, *Righteous Discontent*, 96–97, and Darlene Clark Hine, "'We Specialize in the Wholly Impossible': The Philanthropic Work of Black Women," in *Lady Bountiful Revisited: Women, Philanthropy, and Power*, Kathleen McCarthy, ed. (New Brunswick: Rutgers University Press, 1990), 70–93.

65. Beverly Guy-Sheftall, *Daughters of Sorrow: Attitudes toward Black Women, 1880–1920* (Brooklyn: Carlsen, 1990), 55–57, 62–73.

66. *National Notes*, March 1899, and Darlene Clark Hine, "Rape and the Inner Lives of Black Women in the Middle West: Preliminary Thoughts on the Culture of Dissemblance," *Signs* 14 (Summer 1989): 292.

67. *The Crisis* 9 (January 1915): 141.

68. Quoted in Bryant Simon, "The Appeal of Cole Blease of South Carolina: Race, Class, and Sex in the New South," *Journal of Southern History* 62 (February 1996): 82–83.

69. Other southern black clubwomen also fought for girls' homes with varied success, Alabama not gaining state support while Virginia did. Cynthia Neverdon-Morton, *Afro-American Women of the South and the Advancement of the Race, 1895–1925* (Knoxville: University of Tennessee Press, 1989), 115–16, 137–38.

Disease, Disorder, and Motherhood

Working-Class Women, Social Welfare, and the Process of Urban Development in Atlanta

GEORGINA HICKEY

Addressing the annual meeting of Atlanta's Associated Charities in 1921, the Secretary of the State Board of Public Welfare Burr Blackburn concluded that "the fierce winds of family disintegration blow over this city without ceasing night and day. As we sit here they are crashing through hundreds of homes."[1] With this statement, Blackburn summed up much of the purpose of the Associated Charities and many other social welfare agencies operating in Atlanta in the early decades of the twentieth century. These agencies concerned themselves with shoring up families against the rapid pace of change in the city. The manner in which such organizations pursued this goal, however, reveals the complexity of debates surrounding urban development during this period and the central role working-class women played in this contested process.

At the turn of the century, Atlanta was a dynamic, vibrant New South city. Its population boomed, while the economy expanded well beyond the railroads that had dominated the city up until that point. The city annexed surrounding areas at a fantastic pace, and new migrants swelled Atlanta's population. While most residents viewed this growth as positive, competing visions appeared over the shape this growth was to take. Who was to control Atlanta's future? How would new migrants and industries be incorporated into a stable urban social structure? One of the strongest voices to emerge in these debates was that of Atlanta's burgeoning social welfare network. In particular these agencies strove to promote the use of city resources in protecting women's rights and public health and safety, to reinforce gender roles in which women's primary duty to family and community was motherhood, and to legitimize the authority of private welfare organizations over the poor and sick of the city.

This essay focuses on the development of the city's charity, welfare, and public health organizations. While all these relief and assistance-oriented organizations focused generally on the working-class communities of Atlanta, most also chose to address these communities through interactions with the poor and working women of the city. Thus, these agencies were largely responsible for creating many of the dominant cultural symbols of Atlanta in the early twentieth century; images that focused on the city's working-class women. While the visibility of working-class women extended across the cultural and social landscape of the city, it was perhaps most apparent in Atlanta's social welfare network.

The images that these agencies promoted, as well as their programs, emphasized the dual nature of the ideology attached to working-class women—as the best hope and the worst danger to the city. These images reinforced gender, racial, and class hierarchies in which white women functioned primarily as mothers and black women were primarily workers. A competing narrative that imaged African American women as mothers, however, did emerge from black civic and welfare agencies. Ultimately the various images and policies produced by these organizations demonstrate the highly gendered and racialized terrain of the city during the early decades of the twentieth century. They also illuminate some of the city's anxieties about a stable social order by reinforcing and reinventing family structures in the changing urban environment.

While little has been published on the social welfare agencies of Atlanta, much has been written on the field of social welfare in general. The origins of welfare history lay in its policy needs and professional movements so, not surprisingly, the field tends to focus on the factors that shaped policy development.[2] In the last several decades welfare history has become a window for examining the lives of the poor, immigrants, racial minorities, and women.[3] A parallel push toward the theorization of welfare history as policy of the state has also appeared in recent years.[4] What remains undertheorized, and is the focus of this essay, are the ways in which welfare history, with its rich case studies and organizational records, can be read as a "weather vane" for urban development.[5] The stories and debates that fill the records of Atlanta's welfare agencies reveal the problems of the city as perceived by both middle-class social workers and poor clients, the power struggles of the era, and the ways in which urban residents defined both themselves and the city.

Gender Roles and Moral Order

Prior to 1900 Atlanta hosted only a few charity organizations that dealt specifically or significantly with working-class women. These included the Home for the Friendless, the Florence Crittenton Home, and Grady Hospital. The groundwork laid by these organizations and their programs to aid working and poor women were expanded and incorporated in the network of agencies that blossomed in the early decades of the twentieth century. The rapid growth of Atlanta's female population, economic pressures that made finding consistent wage labor difficult for both men and women, and the lack of kinship structures for many recent migrants all contributed to the focus of early welfare organizations on poor women being adopted by the network of agencies that spread across the city after the turn of the century.

The range of organizations that appeared had a widespread impact on the lives of poor women, influencing everything from their living situations and family structures to diet and health care. Many of the white-run organizations shared case files and resources, but more than that, they shared a vision of welfare that brought poor white women to the forefront as mothers caring for families. Within this philosophy, women became prospects for aid by virtue of their position as primary caregivers for children. These mothers also represented the best hope for stabilizing family structures in the rapidly changing urban environment. Supporting a woman in her role of mother allowed welfare agencies to maintain gender roles and family structures in the face of rapid urbanization, keeping children at home under the supervision of a female parent and keeping men working as the family breadwinner.

The Associated Charities, a progressive, citywide organization, for example, relied heavily on images of motherhood. The images of white women recorded in organizational case studies tended to portray the fine line between danger and protection that mothers represented at the turn of the century. A mother who was honest, moral, and worked hard could ensure the future of her family. A woman who did not embody these qualities could easily destroy her family. While many cases of the latter type were discussed at board meetings and among social workers, it was usually only the more positive images of women struggling to keep their families together that appeared in annual reports and newspaper articles produced by the organizations.

As was common in the publicity of the Associated Charities, the annual report for 1910 alternately described women as, "honest and industrious," or "industrious and a good mother."[6] The women who did not fit this positive description functioned outside the role of motherhood. In many cases negative images were applied to women who surrendered their children to the care of others, exploited their children by allowing them to beg or work for wages, or neglected their children because of alcoholism and other vices.[7] Also reinforcing the controlling and stabilizing effects of motherhood as a primary role for urban working-class white women was the portrayal of single women as potential infectors of men with the "diseases of the street."[8] In these notions of danger, the lines blurred between "women adrift" and mothers who did not meet middle-class standards of respectability or ideas about gender roles.

Throughout these case studies, social workers and reformers promoted the image of women as the key to a family's survival; men only appear peripherally in these stories. This may be due, in part, to the practice of case workers using the home as the site of intervention, evaluation, and assistance. Mothers then became the brokers through which welfare agencies reached other members of the family. Case histories emphasizing the key role women played in working-class families ranged from the deserted wife who, "with true mother instinct," worked to support her three tubercular children, to a woman who, with the help of the Associated Charities, moved her family to a farm that she worked single-handedly in order to care for a sick husband and two children.[9] This focus on mothers and the home reveals social workers' consistent belief that stable families held the key to moral order in the midst of urban growth.

Whether or not a husband or father was present, the pictures painted by these social welfare agencies emphasized women in their role as mothers, even though this role often did include wage work, as the last bulwark between respectable poverty and absolute destitution and immorality.[10] Consequently most of the charity and assistance agencies in Atlanta were quite active in training women and securing employment for them. One white woman, with a sick husband and no income, was loaned a small sum of money to buy supplies so she could take in washing, a job that would allow her to care for her husband while earning money. In recording this woman's case history, the Associated Charities social worker noted, "Her husband finally died, but the wife paid back the forty dollars."[11] Since many of Atlanta's social workers hoped to prod poor women into adopting a strong work ethic, which would encourage them to sacrifice for their children, this woman was praised for repaying the money she had borrowed. Typical of welfare agency policy, she was encouraged to support her family through a gender-specific occupation, such as laundry work, which would reify gender roles in a city where women, a growing number of whom were married, increasingly worked for wages. In some instances, however, this support of women's employment crossed the line of helpfulness into coercion. In cases where single mothers were reluctant or unwilling to work, agencies often removed the children from the home until the women would work steadily in agency-approved occupations and support their families without assistance.[12]

Social workers encouraged "respectable" poverty by pushing the needy, especially women, into wage work. In seeking to remove women from the relief rolls of the city, social workers sought to support women in searching and training for work. The types of wage work encouraged by these agencies is very telling. The few black women with which white welfare organizations dealt were, without exception, fitted with domestic work, either in the homes of whites or as laundry workers. White women were also encouraged and placed in these professions. The Martha's Home, which housed reforming prostitutes and women on probation, regularly received and fulfilled requests by middle-class families for white servants. The settlement houses and some of the churches of the city taught women sewing in hopes of outfitting them to work as seamstresses, an occupation that would allow them to remain in their homes and care for their children.

The dealings of visiting social workers with poor women rewarded evidence of respectability while punishing those who they felt were too ostentatious in their living conditions, dress, or actions. Rarely defined outright, social workers expected poor white women to dedicate themselves to the maintenance of their families without resorting to begging, prostitution, or other illicit behavior. Day-nursery workers, for example, investigated all mothers who requested child care through an "interview with the mother at the nursery, a visit to the home . . . and consultation with other agencies knowing [whether] the family is desirable." These workers hoped to offer "the constructive service which the poor may properly expect" after determining the "true" reason why the mother could not care for the children herself.[13] Social workers took great pride in finding that families with whom they had worked were self-maintaining. One teacher from an industrial school that worked with mill girls reflected, "After eight years of constant labor in these schools I began to see improvement. Many of the girls, now grown up, are making their living sewing, some have married and are sewing for their own little family. Many have come in to the church and Sunday school, and are living good and useful lives."[14]

Beyond promoting narrowly defined gender roles for working-class women, the relationship of poor women to the social welfare network in Atlanta also reinforced social and economic class relations. As new, and usually poor, migrants poured into the city after the turn of the century, social distance between classes was in part maintained by the work of social welfare agencies in the working-class neighborhoods of the city. The predominance of private agencies that relied heavily on volunteers from the city's middle class and the invocation of "civic duty" as a reason to aid the poor reinforced class lines that divided the city. Both the growing middle class and the organized labor community in Atlanta were encouraged to contribute to welfare work. By invoking a sense of duty, however, these groups were presumed safe from the forces that brought the destitute to their state of poverty.[15]

The distance social workers enforced between themselves and their clients was often most evident in the language of pity and contempt they employed in their case studies. Applicants were frequently described as "lazy," "heart broken," and "feeble-minded."[16] A Wesley House worker considered her clients "ignorant of the details of any life different from their own, unacquainted with the usual comforts and pleasures that may belong to any one and above all they were contented to live in filth, endure ill-health and suffered for a wholesome, social and spiritual expression."[17] Social workers' sympathy and desire to assist the impoverished of the city was embedded in language that reinforced Atlanta's socioeconomic class divisions.

The language and actions of the welfare network in many cases reinforced social relations, which were clearly delineated along racial lines, revealing much of the shape of Atlanta's racial order in the early twentieth century. For the most part, Atlanta's white-run welfare agencies were willing to leave the aid of African Americans to the city warden's office or organizations in the black community. The one exception to this trend came in the field of public health. The majority of relief distributed to black residents by white social workers in Atlanta before World War I was handled by the Anti-Tuberculosis Association through medical clinics and visiting nurse programs. The Atlanta Anti-Tuberculosis Association, like most white-run welfare agencies in the city, emphasized assistance to poor and working African American women in their role as domestic workers. The organization often espoused a democratized language of equality that stressed the dire need of blacks as well as whites for health care and relief. Contradicting these ideals, however, the work of the Anti-Tuberculosis Association also contributed to generalized fears many whites held of black women as agents of contagion. Case histories kept by Secretary Rosa Lowe and the agency's visiting nurses reveal a prevalent conception of washerwomen as dangerous and ignorant. Atlantan Minnie Freeman, for example, suffered from tuberculosis for two years before her death at age twenty-two. Her mother scrubbed both Minnie's clothes and bedding and white families' washings in the same tubs. In describing this case the visiting nurse noted with certain disgust, "She should have been placed in a hospital, where she would not have been a menace to others."[18]

In order to solicit funds, the Anti-Tuberculosis Association often played on whites' fear of infection, represented in the figure of the domestic worker. In 1909 the organization included in their plea for financial support the story of a young black woman, releasing her story to the newspapers and emphasizing that "she had up until a week past been in the daily service of a white family, cleaning the house, waiting on the table, nursing the children."[19] Another published meeting report from 1909 brought out the opinion of the association's visiting nurses that, "If the environments of many of the servants, washerwomen and a large majority of the negroes were known to their employers they would be aroused to action, and before employing a servant would investigate the location of the home, the inmates, etc."[20]

Rarely do these documents produced by white-run welfare agencies highlight any other aspect of African American women's lives besides their work as domestics for the city's white residents. Black benevolent and civic organizations of the city, however, promoted competing images of these poor women as mothers. The descriptions that appear in the records of these organizations are remarkably similar at times in tone, language, and content to the descriptions of white mothers created by the white social workers. Both white welfare agencies and black organizations reinforced a specifically gendered social order through the promotion of the role of motherhood while maintaining distinctions in class between reformers and clients. The images produced by black agencies, however, also promoted ideologies of racial uplift and respectability among many in Atlanta's African American population.

The most active organization in Atlanta's black communities that promoted poor black women in their role as mothers was the Neighborhood Union. Even the story of the founding of this group in 1908 used the image of women as the caretakers of the family to justify the necessity of the organization. This often-invoked story focused on a woman whom neighbors often saw but did not know. After a several-day absence from her porch, where she was usually seen sitting in the afternoon, neighbors went to investigate. They found her critically ill, too late to do anything for her, and she died shortly thereafter, leaving three children. Upon hearing this story, Lugenia Burns Hope called together other elite black women in the neighborhood to form an organization to "build the sort of ethnic pride that would take delight in constructive citizenship and happy family life" and would not allow neighbors to become terminally ill without anyone noticing.[21]

The range of programs this community organization hosted included mother's meetings, free clinics, recreational activities, and classes in nursing, home hygiene, sewing, and cooking.[22] Neighborhood Union organizers sought to "elevate the moral, social, intellectual, and spiritual standards of each neighborhood" as a means of both improving the community in which these women lived and earning the cooperation and respect of white communities.[23] Just as poor white women were understood to be the key to family survival by white relief agencies, the Neighborhood Union emphasized black working-class women as critical to community improvement in African American neighborhoods. Neighborhood Union workers hoped to rally the forces of "purity, virility and aspiration of the home" against the "problems of disease, vice, crime and inefficiency, if the Negro race is ever to solve its own problems."[24] Consequently most of the organizations' efforts were directed toward the caretakers of these homes, African American mothers. Programs encouraged cleanliness, efficiency, and morality, which it was hoped would be values that mothers would pass on to their children. Understanding that "the parents of these children are poor but hard working people—[standing] over the wash tub all day and the ironing board most of the night," the Neighborhood Union also offered material relief and child care to weary mothers.[25]

This approach, which took women's wage work for granted and promoted motherhood as African American women's primary role, also spilled over into the organization's dealings with the children of the neighborhood.[26] The Neighborhood Union "endeavored also to train the children to be little helpers in their own homes and the mothers how to make homes. This is done through our little housekeepers' clubs, little mothers' leagues, and other clubs."[27] While the black neighborhoods of the city, especially those surrounding Atlanta's black colleges, were more socioeconomically mixed than the white areas of the city, the language of class distinction also appears in records of the Neighborhood Union as the diminutive descriptions of work with children mixed with descriptions of programs for poor adult mothers.

Ideals of motherhood were even incorporated into a favorite fundraising event of the Neighborhood Union, the carnival. The homes of working-class women were opened up to the community in order to display proper housework techniques, wholesome entertainments, and appropriate play. The event required an entire block to open their homes for each other and the whole community to evaluate, institutionalizing the kind of observant neighborliness the union practiced and encouraged on a daily basis. In the Neighborhood Union's carnivals, middle-class black standards were being demonstrated to the rest of the community. What these carnivals provided, then, rather than an opportunity for disobedience without repercussions, was a space for poor women to temporarily erase class lines and take on a kind of middle-class respectability. In most cases the Neighborhood Union provided appropriate furniture for the homes and clothing for the women on display, as well as assistance in cleaning and organizing for which many working-class women would not regularly have had time. In one extraordinary case, a poor woman who desperately wanted to participate in the carnival was "loaned" the husband of a Neighborhood Union organizer. The woman could then open her home as a "health house" because her "husband" was a dentist.[28]

In promoting working-class black women as mothers, Neighborhood Union organizers not only created a competing narrative to that promoted by the primarily white social welfare and public health movements, they also furthered their own vision of social order for the black community. This vision included a strong sense of mutual cooperation among a community of moral and law-abiding families. Motherhood, consequently, meant not only caring for one's own family. The Neighborhood Union encouraged a kind of community mothering, accepting that most parents worked for wages, the entire neighborhood took responsibility for all the children and made the neighborhood safe in the way a mother would make a home safe.

The activities of welfare organizations, whether black or white, provided both opportunities and restrictions in the daily lives of the working-class and poor women they served. In part these women were empowered by their relationships with social workers and visiting nurses because social welfare agencies used them as an entrée to the laboring and poor classes of the city. Dealings with social workers often inadvertently supported poor women who sought to maintain family integrity, to take pride in their work, or otherwise to define themselves and their place in the city. Organizational records, however, show that poor women were rarely passive clients for charity workers. Poor women used the attention focused on them to create a space in which to bargain for care and support that most closely met their own values, needs, and conceptions of the city.

Throughout the case studies and personal letters of Atlanta's welfare organizations, social workers and reformers complained of the incessant demands women made on their organizations. These stories of women who asserted themselves into the relief process rarely appeared in the annual reports or newspaper accounts of social welfare work in the city. These women undermined the image of professionalism and authority created by the social welfare organizations because they refused to defer to social workers on issues related to home, work, family, or health. In typically frustrated language, one social worker concluded that her client on that day had been particularly "stubborn and felt that rather than do something she didn't want to do it was the duty of the public to supplement her wages to meet family expenses."[29]

Demands for aid ranged from requests for specific jobs to new housing. A woman who came to the Associated Charities in 1921 requested that the organization find her a rental home in which she could take in washing, sell lunches and drinks to railroad men, as well as be near her friends.[30] One of the most successful means clients had for attaining desired relief was playing agencies off one another. Social welfare agencies complained relentlessly over this practice, but the poor still found it a useful way of meeting their needs. Georgia Moore requested aid from both the Associated Charities and the North Avenue Presbyterian Church on the same day. She told each organization that the other had refused her aid and that "[s]he did not have anything at the house to eat." Even though the organizations discovered her duplicity, the Associated Charities still issued her a grocery order in the amount of $2.50.[31] The Associated Charities, like most welfare organizations, found contrary clients to be an almost constant presence on their relief rolls. The agency understood that "a few of them do not come to us anymore because we will not aid them in the way they *wish* to be aided."[32] Interestingly there seems to have been little variation in the techniques used by poor women across racial lines—black and white women alike were vocal and active in defining their own needs. Whatever strategy women employed, it appears that few of them were docile vessels for the lessons and lifestyles advocated by Atlanta's social workers.

While most of the demands of women involved material support in the form of food, shelter, or medical treatment, working-class women could also be quite vocal in their desire to maintain dignity and respectability or to defend their families. In Atlanta's mill villages, for example, women were often reluctant to send their children to the day nursery, fearing it "was only a trick to get their children away from them and give them away or put them in homes."[33] When advising a group of church women regarding Anti-Tuberculosis Association clients they might visit, Secretary Rosa Lowe cautioned that one client in particular, Mrs. LeRoy, was "very sensitive, and if the ladies visit her it will be necessary to bear that in mind and not allow her to know that her name was suggested by this office." Apparently Mrs. LeRoy was "very proud and wants to pay for everything that she gets."[34] When the Associated Charities received a report that Mrs. Jennie Binder was in need, a social worker was sent to her home. That visitor reported, Binder "seemed outraged at my visit, and said to please tell . . . anyone else interested she was not in need, and did not care for a visitor of the Associated Charities to be coming to her house."[35] In these ways, many working-class women of both races were able to articulate a different understanding of respectability from that endorsed by middle-class social workers.

In the eyes of Atlanta's social welfare agencies, poor and working-class women represented a means through which they could promote ideas about urban development. Social workers used images of these women to promote both the work of these relatively new agencies and reinforce a gendered and often racialized script in which motherhood took precedence over all other identities for poor women. Both positive images of women as the best hope for their families and negative images in which women who did not adhere to the script posed danger to the community, reinforced this message. As many of the clients of the welfare agencies proved, however, poor women often defined themselves and prioritized their needs differently than the middle-class social workers. Read in their broadest context, these competing images and ideas surrounding welfare in the city hint at the complexity of debates over the development of the city. While working-class women struggled to thrive as women, workers, mothers, and wives in the city, the welfare organizations struggled to define their territory within Atlanta's power structures.

Authority of Social Welfare

Social welfare organizations, functioning without official municipal support until the 1920s, successfully established themselves as the experts in the realm of working-class families and neighborhoods during the early decades of the twentieth century.[36] Through this unique position, social workers were able to contribute to many of the larger questions plaguing Atlanta in the early years of the twentieth century. Issues related to new uses of urban space and a changing occupational structure in which women increasingly worked for wages became the special purview of welfare agencies. Perhaps more important to the network of agencies, however, was the shifting structure of social work in which there were increasing tensions between public and private relief and a definitive move toward establishing the authority of private welfare agencies in Atlanta.

Some of the earliest progressive reforms in the realm of social work in Atlanta were embodied in this move toward professionalization. Later reforms, in the mid-1920s, would include a reorganization and centralization of the social welfare network. For Atlanta's social workers, the rise of professionalism meant standardization, authority-building, and new forms of intense training. Case histories and record-keeping in general were centralized and transferred to forms. The lengthy, impressionistic descriptions that had characterized clients' records in the early decades of the twentieth century were replaced with a standardized language of scientific diagnosis. Social workers began to rely on standardized "mental tests" to judge the intelligence, emotionality, and memory of clients.[37] Volunteers were purged from the organizations, which led this movement toward professionalization as requirements for necessary training were raised.[38] And benevolent organizations, like the Wesley Settlement House, left the field of welfare work entirely.[39]

Many welfare organizations' attempts to control access to the poor and create a script of expertise and authority in dealing with the poor were aimed at controlling the work of benevolent organizations, particularly those run by local churches. Professional welfare agencies bristled at attempts by other organizations to work directly with the populations they considered clients. In one case, the Associated Charities upbraided a church group that had passed out Christmas baskets of food to poor families in a neighborhood the Associated Charities considered its territory. The Associated Charities insisted that the church group was trying to draw distinctions of worthy and unworthy poor between families who had already been evaluated and properly assisted—implying that only the staff of the Associated Charities was qualified to decide who should receive relief.[40]

The newspapers served as one of the most influential mediums through which social workers could articulate the new professionalism of the field. In this realm too, the stories of working-class women were used to convey messages proselytizing the harm of individual or untrained giving to the poor. Newspapers also allowed social workers to combat negative images of themselves as "officious meddlers," which began to appear in the media during this period.[41] The *Atlanta Journal* in 1915 gave the Associated Charities a weekly space in the paper to run a "Column for the Needy," in which the organization described select cases and explained the methods used to relieve them. The most popular script that appeared in these columns told the story of a woman begging on the street; she was given some change by a well-meaning resident only to spend it frivolously and then sink into even darker circumstances when the money was gone. The solution to this woman's problems was always provided by an "efficient" social worker who would locate the missing husband, contact the long-lost family, or place the children in an institution so the woman could go to work—all without a dime being directly passed into the hand of the beggar.[42]

In addition to regularly publishing the annual reports of social welfare organizations, the local newspapers also frequently printed letters to the editor that defended scientific social work. In 1920 a piece appeared in the *Atlanta Constitution* that decried the lack of hospital care and recommended that anyone in doubt of this fact visit an ill woman who had been turned away from every hospital in the city.[43] R. C. Dexter of the Associated Charities wrote an emphatic letter to the editor defending the work of his organization with the woman in question and denying that anyone could understand or assist her case without consulting his office.[44] This "technical and cultural gatekeeping," with its appearance of objective and rational expertise, which was so often demonstrated through the cases of poor women, was largely effective in elevating the Associated Charities to the foremost position in Atlanta's social welfare network by the 1920s and reinforcing the expertise of private welfare agencies on policy toward the poor.[45]

Similar trends of professionalization and expertise developed in the black community, though these organizations also found welfare issues served them well in promoting their goals for racial justice. The enlarged conception of motherhood developed by the Neighborhood Union and other African American institutions, for example, provided a justification for the role elite black women of Atlanta were claiming for themselves. By promoting the crucial role poor black women had to play in the community, Neighborhood Union organizers were elevating their own status within both the community and the city as well. Finally the imaging of African American working-class women as mothers played a central role in the "politics of respectability" asserted by black middle-class women as means of improving race relations in the city.[46]

African American organizers also used the poor women they imaged as mothers as a rallying point for women of their own class. By repeating the story of the founding of the Neighborhood Union over and over again, in which the story of a working-class mother played the central role, it became something of a mantra that called middle-class and elite women to the duty of serving their race. In the draft of a speech, Lugenia Burns Hope outlined the particular role she felt women fulfilled in the uplift of the race: "The prevention of crime—training and reformation of law breakers— who knows more about the beginning of crime than a mother—who can better train and reform than a woman. What does a father know about the need of play grounds and recreation centers—when he is away from the children all day—what does he care about child labor and the exploitations of women—so long as he is a successful business man. He is perfectly willing to make her do a man's work and pay her half his salary."[47] By emphasizing the need to teach the poorer women of the community how to care properly for their homes and families, the women of the Neighborhood Union were also establishing their own station and duty vis-à-vis both the working classes of their race as well as the men of their class.

The efforts of the Neighborhood Union organizers to create a virtuous working class in the black communities of Atlanta resembles historian Evelyn Brooks Higginbotham's description of black Baptist women. Higginbotham's analysis of middle-class women's moves toward establishing respectability illuminates the key role working-class women, promoted as competent and moral mothers, played in undermining the arguments of white supremacists while directly challenging the negative images of black women. Middle-class black women expressed their commitment to "self-respect, self-sufficiency, racial pride and solidarity, and a strong sense of noblesse oblige," by both living their lives as examples to the rest of the community and working to instill like values in others.[48] By living clean, moral, and temperate lives, these "race women" believed the black communities could contradict the stereotypes that maintained racial divisions in the South. With this understanding, the emphasis members of the Neighborhood Union placed on the manners and morals of poor black women in particular can be read as resistance similar to other more traditional forms of protest.[49] "By privileging respectability, and particularly the capacity and worthiness of poor, working-class black women for respect," these race women also promoted the ideals of self-esteem and self-determination.[50]

The organizers of the Neighborhood Union created and reinforced images of black women as mothers in contradiction to the dominant images of black women as domestic workers presented by primarily white social welfare and public health organizations. For middle-class black women, the issues at stake involved not only material relief to the poor but also community reform and the reorganization of race relations in the city. The issues at stake for white social workers and reformers, who relied heavily on the images of white women as mothers, were quite different. Professionalization of the field for white social workers in the 1910s and early 1920s was furthered by the policies and notions associated with female clients. In essence, then, this move toward professionalization fed the growing visibility of working-class women in the city and the authority of private welfare organizations by promoting solutions to poverty that directly involved Atlanta's poor women.

In promoting the professionalization of welfare work in Atlanta during the early years of the twentieth century, these agencies were also defining a unique place for themselves in the power structures of the city. Social welfare agencies and their workers successfully positioned themselves as the experts on the city's poor. From this position, welfare organizations on both sides of the racial divide sought to control what they perceived to be the negative effects of urbanization by lobbying the municipal government for the distribution of city resources in the areas of direct relief, public health, and material improvements for the "dangerous" neighborhoods where the laboring classes resided.

Public Resources

As the social welfare network grew in the decades following the turn of the century, it frequently turned to images of working-class and poor women. Through these images, social workers from private agencies sought to legitimize their control over the relationship between the city's poor and the municipal government. Social workers made their claims as experts on the needs of the city's poor in front of the state legislature, the county courts, and the city council. Atlanta sponsored only limited work with the needy through the city warden's office, the police department, and court system, and, in many cases, public officials appeared only too happy to turn over expert status and relief duties to private organizations, accepting wholesale both the problems and solutions offered by the social welfare network.

One of the few public offices dealing with Atlanta's poor, the city warden provided food and fuel to people who needed only basic economic assistance. This office worked closely with the private agencies of the city, often providing direct relief to clients recommended by the Associated Charities, the Neighborhood Union, and the Wesley House. These agencies, however, often became embroiled in territorial disputes with the city and its only official relief office. Attempting to protect their position as experts on the poor, the leadership of the Associated Charities consistently attacked the city warden.

The antagonism that existed between private welfare organizations in Atlanta and the city warden's office hinged, in part, on the issues of respectability and expertise. Early in its existence the Associated Charities stated its unwillingness to help those whom they felt were living beyond the means of their station like the young woman who "dressed better than her hard-working neighbors," or the family that "had ice cream every other day in the summer."[51] Insinuating that the city's relief officers underestimated the importance of their job and did not have the proper training, the Associated Charities critiqued the city warden for giving aid indiscriminately to all those who applied. They claimed that "material gifts alone, instead of helping others to help themselves, . . . have resulted in maintaining many people in misery of body and soul."[52] In 1922 the Associated Charities again attacked the city's efforts to aid the poor directly by helping a disgruntled client sue the warden's office. With the assistance of the Associated Charities, Hattie Harper accused the city warden of making sexual advances toward her, promising her relief money if she would be a "good sport."[53]

The relationship of the police department and local court system to Atlanta's welfare agencies was less antagonistic but no less important. In many ways, these public institutions often functioned as part of the larger network that aided and "rescued" women in Atlanta. Police commonly took women into custody, without formally arresting them, as a means of removing women from the street. They were then released to one of the private agencies in town, usually the Associated Charities, which would find them housing and work or return them to their families. This release was often contingent upon the women agreeing to fulfill the recommendations of the welfare agency, such as placing their children in the Home for the Friendless or seeking employment.[54]

Reflecting the latitude in the city's police and court system when dealing with women, the boundaries between public and private organizations often blurred. Women who were charged and appeared in recorder's court were often released to probation officers who worked for private organizations. Between 1913 and 1915, a private organization called the Men and Religion Forward Movement, hired a woman to act as probation officer for those white women released from the recorder's court. This woman kept track of probationers, often arranging living spaces and employment for them, as well as reporting legal and moral violations committed by the women while on probation. This probation work also included trips to the city stockade to visit women prisoners and aid to women whose husbands were imprisoned. In 1914 funds were raised to hire a black probation officer to perform essentially the same work with African American women arrested in the city.[55]

The work of probation officers with women who had not gone to court or even been arrested further blurred the lines between private welfare agencies and public institutions in the early twentieth century. Annie Bond, a witness in a federal case, was under the care of the probation officer who in turn placed Bond in the Martha's Home, a refuge for reforming prostitutes, which was also run by the Men and Religion Forward Movement.[56] Another young woman placed herself on probation. Once under the care of the home, the officer proclaimed Bond "quite a bad girl and must either reform or give her child away."[57] Women under the supervision of a privately funded probation officer were routinely reported to court officials for not carrying out the wishes of the probation officer. Elma Straine was reported for not attending a training program at Crenshaw Hospital, Lulu Bell Brown for lying about her age and running away from home, and Fannie Hicks for using cocaine.[58] Women who appeared in court usually represented middle-class fears of danger associated with women. When moral coercion was not enough, social workers could turn to the punitive measures at the courts' disposal. Primary among these was the power of judges to remove women's custody of their children.

This intimate relationship between the legal structures of the city and Atlanta's social welfare network continued even after 1915 when the city hired its first police matron, Mamie Heard, to oversee both the incarceration of white women prisoners and to function as a social worker. In her first four months on the job, Heard handled 537 cases, 130 of whom were found jobs, sent to institutions, or returned to their families.[59] By 1919 the city had hired two policewomen to "work with prostitutes, wayward girls and [keep] young girls off the streets and from being approached by the so-called 'JOHNNIES.'"[60] These policewomen also investigated cheap theaters, amusements, and boardinghouses that catered to young working-class women. That same year Eliza Baldwin was hired by the city to work with black women who had been arrested. While private agencies lost much of the direct interaction they had established with the city's police force, these new matrons continued welfare work among women in the legal system, serving as social workers as well as court officials and police officers until the early 1920s.

Throughout the early decades of the twentieth century, the Associated Charities and other private relief organizations also tried to usher women through the court systems of the city and county. Many of the women found by these agencies were abused and deserted. Social workers from the Associated Charities encouraged and helped secure divorces for women if it provided some social benefit, such as enabling a client to "remarry and better her economic condition," "marry the person she is living with," or give her "freedom in planning a life for herself and children which she is unable to do as long as [the] marital relationship exists."[61] In cases where the husband had deserted or contributed only irregularly to the family, the Associated Charities helped women sue their husbands in superior court for alimony. A slightly unusual case, but one that demonstrates the willingness of the agency to use the court system on behalf of women, involved a morphine-addicted husband and a destitute wife. According to the case worker, "The Associated Charities tried several plans to keep the family together, but finally ordered the man arrested for vagrancy."[62]

Also during the 1910s, the Associated Charities poured much effort into legislative campaigns, which drew on their expert standing in supporting the rights of working-class women in family relationships. For instance, the organization, in conjunction with other civic and state groups, fought to raise the age of consent for girls in Georgia above the age of ten.[63] The Associated Charities also supported the passage of a liberalized divorce code that would expand the grounds for granting divorce. Finally the "Wife Desertion Bill" of 1919 received the support of the board members who understood "the serious burden of deserting and non-supporting husbands on societies like ours and on the charitable people of Atlanta generally."[64]

Less focused on legal aid and legislative lobbying in order to meet their goals, the Neighborhood Union translated goals to raise the moral standards of African American communities in Atlanta into attempts to alter the physical state of these neighborhoods. These efforts relied on a combination of private and public support. In the 1910s the Neighborhood Union began annual "clean-up" campaigns, which soon became a citywide and publicly supported movement. In the black sections of town, efforts focused on removing rubbish from under and around homes, scrubbing floors, walls, and windows, and transporting sick residents to clinics and hospitals for treatment.[65] Similar to the demands of direct relief, much of the responsibility for this clean-up work fell to mothers. Women were pressured through this intense, week-long campaign every spring, as well as in the classes offered by the Neighborhood Union, to change their standards and practices of housekeeping, reinforcing the Neighborhood Union's long-standing belief that moral status could be judged by "the general external appearance of the several communities and their inhabitants."[66]

In trying to raise the moral standards of the community, Neighborhood Union workers were quick to attack women who refused to fit the model of morality promoted in their conceptualization of motherhood and neighborhood, and here again the agency placed demands on the city government to meet their goals. In the earliest records of the organization there appear requests made to the city council and the police department for the removal of specific women and families. The Neighborhood Union justified its actions by arguing, "We were not helping our neighbor when we failed to tell the mother of the evil company her daughter was keeping while she was away trying to make a living. Blind tigers, houses of ill repute, dance halls, and loud and disturbing gatherings are among the cases which come before the Union frequently." Members found support for these campaigns among municipal agencies, reporting, "The police department has backed us when we have called on them. They say they are glad to assist us in our efforts to have a clean community."[67]

By and large the efforts of Atlanta's private welfare organizations to establish their authority over the poor of the city were successful. During the early decades of the twentieth century, these agencies effectively used female clients and images of poor women to lobby for government resources and policies that adhered to the new professional standards of social work and local agencies' theories on poverty. The 1920s, however, would prove to be a time of transition as the city and state finally became more involved in the lives of their poor residents, and the focus of the city shifted away from moral order to politics and economics. The authority private Atlanta agencies had already established, however, meant that many of these new public institutions followed the lead set by the Associated Charities, Neighborhood Union, and other organizations.

Shifting Terrain of the 1920s and 1930s

For welfare workers, reformers, and public health nurses in early twentieth-century Atlanta, poor women proved to be a useful group on which to focus their efforts. As mothers and workers, the women themselves represented key positions in the city's racial and gender structures—structures that middle-class Atlantans perceived as endangered with the rapid expansion of the city during this period. By emphasizing these roles, then, white social workers shored up a social order in which women were dependents, integrated either into a family unit or a necessary employment situation. Black reformers, through their notions of respectability, also reinforced a particular gender structure in the African American community, which ordered not only relations between men and women but also those between classes and races. This private welfare network and its particular orientation was one response to the problems experienced by the city during these years. With the coming of the 1920s, however, these organizations shifted their focus to the plight of poor and sick children.

Sweeping histories of social welfare, like those by Michael Katz and William Trattner, point to the child-saving of the Progressive Era, but a narrower focus on this period reveals that concern for children was interwoven with other concerns for the poorer classes. In Atlanta a child-centered movement only reached ascendancy in the mid- to late 1920s.[68] Attendant to this shift was a move toward centralization of the private social welfare network of Atlanta and the development of new county and state agencies. The net result of these changes amounted to a dearth of support for the poor women of the city, where there once had been an abundance. Undoubtedly the reluctance of most female welfare recipients to conform to social workers' mandates encouraged social workers to focus their efforts elsewhere. As welfare agencies sought to continually prove themselves efficient and successful entities, children represented more pliable subjects who could be easily reached through schools instead of costly and time-consuming home visits.

As public welfare agencies in the state were organized in the 1920s, a definite split developed between public and private organizations. Private agencies leapt to the defense and reformation of children of "pathological" families, abandoning direct relief altogether except in extreme cases. Public agencies adopted both a focus on children and, as seasonal depressions struck in the late 1920s, a developing interest in temporary material relief for out-of-work men. As private and public organizations negotiated their distinct territories, working and poor women, who had been so crucial to the development of the social welfare network in Atlanta after the turn of the century, fell through cracks in the network with virtually all relief being channeled to children.

The meaning for women of this changing focus of social welfare organizations in the 1920s was somewhat contradictory. Women still represented the largest portion of the population during this decade, and while the trend had slowed, women were still increasing their numbers in the paid workforce.[69] But as the 1920s pressed on, women's experiences in the city were less sensationalized and more regularized. Women's experiences were incorporated into city structures in ways similar to those of working-class men. Women's poverty became more normalized, as the lives of at risk children were invested with anxieties about moral decay and individual pathologies. The network of social welfare organizations that had developed in relation to these women still existed, though, and in some cases was still used to help them, even if its focus had changed. What is most different about the 1920s in Atlanta, it seems, is that sense of danger and hope that had been invested in poor women in the two decades preceding it was now invested primarily in the children of those women.

In the end, the first two decades of the twentieth century represented a unique moment in the development of Atlanta. During these years of rapid growth and economic prosperity, social welfare agencies provided some of the strongest middle-class voices in articulating and promoting conceptions of moral order developed in and through their work with the poor women of the city. In the process, the lives working-class women received widespread scrutinization while reformers and social workers positioned themselves as experts within the power structures of the city. In general early twentieth-century Atlantans endorsed the growth of the city—where residents differed, however, was in their conceptions of exactly what shape this growth should take. The records of Atlanta's social welfare network reveal the contours of at least some of these debates, especially the disparate views of black and white, middle class and working class, and public and private as all manner of urbanites sought to define themselves and their city.

NOTES

1. "The Unification of Atlanta's Social Forces," address delivered by Burr Blackburn at the Annual Meeting of the Associated Charities, February 8, 1921, Child Services and Family Counseling, Atlanta History Center (hereafter CSFC).

2. Clarke A. Chambers, "Toward a Redefinition of Welfare History," *Journal of American History* 73 (September 1986): 407–33, provides a survey and full citations of this literature.

3. For example, Michael B. Katz, *In the Shadow of the Poorhouse: A Social History of Welfare in America* (New York: Basic Books, Inc., 1986); Elisabeth Lasch-Quinn, *Black Neighbors: Race and the Limits of Reform in the American Settlement House Movement, 1890–1945* (Chapel Hill: University of North Carolina Press, 1993).

4. For example, Linda Gordon, ed., *Women, the State, and Welfare* (Madison: University of Wisconsin Press, 1990).

5. I am borrowing this phrase from Linda Gordon, *Heroes of Their Own Lives: The Politics and History of Family History, Boston, 1880–1960* (New York: Viking, 1988), 2.

6. Annual Report of the Associated Charities for 1910, pp. 16, 10, CSFC.

7. One settlement worker reported a new mother had asked to have her baby placed in an orphanage, explaining "her husband had brought her here from another city and placed her in this boarding house and had run away and left her, that she wanted to go back home but could not make her living with the baby." The appalled visitor replied that "there were many mothers who made their living with many more little children and never think of giving them away." E. M. Evans, *Living for Jesus or a Sketch of My City Mission Work in Atlanta* (Atlanta: Evans Printing Co., n.d.), 69. The Associated Charities convinced the juvenile court to remove the children from one woman who "did not scruple to send them out to beg on the streets when the meal got low in the bag." Annual Report of the Associated Charities, 1915, CSFC.

8. Annual Report of the Associated Charities, 1911, CSFC.

9. "Anti-Tuberculosis Association 1909 photographs," Patient Scrapbook, Atlanta Lung Association, Atlanta History Center, 7. Untitled typed report of the Associated Charities, 1909, Atlanta Lung Association, Atlanta History Center (hereafter ALA).

10. It was in the name of protecting and encouraging proper motherhood, and what Mimi Abramovitz has referred to as the "family ethic," that reformers justified their intervention into the lives of poor women and "helped to meet the economy's need for women's unpaid labor in the home and their low-paid labor in the market." Abramovitz, *Regulating*

the Lives of Women: Social Welfare Policy from Colonial Times to the Present (Boston: South End Press, 1996), 3, 4.

11. Annual Report of the Associated Charities for 1906, CSFC.

12. A woman with the Associated Charities referred to as "Mrs. L" refused to work at a job the agency had secured for her. Her children were remanded to a local orphanage. The case worker then reported, "Work again secured for woman, who was given to understand she must make good in three months or the Orphanage would be given legal control of the children." At the time of this report, the woman was working steadily and well on her way to "earning" her children back. Annual Report of the Associated Charities, 1915, CSFC.

13. Untitled report, 1918–30, CSFC.

14. Evans, Living for Jesus, 24.

15. See, for example, the editorial page, Journal of Labor, October 21, 1927.

16. Evans, Living for Jesus, 58. "Relief vs. Service," 1916, CSFC.

17. Wesley House Bulletin, 1903–1907, 20.

18. "Anti-Tuberculosis Association 1909 photographs," Patient Scrapbook, 17, ALA.

19. "Free Dispensary Opened to Treat Tuberculosis," Atlanta Journal, March 18, 1909.

20. "Negroes Rally to Science in Campaign That is Made to Stamp Out Tuberculosis," Atlanta Journal, November 30, 1909.

21. "The Neighborhood Union: An Experiment in Community Cooperation," Neighborhood Union Collection, Woodruff Library, Atlanta University Center (hereafter NU). See also Cynthia Neverdon-Morton, Afro-American Women of the South and the Advancement of the Race, 1895–1925 (Knoxville: University of Tennessee Press, 1989), 145.

22. Unlike white agencies, the Neighborhood Union incorporated working-class women of the community into its organizational structure. Draft of the Annual Report of the Neighborhood Union, 1912, NU.

23. Undated newspaper clipping, Atlanta Journal, NU.

24. Neighborhood Union quoted in undated newspaper clipping, Atlanta Constitution, 1911, NU.

25. Draft of speech by Lugenia Burns Hope on poor housing, 1909, NU.

26. With this argument I am departing from recent interpretations advanced by Elizabeth Lasch-Quinn. Lasch-Quinn has argued that black settlement-house workers, such as Hope and her associates at the Neighborhood Union, were trying to distance themselves from their positions as wives and mothers to instead focus on citizenship rights. I believe that the NU actually sought to both use maternalism and social justice arguments. NU leaders revalued black motherhood, in particular, through the promotion of working women. Lasch-Quinn, Black Neighbors, 112–13, 120.

27. "Work of the Neighborhood Union," Spelman Messenger, November 1916.

28. Louie D. Shivery, "The History of Organized Social Work among Atlanta Negroes, 1890–1935" (M.A. thesis, Atlanta University, 1936), 177.

29. "Report in Sociology 10 on Desertion Case from Case No. 11432, Family Welfare Society," by Willard C. Hay, Woodward Collection, Robert W. Woodruff Library, Special Collections Department, Emory University (hereafter WC).

30. "Vancott Family," by Evelyn Alexander, case history, WC.

31. "Georgia Moore, #5," July 12, 1907, case history, CSFC. Joseph Logan, one of the

founders, attached a note to this case history, writing, "Our longest and most difficult case." Associated Charities to Mr. A. H. Spain, November 25, 1907. In this letter, the case worker wrote of Moore, "If she should come to you at all, please send her to us without doing anything for her. She does seem incorrigible [sic] in some ways, is really one of the hardest cases we have had since the opening of this office, her case is #5 in the files. She is the main wage earner in her family, and she will piece quilts and sell them, tho' we have never been able to induce her to do any sort of factory work. We hope to have better results with her this winter."

32. "Fourth Annual Report, Associated Charities of Atlanta, January 1 1909–January 1, 1910," ALA.

33. Evans, *Living for Jesus*, 34.

34. Rosa Lowe to Mrs. E. M. Chapman, November 9, 1911, ALA. Mrs. LeRoy contributed to the support of the family by working as a palmist despite her tubercular condition. Lowe suggested that the church ladies help LeRoy maintain her dignity by allowing her to read their palms.

35. Associated Charities to Edward Alfriend, October 26, 1910, CSFC.

36. The lack of public aid for welfare efforts in Atlanta is one of the few striking differences between the South and the North. Welfare networks in northern cities were not as solidly private in the decades around the turn of the century as networks in the South appear to have been. Beyond a lack of support from the municipal government, Atlanta's agencies also faced open hostility from the state government. Districting in Georgia gave the rural parts of the state the upper hand in the state legislature, and while the capital was located in Atlanta, legislators tended to be profoundly unsympathetic to the particularly urban problems facing the city.

37. Lois Vancott, for example, was judged through these tests to have mental age of less than twelve years and the reasoning ability of a thirteen-year-old. The social work student analyzing this case concluded from that "to overcome her weak points Mrs. Vancott must have constant supervision and training." "Vancott Family," by Evelyn Alexander, WC.

38. Apparently this move was not understood or accepted by wealthy contributors to charity organizations in the city. The Associated Charities tried to explain social work as a "growing profession" by arguing: "When there is a clearer understanding of the causes of economic need, and of successful methods of its relief, a satisfactory answer to the question why salaries are paid to Associated Charities employees, will be simply that they minister to the poor." Annual Report of the Associated Charities, 1910, CSFC.

39. In the case of Wesley House, the board of city missions voted 1919 to close its night schools, feeling this type of program should fall under the responsibilities of the public board of education. In 1920 the board voted to abandon all "welfare work," close the settlement house, and instead focus their outreach efforts on being missionaries for Christianity. "A Story of Wesley Community House and of Some of the Peoples it has Served," unpublished manuscript, Board of City Missions, Wesley Community House, Atlanta, Georgia.

40. Minutes of the General Staff Conference, December 31, 1931, CSFC.

41. Daniel J. Walkowitz, "The Making of a Feminine Professional Ideal: Social Workers in the 1920s," *American Historical Review* 95 (October 1990): 1067.

42. "Column for the Needy" *Atlanta Journal*, 1915.

43. *Atlanta Constitution*, May 25, 1920.
44. R. C. Dexter to Editor, *Atlanta Constitution*, May 25, 1920, CSFC.
45. Jean-Christopher Agnew, "A Touch of Class" *Democracy* 3 (Spring 1983): 59–72.
46. I am borrowing this phrase from Evelyn Brooks Higginbotham, *Righteous Discontent: The Women's Movement in the Black Baptist Church, 1880–1920* (Cambridge: Harvard University Press, 1993), see chap. 7.
47. Handwritten, untitled speech, Lugenia Burns Hope, NU.
48. Jacqueline A. Rouse, *Lugenia Burns Hope: Black Southern Reformer* (Athens, Ga.: University of Georgia Press, 1989), 7.
49. Higginbotham, *Righteous Discontent*, 187.
50. Ibid., 191.
51. Annual Report of the Associated Charities, 1906, CSFC.
52. Annual Report of the Associated Charities, 1910, CSFC. Joseph Logan, head of the Associated Charities, complained that the methods of the city warden displayed a "serious lack of appreciation of almost universally accepted methods of charitable relief." Joseph Logan to J. H. Lewis, June 25, 1915, CSFC.
53. Quoted in "Slander Charges Made by Woman, Denied by Warden," *Atlanta Journal*, January 1922, clipping file, CSFC. Once the press printed Harper's side of the story in a sympathetic light, she withdrew the charges—to the dismay of the Associated Charities.
54. In 1909 a woman migrated to Atlanta from the country with her three children. After the death of her youngest child, the other children were removed from her custody. She was arrested shortly after when she refused to take a job, choosing to beg instead. She was arrested for vagrancy but released into the custody of the Associated Charities when she agreed to take a job at the Decatur Orphanage. Annual Report of the Associated Charities, 1910, CSFC.
55. Minutes of the Men and Religion Forward Movement, January 26, 1914, Christian Council Collection, Atlanta History Center (hereafter CCC).
56. Report of the Martha Home, January 30 to February 5, 1914, CCC.
57. Report of Probation Work, April 11 to April 16, 1914, CCC.
58. Report of Probation Work, January 16, February 12, and October 2, 1914, CCC.
59. Matron's Report, Annual Report of the Chief of Police of the City of Atlanta, Georgia, for the year ending December 31, 1915, Herbert T. Jenkins Collection, Atlanta History Center (hereafter JC).
60. Annual Report of the Chief of Police of the City of Atlanta, Georgia, for the year ending December 31, 1919, JC.
61. "Divorce cases represent 4% of our work," report of the Legal Aid Society, August 1938, CSFC. While this report was obviously written much later than period of this chapter, I cite it here as the most clear and complete articulation of a policy followed by the Associated Charities before 1920 and adopted in the 1930s by the Legal Aid Society in conjunction with that organization.
62. Annual Report of the Associated Charities for 1906, CSFC.
63. Darlene Roth, "Matronage: Patterns in Women's Organizations, Atlanta, 1890–1940" (Ph.D. diss., George Washington University, 1978).
64. R. C. Dexter to J. M. B. Hoxsey, June 12, 1920, CSFC.

65. Shivery, "The History of Organized Social Work among Atlanta Negroes," 138.

66. Professor Watson, Survey by the Sociological Department of Morehouse College, appendix no. 2, in Shivery, "The History of Organized Social Work among Atlanta Negroes," 432.

67. "Work of the Neighborhood Union," *Spelman Messenger,* November 1916.

68. Michael Katz and William Trattner in their studies of the social welfare history of the United States found evidence of this "child-saving" movement beginning in the 1880s, at least in the Northeast. Katz, *In the Shadow of the Poorhouse,* chap. 5; and William Trattner, *From Poor Law to Welfare State: A History of Social Welfare in America* (New York: Free Press, 1974; reprint, 1989), 114–20.

69. Julia Kirk Blackwelder, "Quiet Suffering: Atlanta Women in the 1930s," *Georgia Historical Quarterly* 61 (Summer 1977): 112–24.

SELECTED BIBLIOGRAPHY

Anderson, James D. *The Education of Blacks in the South, 1860–1935.* Chapel Hill: University of North Carolina Press, 1988.

Baine, Eunice V. "The History of the Family Service Agency, Memphis, Tennessee." M.A. thesis, Tulane University, 1942.

Barr, Alwyn. "The Other Texas: Charities and Community in the Lone Star State," *Southwestern Historical Quarterly* 97 (July 1993): 1–10.

Beardsley, Edward H. *A History of Neglect: Health Care for Blacks and Mill Workers in the Twentieth-Century South.* Knoxville: University of Tennessee Press, 1987.

Bellows, Barbara. *Benevolence among Slaveholders: Assisting the Poor in Charleston, 1670–1860.* Baton Rouge: Louisiana State University Press, 1993.

Berkley, Kathleen. "Colored Ladies Also Contributed: Black Women's Activities from Benevolence to Social Welfare, 1866–1896," in *The Web of Southern Social Relations: Women, Family, and Education,* Walter J. Fraser et al., eds. Athens: University of Georgia Press, 1985.

Bernhard, Virginia. "Poverty and the Social Order in Seventeenth-Century Virginia." *Virginia Magazine of History and Biography* 85 (April 1977): 141–55.

Berry, Benjamin. "Plymouth Settlement House and the Development of Black Louisville, 1900–1930." Ph.D. diss., Case Western Reserve University, 1977.

Bond, Nathaniel B. "The Treatment of the Dependent, Defective, and Delinquent Classes in Mississippi." Ph.D. diss., Tulane University, 1923.

Brown, Roy M. *Public Poor Relief in North Carolina.* Chapel Hill: University of North Carolina Press, 1928.

Burwell, N. Yolanda. "Lawrence Oxley and Locality Development: Black Self-Help in North Carolina, 1925–1928," in *African American Community Practice Models: Historical and Contemporary Responses,* Iris Carlton-LaNey and N. Yolanda Burwell, eds. New York: Haworth Press, 1996.

Butchart, Ronald E. *Northern Schools, Southern Blacks, and Reconstruction: Freedmen's Education, 1862–1875.* Westport, Conn.: Greenwood Press, 1980.

Byrd, Michael D. "Ye Have the Poor Always with You: Attitudes towards Poor Relief in Colonial Charles Town." M.A. thesis, University of South Carolina, 1973.

Carleton, David L., and Peter A. Coclanis, eds. *Confronting Southern Poverty in the Great Depression: The Report of Economic Conditions of the South.* New York: Bedford Books, 1996.

Coddington, Edwin Broughton. "Soldiers' Relief in the Seaboard States of the

Southern Confederacy." *Mississippi Valley Historical Review* 37 (June 1950): 17–38.

Colby, Ira. "The Freedmen's Bureau in Texas and Its Impact on the Emerging Social Welfare System and Black-White Social Relations, 1865–1885." Ph.D. diss., University of Pennsylvania, 1984.

———. "The Freedman's Bureau: From Social Welfare to Segregation." *Phylon* 46 (September 1985): 219–30.

Cole, William Earle. *Almshouse Policies and Almshouse Care of the Indigent in Tennessee*. Knoxville: Research Council, University of Tennessee, 1938.

Cottrell, Debbie Mauldin. "The County Poor Farm System in Texas." *Southwestern Historical Quarterly* 93 (October 1989): 169–91.

Dain, Norman. *Disordered Minds: The First Century of Eastern State Hospital in Williamsburg, Virginia 1766–1866*. Williamsburg, Va.: Colonial Williamsburg Foundation, 1971.

Dann, John C. "Humanitarianism, Reform, and Organized Benevolence in the Southern United States, 1780–1830." Ph.D. diss., College of William and Mary, 1975.

Davis, Cleta Weatherby. "History of Public Welfare Administration in Florida." M.A. thesis, University of Chicago, 1936.

Ellis, John H. *Yellow Fever and Public Health in the New South*. Lexington: University Press of Kentucky, 1992.

Escott, Paul D. "The Cry of the Sufferers: The Problem of Welfare in the Confederacy." *Civil War History* 23 (September 1977): 228–40.

Etheridge, Elizabeth. *The Butterfly Caste: A Social History of Pellagra in the South*. Westport: Greenwood Press, 1972.

Ettling, John. *The Germ of Laziness: Rockefeller Philanthropy and Public Health in the New South*. Cambridge: Harvard University Press, 1981.

Evans, Helen. "Provisions for Public Relief in Texas, 1841–1937." M.A. thesis, Tulane University School of Social Work, 1941.

Franklin, John Hope. "Public Welfare in the South during Reconstruction, 1865–1880." *Social Service Review* 44 (December 1970): 379–92.

Fraser, Walter J., Jr. "Controlling the Poor in Colonial Charleston." *Proceedings of the South Carolina Historical Association* (1980): 13–18.

Grantham, Dewey W. *Southern Progressivism: The Reconciliation of Progress and Tradition*. Knoxville: University of Tennessee Press, 1983.

Gregory, James N. "The Southern Diaspora and the Urban Dispossessed." *Journal of American History* 82 (June 1995): 111–35.

Hamilton, Alice R. "The History of the Department of Public Welfare of Georgia, 1919–1937." M.A. thesis, Tulane University, 1939.

Hamm, Dorothy Ann. "A Study of the Influence of Public Assistance Legislation on the Almshouse Population in Mississippi." M.A. thesis, Tulane University, 1947.

Harlan, Louis R. *Separate and Unequal: Public School Campaigns and Racism in the Southern Seaboard States, 1901–1915.* Chapel Hill: University of North Carolina Press, 1958.

Hasson, Gail Snowden. "The Medical Activities of the Freedmen's Bureau in Reconstruction Alabama, 1865–1868." Ph.D. diss., University of Alabama, 1982.

Herring, Harriet. *Welfare Work in Mill Villages: The Story of Extra Mill Activities in North Carolina.* New York: Arno Reprints, 1929.

Hine, Darlene Clark, "'We Specialize in the Wholly Impossible': The Philanthropic Work of Black Women," in *Lady Bountiful Revisited: Women, Philanthropy, and Power,* Kathleen McCarthy, ed. New Brunswick: Rutgers University Press, 1990.

Hughes, John S. "Labeling and Treating Black Mental Illness in Alabama, 1861–1910," *Journal of Southern History* 58 (August 1992): 435–60.

Humphreys, Margaret. *Yellow Fever and the South.* New Brunswick: Rutgers University Press, 1992.

Hutchins, Myldred F. "The History of the Poor Law Legislation in Georgia, 1733–1919." M.A. thesis, Tulane University, 1940.

Johnson, Christopher. "Poverty and Dependency in Antebellum Mississippi." Ph.D. diss., University of California, Riverside, 1988.

Jones, James H. *Bad Blood: The Tuskeegee Syphilis Experiment.* New York: Free Press, 1981.

LaMonte, Edward. *Politics and Welfare in Birmingham, 1900–1975.* Tuscaloosa: University of Alabama, 1995.

Larson, Edward J. "'In the Finest, Most Womanly Way': Women in the Southern Eugenics Movement." *The American Journal of Legal History* 39 (April 1995): 119–47.

Lasch-Quinn, Elisabeth. *Black Neighbors, Race, and the Limits of Reform in the American Settlement House Movement, 1890–1945.* Chapel Hill: University of North Carolina Press, 1993.

Leeman, Minnie Elliott. "The History of the Family Service Bureau of Houston, Texas, 1904–1943." M.A. thesis, Tulane University, 1946.

Levine, Daniel. "A Single Standard of Civilization: Black Private Social Welfare Institutions in the South, 1880s-1920s." *Georgia Historical Quarterly* 81 (Spring 1997): 52–77.

Link, William A. *A Hard Country and a Lonely Place: Schooling, Society, and Reform in Rural Virginia, 1870–1920.* Chapel Hill: University of North Carolina Press, 1986.

———. *The Paradox of Southern Progressivism, 1880–1930.* Chapel Hill: University of North Carolina Press, 1992.

———. "Privies, Progressivism, and Public Schools: Health Reform and Education in the Rural South, 1909–1920." *Journal of Southern History* 54 (November 1988): 623–42.

Mackey, Howard. "The Operation of the English Old Poor Law in Colonial Virginia," *Virginia Magazine of History and Biography* 73 (January 1965): 29–40.

Margo, Robert A. *Race and Schooling in the South, 1880–1950: An Economic History.* Chicago: University of Chicago Press, 1990.

Martin, Josephine Walker. "The Educational Efforts of the Major Freedmen's Aid Societies and the Freedmen's Bureau in South Carolina, 1862–1870." Ph.D. diss., University of South Carolina, 1972.

McCandless, Peter. "'A House of Cure': The AnteBellum South Carolina Lunatic Asylum." *Bulletin of the History of Medicine* 64 (1990): 220–42.

———. *Moonlight, Magnolias, and Madness: Insanity in South Carolina from the Colonial Period to the Progressive Era.* Chapel Hill: University of North Carolina Press, 1996.

McDowell, John P. *The Social Gospel Movement in the South: The Women's Home Mission Movement in the Methodist Episcopal Church, South, 1886–1939.* Baton Rouge: Louisiana State University Press, 1982.

Moran, Robert. "The Negro Dependent Child in Louisiana, 1800–1935." *Social Service Review* 45 (March 1971): 53–61.

Morrison, Joseph. "Illegitimacy, Sterilization, and Racism: A North Carolina Case Study." *Social Service Review* 39 (1976): 559–69.

Murray, Gail S. "Charity within the Bounds of Race and Class: Female Benevolence in the Old South." *South Carolina Historical Magazine* 96 (January 1995): 54–70.

Nieman, Donald G. *African Americans and Education in the South, 1865–1900.* New York: Garland, 1994.

Noll, Steven. *Feeble-Minded in Our Midst: Institutions for the Mentally Retarded in the South, 1900–1940.* Chapel Hill: University of North Carolina Press, 1995.

Oliver, Robert. "A Crumbling Fortress: The Tennessee Lunatic Asylum, 1837–1865." *Tennessee Historical Quarterly* 54 (Summer 1995): 124–39.

Rabinowitz, Howard N. "From Exclusion to Segregation: Health and Welfare Services for Southern Blacks, 1865–1890." *Social Service Review* 48 (September 1974): 565–94.

Ratcliffe, Bernice Greaves. "100 Years of Poor Relief Administration in Arkansas, 1836–1936." M.A. thesis, Tulane University, 1947.

Rosenburg, R. B. *Living Monuments: Confederate Soldiers' Homes in the New South.* Chapel Hill: University of North Carolina Press, 1993.

Ross, Edyth L. "The Black Heritage in Social Welfare: A Case Study of Atlanta." *Phylon* 37 (Winter 1976): 297–307.

———. *Black Heritage in Social Welfare, 1860–1930.* Metuchen, N.J.: Scarecrow Press, 1978.

Rouse, Jacquelyn Anne. *Lugenia Burns Hope, Black Southern Reformer.* Athens: University of Georgia Press, 1992.

Savitt, Todd Lee. *Medicine and Slavery: The Diseases and Health Care of Blacks in Antebellum Virginia.* Urbana: University of Illinois Press, 1978.

Schoen, Johanna. "'A Great Thing for Poor Folks': Birth Control, Sterilization, and Abortion in Public Health and Welfare in the Twentieth Century." Ph.D. diss., University of North Carolina at Chapel Hill, 1996.

Shivers, Lydia Gordon. "The Social Welfare Movement in the South: A Study of Regional Culture and Social Organization." Ph.D. diss., University of North Carolina, 1935.

Shivery, Louie. "The Neighborhood Union: A Survey of the Beginnings of Social Welfare Movements among Negroes in Atlanta." *Phylon* 3 (Spring 1942): 149–62.

Sims, Anastatia. *The Power of Femininity in the New South: Women's Organizations and Politics in North Carolina, 1880–1930.* Columbia: University of South Carolina Press, 1997.

Speizman, Milton. "The Movement of the Settlement House Idea into the South." *Southwestern Social Science Quarterly* 44 (December 1963): 237–46.

Stone, Olive Mathews. "Poor Relief in Alabama." M.A. thesis, University of Chicago, 1929.

Stuart, Paul H. "The Kingsley House Extension Program: Racial Segregation in a 1940s Settlement Program." *Social Service Review* 66 (March 1992): 112–20.

Thielman, Samuel. "Southern Madness: The Shape of Mental Health Care in the Old South," in *Science and Medicine in the Old South,* Ronald Numbers and Todd Savitt, eds. Baton Rouge: Louisiana State University Press, 1989.

Thomas, Emory. "To Feed the Citizens: Welfare in Wartime Richmond, 1861–1865." *Virginia Cavalcade* 22 (Summer 1972): 22–29.

Turner, Elizabeth Hayes. *Women, Culture, and Community: Religion and Reform in Galveston, 1880–1923.* New York: Oxford University Press, 1997.

Vandal, Gilles. "Nineteenth Century Municipal Responses to the Problem of Poverty: New Orleans' Free Lodgers 1850–1880." *Journal of Urban History* 19 (November 1992): 30–59.

Van de Voort, Anita. "Public Welfare Administration in Jefferson County, Alabama." M.A. thesis, Tulane University, 1934.

Vouga, Anne F. "Presbyterian Missions and Louisville Blacks: The Early Years, 1898–1910." *Filson Club Historical Quarterly* 58 (July 1984): 310–35.

Wallace, Ellen Barbour. "History of Legal Provision for the Poor and of Public Welfare Administration in Tennessee." M.A. thesis, University of Chicago, 1927.

Wallenstein, Peter. *From Slave South to New South: Public Policy in Georgia in the Nineteenth Century.* Chapel Hill: University of North Carolina Press, 1987.

Warner, Margaret. "Local Control versus National Interest: The Debate over Southern Public Health, 1878–1884." *Journal of Southern History* 50 (August 1984): 407–28.

Washburn, Benjamin Earle. *A History of the North Carolina State Board of Health, 1877–1925.* Raleigh: North Carolina State Board of Health, 1966.

Weaver, H. N. "African Americans and Social Work: An Overview of the Antebellum through Progressive Eras." *Journal of Multicultural Social Work* 2 (1992): 91–102.

Wedell, Marsha. *Elite Women and the Reform Impulse in Memphis, 1875–1915.* Knoxville: University of Tennessee Press, 1991.

Whites, LeeAnn. "The Charitable and the Poor: The Emergence of Domestic Politics in Augusta, Georgia, 1860–1880." *Journal of Social History* 17 (Summer 1984): 601–15.

Wisner, Elizabeth. "The Howard Association of New Orleans." *Social Service Review* 41 (1967): 411–18.

———. *Public Welfare Administration in Louisiana.* Chicago: University of Chicago, 1930.

———. *Social Welfare in the South: From Colonial Times to World War I.* Baton Rouge: Louisiana State University Press, 1970.

Young, James R. "Confederate Pensions in Georgia, 1886–1929." *Georgia Historical Quarterly* 66 (1982): 47–52.

———. "Malaria in the South, 1900–1930." Ph.D. diss., University of North Carolina, 1972.

Zmora, Nurith. *Orphanages Reconsidered: Child Care Institutions in Progressive Era Baltimore.* Philadelphia: Temple University Press, 1994.

Zornow, William F. "Aid for Indigent Families of Soldiers in Virginia, 1861–1865." *Virginia Magazine of History and Biography* 66 (1958): 454–58.

CONTRIBUTORS

E. Susan Barber, assistant professor of history at the College of Notre Dame of Maryland, received her Ph.D. from the University of Maryland, College Park.

Kathleen Gorman received her Ph.D. from the University of California, Riverside. She is currently a lecturer at California State University, San Marcos.

Elna C. Green is the Allen Morris Associate Professor of History at Florida State University. She received her Ph.D. from Tulane University and is the author of *Southern Strategies: Southern Women and the Woman Suffrage Question*.

Susan Hamburger received her Ph.D. from Florida State University. She is manuscripts librarian at Pennsylvania State University.

Georgina Hickey is assistant professor of history at Georgia Southern University. She received her Ph.D. from the University of Michigan.

Mazie Hough received her Ph.D. from the University of Maine. She is currently a staff associate at the Women in the Curriculum and Women's Studies Program at the University of Maine.

Joan Marie Johnson received her Ph.D. from University of California, Los Angeles, and is currently assistant professor of history at Miami University, Middletown.

Lee S. Polansky is a doctoral candidate at Emory University and works as senior research manager for a Washington, D.C., nonprofit organization.

James H. Tuten is a doctoral candidate at Emory University and is visiting instructor of history at Juniata College.

Peter Wallenstein is associate professor of history at Virginia Polytechnic Institute and State University. He received his Ph.D. from the Johns Hopkins University and is the author of *From Slave South to New South: Public Policy in Nineteenth-Century Georgia*.

INDEX

Academy for the Blind, 11, 13–14, 18
African Americans, xvi, 56, 103, 109, 124–25, 166, 201; churches of, xi; and education, 144, 164, 165; self-help activities of, xi, 84–85; and social welfare, xv, 12, 15, 86, 90, 150, 171–77, 187–90, 194–96, 200
Alabama, xv, 125; poorhouses in, xvi, 40–57; during Civil War, xiv
Almshouses. *See* poorhouses
American Asylum at Hartford for the Education and Instruction of the Deaf and Dumb, 8, 10
American Mercury, xxii
American Poor Farm and Its Inmates (Evans), 48, 51
Anti-Tuberculosis Association, 187, 191
Associated Charities, 181, 183–85, 191–94, 197, 199, 201
asylums, xii; in Georgia, 5, 11, 12; impact of Civil War on, 13; insane, 5, 9
Atlanta, 69, 138–43, 150–52, 181–203
Atlanta Constitution, 194
Atlanta Journal, 193
Atlanta University, 172
Atlanta Women's Club (AWC), 143

Baptists, 121, 195
Beard, Mary Ritter, 101
Bellows, Barbara, xiv
Bernhard, Virginia, x–xi
Berry, Martha, 166
Bethune, Mary McLeod, 175

Birmingham, 41, 42
Birmingham News, 50, 51
Blasingame, C. P., 35
Blassingame, John, 84
Blease, Coleman, 177
Boston, 139
Bread riots, xiv

Charities, xxii
Charity Organization Society, 85–95
Charleston, x, xii–xiii, 171
Chicago, 139
child labor, 168
children: in poorhouses, 43; and social welfare, 120–33, 144–45, 202
child-saving, 201
Christian Woman's Exchange, 90
churches, xii, 112, 121, 174, 191; and social welfare, x, xi, 107–8
Civil War, xvii; effects of, on unwed mothers, 102–3; orphans of, 120–33; and social welfare, xiv, xv, xvi, 12, 13, 15, 127; veterans of, 24–37
class, xii, 140, 145, 181, 182, 202; and gender, 192; and race, 176, 194; and social welfare, viii, 34, 71, 90, 105, 106, 112, 140–41, 146, 165–66, 192, 202
Cobb, Howell, 7, 12
Columbia, 171, 173, 174
Community Chest, 93
Confederacy, xiv, 24–37, 65–66
Conference of Charities, 86
Connecticut, 8, 10
Current Opinion, xxii

217

Daniel, Jean Moncure, 122
de l'Epeé, Abbé Charles Michel, 7
Discovery of the Asylum (Rothman), 5
Dix, Dorothea, xiii, 10
Dozier, James C., 174
Duke Foundation, 174–75

education, xv, 164–68, 169, 170, 172
Emancipation, 13
Embree, Cynthia, 152–55
Escott, Paul, xiv
ethnicity, viii, 81
Evans, Harry, 40, 48, 54–55

Fairwold Home for Delinquent Girls, 173–75
Falconer, Martha, 155
fallen women, 88–89, 100–117
Fannin, Oliver P., 10
Federal government: and poor relief, xv, xvi, 17, 83; and Freedmen's Bureau, xv, xxi, 17; New Deal programs of, xviii, 54–55, 57
Female Domestic Missionary Society, xiii
Female Humane Association, xiii, 120–33
Feminism, xiii
Florence Crittenton Homes, 103, 183
Florida, 25
Flynt, Wayne, xvi
Fortescue, Walter S., 11
Foster, Betty, 138, 139, 141, 142, 147, 148, 151, 155
Foster, Ira, 41
Foster, John, 41–42
France, institutions in, 7
Franklin, John Hope, xv, xviii
Freedman's Bureau, xv, xxi, 17
free kindergartens, 167

Gallaudet, Thomas Hopkins, 8
Garrett, G. A., 31, 34
Garrett, James J., 24, 32–34
gender, viii, xiii, 89, 155; and class, 181–203; and race, 195; and social welfare, 18, 40–41, 42, 43, 46, 52, 62, 74, 82, 106, 151, 169
gender roles, 140, 182, 184, 186, 201
Georgia, 3–21, 138–56, 166; institutions in, xii, xvi, 3, 10, 13, 142, 150, 151, 152, 181; social welfare for children in, 144, 145; Civil War veterans in, 24–37; "girl problem" in, 139–41
Georgia Asylum for the Education of the Deaf and Dumb, 11, 17–18
Georgia Training School for Girls, 148, 149, 151–55
German Protestant Home, 81
Gleaner, The, 107, 109
Glenn, Evelyn Nakano, 101
Goldman, Julius, 93
Grady, Sarah Frances, 65
Great Depression, 28, 49, 53, 56, 69
Green, Thomas F., 10, 16

Hauy, Valentin, 7
Hearn Manual-Training School, 10
Hebrew Benevolent Society, 81
Higginbotham, Evelyn Brooks, 176, 195
Hill, Edna, 153, 154
Hill, Jewel, 151, 153, 154
Home for the Friendless, 183, 197
Home for Homeless Young Women, 91
Home for Needy Confederate Women, 61–74
Howe, Samuel Gridley, 8
Huey, Thomas, 51
Huntington, Arabella Yarrington, 66
Hutchins, Minerva L., 67

immigrants, xiii, 81, 103, 124, 139
Indiana, 8
indoor relief, x, 51, 84
Interpreting Southern History (Boles and Nolen), xviii

Jacksonian America, 3–5
Jefferson County Community Chest, 53
Jefferson County Poor Farm, xviii, 40–60
Jenkins, Charles J., 14, 15
Johnson, Elizabeth Fischer, 104–5, 111, 112
juvenile delinquency, 138–56

Katz, Michael, xii
Kaufman, Rhoda, 139–42, 147–49
Kentucky, xii, xvi, 8
Keystone, The, 162, 164, 166, 169, 170, 171
Kingsley House, 81, 92, 93, 94
Knight, R. C., 31, 35
Ku Klux Klan, 170, 171
Kunzel, Regina, 94
Kurtagh, Emeric, 95

Ladies' Auxiliary of George E. Pickett Camp, Confederate Veterans, 62–63
Ladies' Unsectarian Aid Society, 89, 91
Lee Camp Soldiers' Home, 67, 68
Leloudis, James, 141
Lindsey, J. W., 31, 36
Lining, Ida, 163, 164
Literary Digest, xxii
Lock, Annie, 152
Lock, Sally, 152
Long, N. M., 113
Lost Cause, 26, 62, 72–73, 160, 162–64, 168, 171, 177
Louisiana, 83

Lubove, Roy, 94
Lumpkin, Wilson, 9
lynching, 109–10, 140, 176

Male Orphan Asylum, 124, 126, 130, 132
Mann, William Hodges, 68
Martha's Home, 198
Martha Washingtonians, 120
Maryland, 18
Massachusetts, x, xvii
McCandless, Peter, 6
McCarthy, Carleton, 63, 64, 67
McClintock, Megan J., 25, 61, 120
McDaniel, Henry D., 33–34, 35
McKissick, Margaret, 168
McMain, Eleanor, 81, 93
Medical College of Virginia, 132
Memorial Home for Girls, 132
Memphis, 100–119
Memphis Bethel, 104
Memphis Daily Appeal, 105, 110–11, 113
Memphis Ledger, 113
Men and Religion Forward Movement, 198
Meriwether, Lide, 100, 106–7, 111, 112
Methodists, 121
Mississippi, 113
Mobile, Ala., xiv
Montague, Elizabeth Lyne Hoskins, 64–72
mutual assistance associations, xi, xx, 84–85

National Association for the Advancement of Colored People (NAACP), xxii
National Association of Colored Women (NACW), 171, 172, 175

National Association of Social Workers, xvii
National Convention of Charities and Corrections, 144
National Negro Digest, 174
National Urban League, xxii
Needham, Rolly, 24, 34–36
Neighborhood Union, 188–90, 194, 195, 197; fundraising by, 189; goals of, 200
New Deal, xviii, 54–55, 57
New England, xi, 8
New England Asylum for the Purpose of Educating the Blind, 8
New Orleans, xiii; cultural diversity in, 81; during Civil War, xiv; social welfare in, 81–95
New South Creed, 26
New York, 8, 121
New York Tribune, 164
Noll, Steven, xvii
North Carolina, xvii, 18
Nunnally, J. E., 35

Ohio, 8
orphanages, xii, 121
orphans, 120–33
Orphans Courts, xxi
outdoor relief, x–xi, xiii, 42, 45, 51, 53–54, 85, 87, 196, 197, 202
Outlook, xxii
Overseers of the Poor, xxi

Palmetto Leader, 174
Pennsylvania, 8
pensions, 25, 29–36, 61
Phyllis Wheatley Club, 85, 92
Pinel, Philippe, 7
Pollard, John Garland, 69
poor farms. *See* poorhouses

poorhouses, xi, xvi, xviii, 84, 88, 124; children in, 43; criticisms of, 48, 51, 54–55; demography of, 43, 46, 51–52; escapes from, 45; inmates with mental disabilities in, 45, 46; mortality rates in, 52–53; organization of, 50; in Charleston, xiii; in Alabama, 40–57
poor laws, ix, x, xiv, 41, 83
Pope, General John, 14
Poppenheim, Louisa, 160, 162, 165, 169, 170
poverty: attitudes toward, x–xi; causes of, 91, 92; in New Orleans, 82; and old age, 42, 43, 51–52, 55; and social welfare, 107
Powell, James R., 41
Poydras Female Orphan Society, xiii
Presbyterians, 112, 121, 191
private charity, 105–6, 200, 201, 202
professionalization, 92, 94, 147, 192–96
Progressive Era, 82, 86, 92, 94, 95, 140, 151, 160, 168, 193, 201; reformers and social welfare in, 40, 48, 51; in Virginia, 68; in South, 95
Progressivism, xix, 45
prostitution, 126, 138, 139, 140, 145, 198, 199
Protecting Soldiers and Mothers (Skocpol), 25
Provident Sewing Association, 87–88, 91
Puritans, x

Quesenbery Commission, 70, 71

Rabinowitz, Howard, 15
race, viii, xiii, 85, 111, 140, 150, 171, 182; and class, 176, 194, 195; and Georgia institutions, 12; and social

reform, 146, 148; and social welfare, xvi, 11, 13, 18–19, 40–41, 42, 43, 46, 50, 52, 73, 81, 84, 106, 120, 153, 160–77, 188
race relations, 194
Reconstruction, xv, xvi
Red Cross, 53
reform schools, 138–56
religion, xii, 83, 84, 101, 124, 155
residency laws, xi
Richmond, 62–74, 120–33
Richmond Examiner, 125
Richmond Professional Institute, xiii, xiv, xxii
Rockefeller Foundation, xvii
Rothman, David, xii, 5–6
Ruger, Thomas H., 15
Rush, Benjamin, 7
Rutherford, Mildred, 68

Sage Foundation, xvii
School of Social Work, Tulane University, xxii, 93–94
scientific charity, 85, 89, 91, 92
Scott, Anne Firor, 130
segregation, 109, 160, 171, 177; and Georgia welfare institutions, 15–16; and social welfare, 84, 86, 185, 187
settlement house movement, 92, 193, 197
Sisters of Charity, 124
Sisters of Temperance, 120
Skocpol, Theda, 25, 61, 120
slavery, xi, xii, xiii–xiv, xviii
social control, viii, 5–6
Social Security Act, xviii, 54–55
social welfare, 153, 168, 171; effects of Depression on, 49; functions of, 42; goals of, 90; historiography of, viii–xxii, 176, 182–83, 201; role of states in, 4; role of taxes in, 6–7, 8, 13–14; and professionalization, 196
Society of Friends, 121, 124
South Carolina, 160–77; and Civil War pensions, 25; seventeenth century, x; institutions in, xii; support for social welfare in, 173
South Carolina Federation of Colored Women's Clubs (SCFCWC), 161, 171, 173–75
South Carolina Federation of Women's Clubs (SCFWC), 160–64, 166–69, 170, 171
South Carolina State College, 172
Southern Association of College Women (SACW), 139, 142
southern distinctiveness, xvii, xviii, xx, 20, 24–37, 56, 61, 82, 94, 95, 150, 160, 162
St. Anna's Asylum, 84
St. Joseph's Female Academy and Orphan Asylum, 124, 126, 132
St. Joseph's Home, 84
Stafford, Maud, 110
state formation, viii–ix
Survey, The, xxii

taxes, 28
Taylor, Helen, 138, 139, 141, 142, 151, 155
Tennessee, xvi, 100–117
Texas, xvi, 25
Tompkins, Captain Sallie, 66
Touro Infirmary, 81
Touro-Shakspeare Home, 84, 88
Treadway, Sandra Gioia, 61–62
Trinkle, Governor Elbert Lee, 68–69, 71
Tuke, William, 7
Tulane University, 93
Turner, George P., 49, 50

Union Benevolent Association, 120
United Daughters of the Confederacy, 65–66, 68, 71, 72, 162
United Hebrew Charities, 92–93
unwed mothers, 88–89, 100–117

Vanderbilt University, 139
veterans, xv, xvii, 24–37; dependents of, 61–74; homes for, xvii, 67–68
Virginia, x, 8, 61–74, 120–33; institutions in, xii, xvi, 65, 68, 69
Visanska, Sarah, 162, 167, 168, 170

Walton County, Ga., 29–36
Washington, Booker T., 166, 167
Washington, D.C., 68, 69
Wedell, Marsha, 105
Wells, Ida B., 109
Wesley Settlement House, 193, 197
Western and Atlantic Railroad, 7, 8, 15
Wife Desertion Bill, 199
Wilkinson, Marion, 171, 172, 173, 175

Wilkinson, Robert, 172, 173
Wirt, Elizabeth, 122
Wisner, Elizabeth, xi, xviii, 84, 95
Woman's Christian Association Mission (WCA), 103–17
Women, xiii, xix; African American, 161, 171, 187–90, 195–96, 199; in Atlanta, 181–203; and charity organizations, 86, 90; and Lost Cause, 162–64; gender roles of, 138–39, 140, 141, 155; in Memphis, 100–119; motivations of, for social work, 160–77; "new southern," 64; reform schools for, 138–56; in Richmond, 120–33; rights of, 101–2, 199; and social welfare, 82, 160–77, 181–203; widowed, 27, 61–74
Women's clubs, 142–43, 160–77
Women's History, xix

yellow fever, 83, 103
Young, Ethel, 154

www.ingramcontent.com/pod-product-compliance
Lightning Source LLC
Chambersburg PA
CBHW011755220426
43672CB00018B/2974